CRE**A**TIVE
HOMEOWNER®

BEST-SELLING
RANCH
HOME PLANS

CREATIVE HOMEOWNER®, Upper Saddle River, New Jersey

COPYRIGHT © 2005

CREATIVE
HOMEOWNER®

A Division of Federal Marketing Corp.
Upper Saddle River, NJ

VP/Publisher: Brian H. Toolan
VP/Editorial Director: Timothy O. Bakke
Production Manager: Kimberly H. Vivas

Home Plans Editor: Kenneth D. Stuts
Home Plans Designer Liaison: Maureen Mulligan

Design and Layout: Arrowhead Direct (David Kroha, Cindy DiPierdomenico, Judith Kroha)

Cover Design: David Geer

Current Printing (last digit)
10 9 8 7 6 5

Best-Selling Ranch Home Plans
Library of Congress Control Number: 2005924174
ISBN: 1-58011-272-2

CREATIVE HOMEOWNER®
A Division of Federal Marketing Corp.
24 Park Way
Upper Saddle River, NJ 07458
www.creativehomeowner.com

Note: The homes as shown in the photographs and renderings in this book may differ from the actual blueprints. When studying the house of your choice, please check the floor plans carefully.

PHOTO CREDITS

Front cover: *top* plan 391034, page 75; *bottom row left to right* plan 161001, page 128; plan 131006, pages 232–233; plan 111004, page 290; plan 271074, page 284 **back cover:** *top* plan 391059, page 234; *center* plan 131006, pages 232–233; *bottom left* plan 161002, pages 184–185; *bottom center* plan 111004, page 290; *bottom right* plan 161002, pages 184–185 **page 1:** plan 391059, page 234 **page 3:** *top* plan 311005, page 267; *center* plan 121051, page 174; *bottom* plan 131007, page 77 **page 4:** plan 391069, page 26 **page 5:** plan 401023, pages 252–253 **page 6:** *top* plan 131003, page 9; *bottom* plan 121056, page 45 **page 7:** 131004, page 10 **page 69:** courtesy of Mannington Floors **page 70:** courtesy of Congoleum **page 71:** *top* courtesy of Congoleum; *bottom* courtesy of Mannington Floors **page 72:** courtesy of Dal-Tile **page 73:** *left* courtesy of Mannington Floors; *right* courtesy of Congoleum **page 74:** *left* courtesy of Mannington Floors; *right* courtesy of Dal-Tile **pages 150–155:** illustrations by Warren Cutler, Tony Davis (site plans), Elizabeth Eaton, Biruta Hansen, Paul Mirocha, Gordon Morrison, Michael Rothman, Michael Wanke **pages 198–199:** *all* courtesy of Sylvania **page 200:** courtesy of Kraftmaid Cabinetry **page 201:** *all* courtesy of Sylvania **page 247:** *top* courtesy of Thomasville *bottom both* courtesy of Rubbermaid **page 248:** courtesy of IKEA **page 249:** courtesy of Closetmaid **page 250:** *top* courtesy of Closetmaid *bottom* courtesy of Rubbermaid **pages 271–272** *both* George Ross/CH **page 273:** Christine Elasigue/CH **page 274:** *top* George Ross/CH; *bottom* Christine Elasigue/CH **page 275:** *top* George Ross/CH; *bottom* Christine Elasigue/CH **pages 276–278:** Christine Elasigue/CH **page 313:** *Top to Bottom* plan 151003, page 83; plan 121004, page 114; plan 161001, page 128 **page 320:** *Top to Bottom* plan 131005, page 140; plan 271077, page 142; plan 151168, page 231

Contents

Getting Started

Maybe you can't wait to bang the first nail. Or you may be just as happy leaving town until the windows are cleaned. The extent of your involvement with the construction phase is up to you. Your time, interests, and abilities can help you decide how to get the project from lines on paper to reality. But building a house requires more than putting pieces together. Whoever is in charge of the process must competently manage people as well as supplies, materials, and construction. He or she will have to

- Make a project schedule to plan the orderly progress of the work. This can be a bar chart that shows the time period of activity by each trade.
- Establish a budget for each category of work, such as foundation, framing, and finish carpentry.
- Arrange for a source of construction financing.
- Get a building permit and post it conspicuously at the construction site.

- Line up supply sources and order materials.
- Find subcontractors and negotiate their contracts.
- Coordinate the work so that it progresses smoothly with the fewest conflicts.
- Notify inspectors at the appropriate milestones.
- Make payments to suppliers and subcontractors.

You as the Builder

You'll have to take care of every logistical detail yourself if you decide to act as your own builder or general contractor. But along with the responsibilities of managing the project, you gain the flexibility to do as much of your own work as you want and subcontract out the rest. Before taking this path, however, be sure you have the time and capabilities. Do you also have the time and ability to schedule the work, hire and coordinate subs, order materials, and keep ahead of the account-

ing required to manage the project successfully? If you do, you stand to save the amount that a general contractor would charge to take on these responsibilities, normally 15 to 30 percent of the construction cost. If you take this responsibility on but mismanage the project, the potential savings will erode and may even cost you more than if you had hired a builder in the first place. A subcontractor might charge extra for having to return to the site to complete work that was originally scheduled for an earlier date. Or perhaps because you didn't order the windows at the beginning, you now have to pay for a recent cost increase. (If you had hired a builder in the first place he or she would absorb the increase.)

Acting as the builder, below, requires the ability to hire and manage subcontractors.

Building a home, opposite, includes the need to schedule building inspections at the appropriate milestones.

Hiring a Builder to Handle Construction

A builder or general contractor will manage every aspect of the construction process. Your role after signing the construction contract will be to make regular progress payments and ensure that the work for which you are paying has been completed. You will also consult with the builder and agree to any changes that may have to be made along the way.

Leads for finding builders might come from friends or neighbors who have had contractors build, remodel, or add to their homes. Real-estate agents and bankers may have some names handy but are more likely familiar with the builder's ability to complete projects on time and budget than the quality of the work itself.

The next step is to narrow your list of candidates to three or four who you think can do a quality job and work harmoniously with you. Phone each builder to see whether he or she is interested in being considered for your project. If so, invite the builder to an interview at your home. The meeting will serve two purposes. You'll be able to ask the candidate about his or her experience, and you'll be able to see whether or not your personalities are compatible. Go over the plans with the builder to make certain that he or she understands the scope of the project. Ask if they have constructed similar houses. Get references, and check the builder's standing with the Better Business Bureau. Develop a short list of builders, say three, and ask them to submit bids for the project.

Contracts

Lump-Sum Contracts

A lump-sum, or fixed-fee, contract lets you know from the beginning just what the project will cost, barring any changes made because of your requests or unforeseen conditions. This form works well for projects that promise few surprises and are well defined from the outset by a complete set of contract documents. You can enter into a fixed-price contract by negotiating with a single builder on your short list or by obtaining bids from three or four builders. If you go the latter route, give each bidder a set of documents and allow at least two weeks for them to submit their bids. When you get the bids, decide who you want and call the others to thank them for their efforts. You don't have to accept the lowest bid, but it probably makes sense to do so since you have already honed the list to builders you trust. Inform this builder of your intentions to finalize a contract.

Cost-Plus-Fee Contracts

Under a cost-plus-fee contract, you agree to pay the builder for the costs of labor and materials, as verified by receipts, plus a fee that represents the builder's overhead and profit. This arrangement is sometimes referred to as "time and materials." The fee can range between 15 and 30 percent of the incurred costs. Because you ultimately pick up the tab—whatever the costs—the contractor is never at risk, as he is with a lump-sum contract. You won't know the final total cost of a cost-plus-fee contract until the project is built and paid for. If you can live with that uncertainty, there are offsetting advantages. First, this form allows you to accommodate unknown conditions much more easily than does a lump-sum contract. And rather than being tied down by the project documents, you will be free to make changes at any point along the way. This can be a trap, though. Watching the project take shape will spark the desire to add something or do something differently. Each change costs more, and the accumulation can easily exceed your budget. Because of the uncertainty of the final tab and the built-in advantage to the contractor, you should think twice before entering into this form of contract.

Contract Content

The conditions of your agreement should be spelled out thoroughly in writing and signed by both parties, whatever contractual arrangement you make with your builder. Your contract should include provisions for the following:

When submitting bids, all of the builders should base their estimates on the same specifications. Once the work begins, communicate with your builder to keep the work proceeding smoothly.

Inspect your newly built home, if possible, before the builder closes it up and finishes it.

- The names and addresses of the owner and builder.
- A description of the work to be included ("As described in the plans and specifications dated . . .").
- The date that the work will be completed if time is of the essence.
- The contract price for lump-sum contracts and the builder's allowed profit and overhead costs for changes.
- The builder's fee for cost-plus-fee contracts and the method of accounting and requesting payment.
- The criteria for progress payments (monthly, by project milestones) and the conditions of final payment.
- A list of each drawing and specification section that is to be included as part of the contract.
- Requirements for guarantees. (One year is the standard period for which contractors guarantee the entire project, but you may require specific guarantees on certain parts of the project, such as a 20-year guarantee on the roofing.)
- Provisions for insurance.
- A description of how changes in the work orders will be handled.

The builder may have a standard contract that you can tailor to the specifics of your project. These contain complete specific conditions with blanks that you can fill in to fit your project and a set of "general conditions" that cover a host of issues from insurance to termination provisions. It's always a good idea to have an attorney review the draft of your completed contract before signing it.

Working with Your Builder

The construction phase officially begins when you have a signed copy of the contract and copies of any insurance required from the builder. It's not unheard of for a builder to request an initial payment of 10 to 20 percent of the total cost to cover mobilization costs, those costs associated with obtaining permits and getting set up to begin the actual construction. If you agree to this, keep a careful eye on the progress of the work to ensure that the total

paid out at any one time doesn't get too far out of sync with the actual work completed.

What about changes? From here on, it's up to you and your builder to proceed in good faith and to keep the channels of communication open. Even so, changes of one sort or another beset every project, and they usually add to its cost.

Light at the End of the Tunnel.

The builder's request for a final inspection marks the end of the construction phase— almost. At the final inspection meeting, you and the builder will inspect the work, noting any defects or incomplete items on a "punch list." When the builder tidies up the punch list items, you should reinspect. Sometimes, builders go on to another job and take forever to clean up the last few details, so only after all items on the list have been completed satisfactorily should you release the final payment, which often accounts for the builder's profit.

Some Final Words

Having a positive attitude is important when undertaking a project as large as building a home. A positive attitude can help you ride out the rigors and stress of the construction process.

Stay Flexible. Expect problems, because they certainly will occur. Weather can upset

the schedule you have established for subcontractors. A supplier may get behind on deliveries, which also affects the schedule. An unexpected pipe may surprise you during excavation. Just as certain, every problem that comes along has a solution if you are open to it.

Be Patient. The extra days it may take to resolve a construction problem will be forgotten once the project is completed.

Express Yourself. If what you see isn't exactly what you thought you were getting, don't be afraid to look into changing it. Or you may spot an unforeseen opportunity for an improvement. Changes usually cost more money, though, so don't make frivolous decisions.

Finally, watching your home go up is exciting, so stay upbeat. Get away from your project from time to time. Dine out. Take time to relax. A positive attitude will make for smoother relations with your builder. An optimistic outlook will yield better-quality work if you are doing your own construction. And though the project might seem endless while it is under way, keep in mind that all the planning and construction will fade to a faint memory at some time in the future, and you will be getting a lifetime of pleasure from a home that is just right for you.

Plan #391008

Dimensions: 50' W x 40' D

Levels: 1

Square Footage: 1,312

Bedrooms: 3

Bathrooms: 2

Foundation: Crawl space, slab, or basement

Materials List Available: Yes

Price Category: B

Images provided by designer/architect.

Here's the sum of brains and beauty, which will please all types of families, from starters and nearly empty nesters to those going golden.

Features:

- **Entry:** This restful fresh-air porch and formal foyer bring you graciously toward the great room, with its fireplace and vaulted ceiling.

- **Dining Room:** This adjacent dining room features sliding doors to the deck and smooth open access to the U-shaped kitchen.

- **Laundry Room:** The laundry area has its own separate landing from the garage, so it's conveniently out of the way.

- **Master Suite:** This master suite with tray ceilings features nearly "limitless" closet space, a private bath, and large hall linen closet.

- Bedrooms: The two secondary bedrooms, also with roomy closets, share a full bath. Bedroom 3 easily becomes a home office with direct foyer access and a window overlooking the porch.

Copyright by designer/architect.

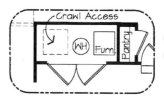

Crawl Space Option

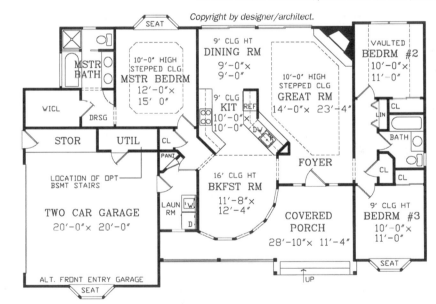

Plan #131003

Dimensions: 60' W x 39'10" D
Levels: 1
Square Footage: 1,466
Bedrooms: 3
Bathrooms: 2
Foundation: Crawl space, slab, or basement
Materials List Available: Yes
Price Category: C

Images provided by designer/architect.
This home, as shown in the photograph, may differ from the actual blueprints.
For more detailed information, please check the floor plans carefully.

Victorian styling adds elegance to this compact and easy-to-maintain ranch design.

Features:

- Ceiling Height: 8 ft.

- Foyer: Bridging between the front door and the great room, this foyer is a surprise feature.

- Great Room: A 10-ft. ceiling adds to the spacious feeling of this room, while the corner fireplace gives it an intimate feeling. Sliding glass doors at the rear of the room open to the backyard.

- Dining Room: This formal room adjoins the great room, allowing guests and family to flow between the rooms.

- Breakfast Room: Turrets add a Victorian feeling to this room that's just off the kitchen and overlooks the front porch.

- Master Suite: Privacy is assured in this suite, which is separated from the main part of the house. A separate toilet room and large walk-in closet add convenience to its beauty.

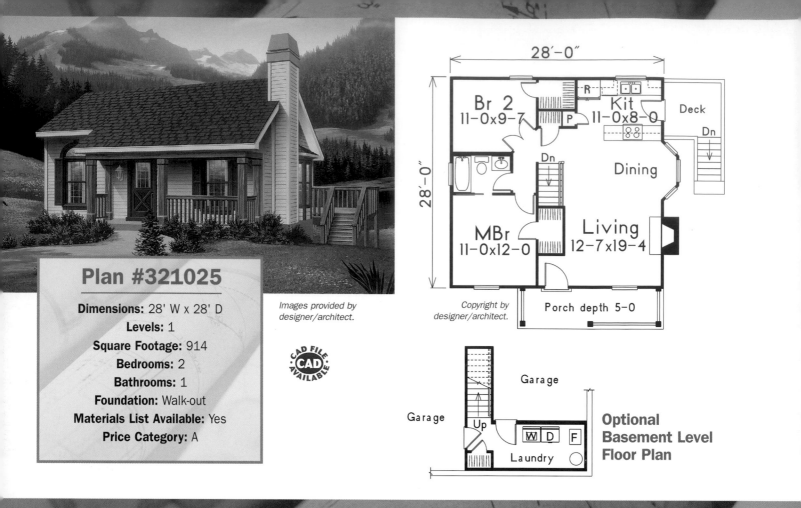

Plan #321025

Dimensions: 28' W x 28' D

Levels: 1

Square Footage: 914

Bedrooms: 2

Bathrooms: 1

Foundation: Walk-out

Materials List Available: Yes

Price Category: A

Images provided by designer/architect.

CAD FILE **CAD** AVAILABLE

Optional Basement Level Floor Plan

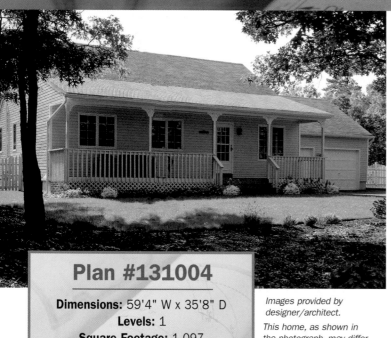

Plan #131004

Dimensions: 59'4" W x 35'8" D

Levels: 1

Square Footage: 1,097

Bedrooms: 3

Bathrooms: 2

Foundation: Crawl space, slab, or basement

Materials List Available: Yes

Price Category: C

Images provided by designer/architect.

This home, as shown in the photograph, may differ from the actual blueprints. For more detailed information, please check the floor plans carefully.

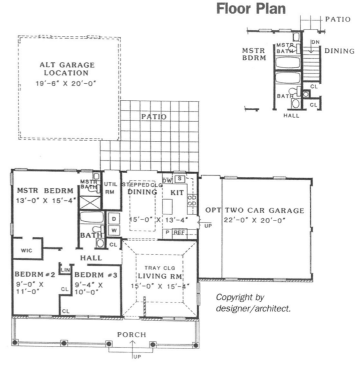

Alternate Basement Floor Plan

Copyright by designer/architect.

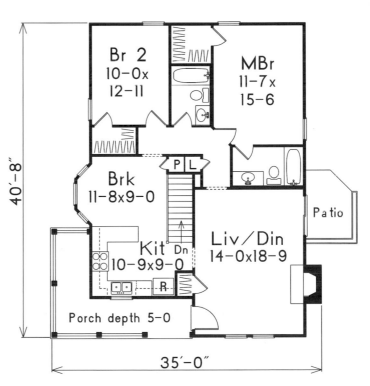

Plan #321040

Dimensions: 35' W x 40'8" D

Levels: 1

Square Footage: 1,084

Bedrooms: 2

Bathrooms: 2

Foundation: Basement

Materials List Available: Yes

Price Category: B

This cute cottage, with its front porch, would make a great starter home or a weekend getaway home.

Features:

- Living Room: This room features an entry closet and a cozy fireplace.

- Kitchen: This well-designed kitchen opens into the breakfast area.

- Master Suite: This retreat has a walk-in closet and a private bath.

- Bedroom: This second bedroom features a walk-in closet and has access to the hall bathroom.

CAD FILE AVAILABLE

Br 2
10-0x
12-11

MBr
11-7 x
15-6

Brk
11-8x9-0

Kit
10-9x9-0

Liv/Din
14-0x18-9

Patio

Dn

Porch depth 5-0

40'-8"

35'-0"

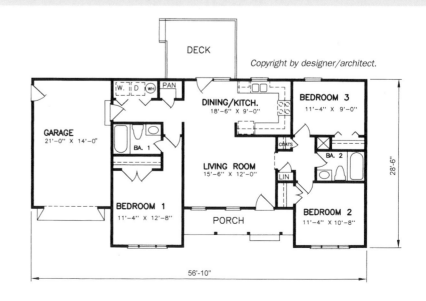

Plan #341004

Dimensions: 56'10" W x 28'6" D
Levels: 1
Square Footage: 1,101
Bedrooms: 3
Bathrooms: 2
Foundation: Crawl space; basement or slab for fee
Materials List Available: Yes
Price Category: B

You'll love the romantic feeling that the gables and front porch give to this well designed home, with its family-oriented layout.

Features:

- Living Room: The open design between this spacious room and the kitchen/dining area makes this home as ideal for family activities as it is for entertaining.

- Outdoor Living Space: French doors open to the back deck, where you're sure to host alfresco dinners or easy summer brunches.

- Kitchen: Designed for the cook's convenience, this kitchen features ample work area as well as excellent storage space in the nearby pantry.

- Laundry Area: Located behind closed doors to shut out the noise, this laundry closet is conveniently placed.

- Master Suite: With triple windows, a wide closet, and a private bath, this is a luxurious suite.

Images provided by designer/architect.

SMARTtip

Creating Depth with Wall Frames

Wall frames create an illusion of depth and density because 1) they are three-dimensional and 2) they divide the wall area into smaller, denser segments. The three-dimensional quality of wall frames is fundamentally different from that of the alternative treatment: raised panels. Despite the name, raised panels actually produce a concave-like, or receding, effect whereas wall frames are more convex, protruding outward. In terms of sculpture, concave units create negative space while convex units create positive space. Raised panels, therefore, deliver a uniform sense of volume, mass, and density, while wall frames create a higher level of tension and dramatic interest.

Copyright by designer/architect.

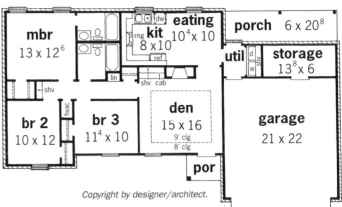

Copyright by designer/architect.

Images provided by designer/architect.

Plan #201004

Dimensions: 60'10" W x 34'10" D

Levels: 1

Square Footage: 1,121

Bedrooms: 3

Bathrooms: 2

Foundation: Crawl space, slab (basement option for fee)

Materials List Available: Yes

Price Category: B

SMARTtip

Color Basics

Use color effectively to enhance the perception of the space itself. Make a large room feel cozy with warm colors, which tend to advance. Conversely, open up a small room with cool colors or neutrals, which tend to recede.

Copyright by designer/architect.

Plan #181021

Dimensions: 37' W x 44' D

Levels: 1

Square Footage: 1,124

Bedrooms: 2

Bathrooms: 1

Foundation: Basement

Materials List Available: Yes

Price Category: B

Images provided by designer/architect.

CAD FILE CAD AVAILABLE

Plan #141001

Dimensions: 48' W x 29' D

Levels: 1

Square Footage: 1,208

Bedrooms: 3

Bathrooms: 2

Foundation: Basement

Materials List Available: Yes

Price Category: B

Images provided by designer/architect.

SMARTtip

Hydro-seeding

An alternative to traditional seeding is hydro-seeding. In this process, a slurry of grass seed, wood fibers, and fertilizer is spray-applied in one step. Hydro-seeding is relatively inexpensive. Compared with seeding by hand, hydro-seeding is also very fast.

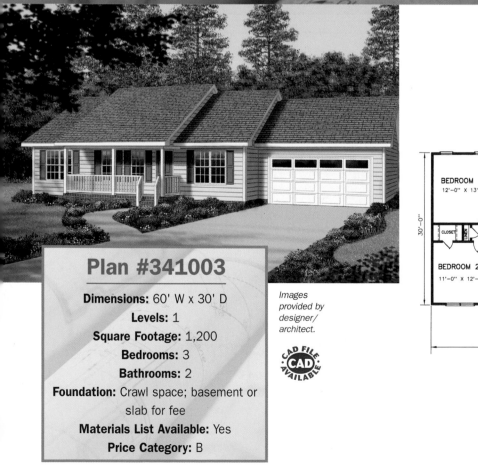

Plan #341003

Dimensions: 60' W x 30' D

Levels: 1

Square Footage: 1,200

Bedrooms: 3

Bathrooms: 2

Foundation: Crawl space; basement or slab for fee

Materials List Available: Yes

Price Category: B

Images provided by designer/architect.

Plan #351013

Dimensions: 30' W x 36' D

Levels: 1

Square Footage: 800

Bedrooms: 2

Bathrooms: 1

Foundation: Crawl space or basement

Materials List Available: Yes

Price Category: B

Images provided by designer/architect.

The design and layout of this home bring back the memories of days gone by and places in which we feel comfortable.

Features:

- **Living Room:** When you enter this room from the front porch, you can feel the warmth from its fireplace.

- **Kitchen:** This kitchen features a raised bar and is open to the living room.

- **Bedrooms:** Two equally sized bedrooms share a common bathroom located in the hall.

- **Screened Porch:** Located in the rear of the home and accessible from bedroom 1 and the kitchen, this area is for relaxing.

Copyright by designer/architect.

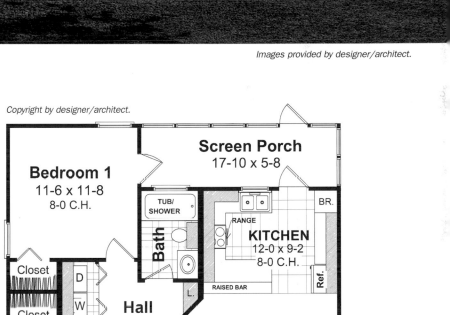

Plan #341123

Dimensions: 44'8" W x 26' D

Levels: 1

Square Footage: 1,154

Bedrooms: 3

Bathrooms: 2

Foundation: Crawl space; basement or slab for fee

Materials List Available: Yes

Price Category: B

With a thoughtfully designed floor plan and a timeless traditional style, this plan is a popular plan among those building their first home.

Features:

- Living Rom: This spacious living room at the front of the house features two single windows and easy traffic flow to the dining/kitchen area.

- Dining/Kitchen Area: A large bay window in this space allows plenty of natural light, wonderful for enjoying your morning cup of coffee by.

- Master Suite: This beautiful master suite, with its private bath, is located on the opposite end of the house from the secondary bedrooms for added privacy.

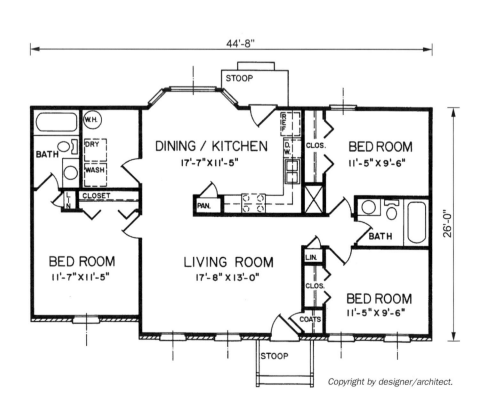

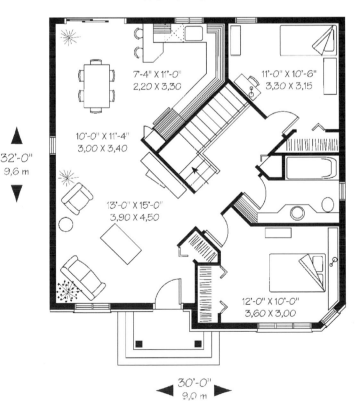

Images provided by designer/architect.

Plan #181215

Dimensions: 30' W x 32' D

Levels: 1

Square Footage: 929

Bedrooms: 2

Bathrooms: 1

Foundation: Basement

Materials List Available: Yes

Price Category: A

Copyright by designer/architect.

Whether just starting out or wrapping it up for the Golden Years, this generous one-level is perfect for two-plus. A peaked roofline, Palladian window, and covered front porch are a visual delight.

Features:

- Entry: An open interior branches out from the entry hall to the family room, where a cathedral ceiling soars to 10'-6¾".

- Dining Room: This room, which adjoins the family room, also embraces openness.

- Kitchen: This cordial kitchen features a breakfast counter for two and sprawling space for food preparation.

- Bedrooms: A full bathroom is nestled between two large bedrooms. Bedroom 1 enjoys a front and side view. Bedroom 2 has an intimate backyard vista.

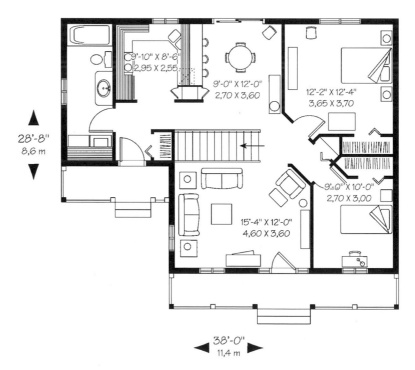

Plan #181218

Dimensions: 38' W x 28'8" D

Levels: 1

Square Footage: 946

Bedrooms: 2

Bathrooms: 1

Foundation: Basement

Materials List Available: Yes

Price Category: A

With a showcase front porch trimmed by quaint railings and carved brackets, this design uses all of its space beautifully and practically.

Features:

- Living room: This company-loving room waits just inside the entrance.

- Kitchen: This creative U-shaped kitchen has a bounty of counter and cabinet space as well as a breakfast counter that stretches into the dining area and doubles as a serving board.

- Utility Areas: The full bathroom is paired with the laundry area, and a side door near the kitchen leads to a smaller covered porch.

- Bedrooms: Two spacious bedrooms sit comfortably beside each other.

Images provided by designer/architect.

Plan #151067

Dimensions: 46'10" W x 54'10" D

Levels: 1

Square Footage: 1,485

Bedrooms: 3

Bathrooms: 2

Foundation: Crawl space, slab (basement option for fee)

CompleteCost List Available: Yes

Price Category: B

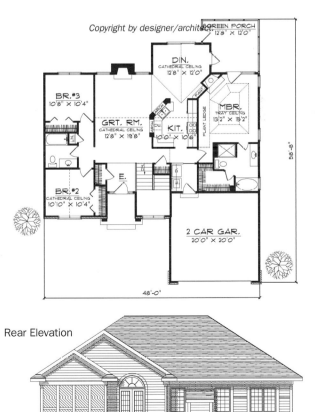

Images provided by designer/architect.

Rear Elevation

Plan #221013

Dimensions: 48' W x 58'8" D

Levels: 1

Square Footage: 1,495

Bedrooms: 3

Bathrooms: 2

Foundation: Basement

Materials List Available: No

Price Category: B

Plan #401043

Dimensions: 38' W x 32' D

Levels: 1

Square Footage: 988

Bedrooms: 3

Bathrooms: 1

Foundation: Basement

Materials List Available: Yes

Price Category: A

Images provided by designer/architect.

Copyright by designer/architect.

This economical, compact home is the ultimate in efficient use of space.

Features:

• **Porch:** The front entry is sheltered by this casual country porch, which also protects the living room windows.

• **Living Room:** This central living room features a cozy fireplace and outdoor access to the front porch.

• **Kitchen:** This U-shaped kitchen serves both a dining area and a breakfast bar. Sliding glass doors lead from here to the rear yard.

• **Master Bedroom:** This room has a walk-in closet and shares a full bathroom with the secondary bedrooms.

• A single or double garage may be built to the side or to the rear of the home.

Right Side Elevation

Rear Elevation

Left Side Elevation

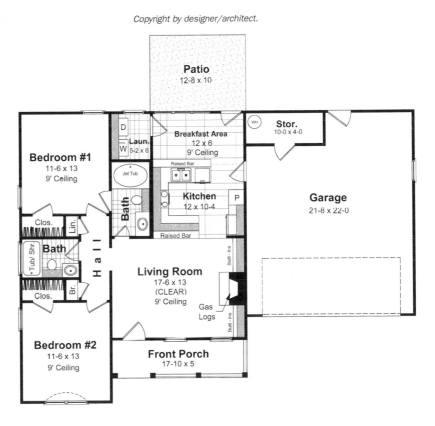

Plan #351016

Dimensions: 52' W x 38'4" D
Levels: 1
Square Footage: 1,002
Bedrooms: 2
Bathrooms: 2
Foundation: Crawl space or slab
Materials List Available: Yes
Price Category: B

This design includes many popular features, including a two-car garage.

Features:

- **Living Room:** This room welcomes you into the cozy home. It features a gas fireplace with built-in shelves on each side.

- **Kitchen:** This kitchen boasts two raised bars. One is open to the breakfast area and the other is open to the living room.

- **Bedrooms:** These two bedrooms have large closets, and bedroom 1 has direct access to the bathroom, which features a jetted tub.

- **Garage:** This two-car garage has a storage area, plus room for two nice-sized cars.

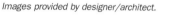

Plan #151218

Dimensions: 48' W x 30'6" D

Levels: 1

Square Footage: 1,008

Bedrooms: 2

Bathrooms: 2

Foundation: Crawl space or slab

CompleteCost List Available: Yes

Price Category: B

Images provided by designer/architect.

This economical home may be just what you're looking for!

Features:

- Great Room: This gathering room has a vaulted ceiling.

- Kitchen: This kitchen boasts an abundant amount of cabinets, and counter space is open to the dining room.

- Master Suite: This retreat area features a large walk-in closet and a private bathroom.

- Bedroom: The second bedroom has its own door into the hall bathroom.

- Carport: This area has room for one car, plus there is a storage area.

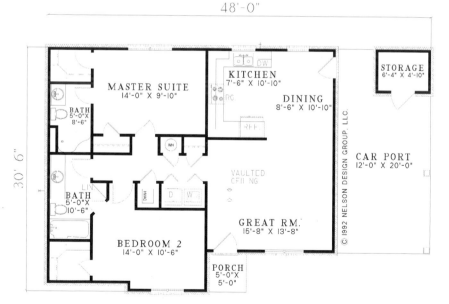

Copyright by designer/architect.

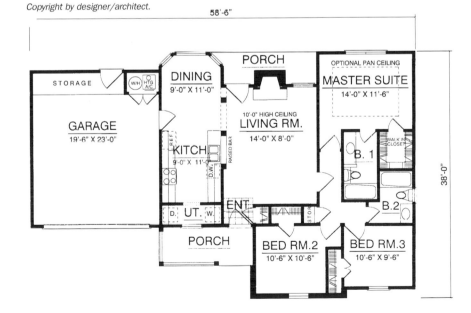

Plan #371047

Dimensions: 58'6" W x 38' D
Levels: 1
Square Footage: 1,222
Bedrooms: 3
Bathrooms: 2
Foundation: Slab
Materials List Available: No
Price Category: B

Images provided by designer/architect.

This cozy country home has all the amenities and is a perfect starter home.

Features:

- **Living Room:** This large room features a 10-foot-high ceiling and a cozy fireplace.

- **Kitchen:** This kitchen has a raised bar that opens into the living room. Located off the kitchen is a handy utility room.

- **Master Suite:** This large suite with optional pan ceiling has a big walk-in closet and its own private bath.

- **Bedrooms:** The two large additional bedrooms share a convenient bathroom in the hall.

Copyright by designer/architect.

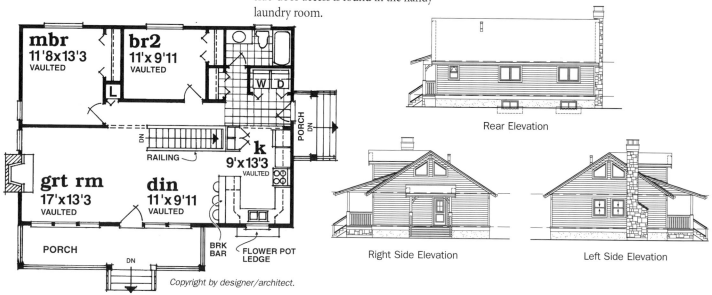

Plan #401047

Dimensions: 38' W x 34' D

Levels: 1

Square Footage: 1,064

Bedrooms: 2

Bathrooms: 1

Foundation: Basement

Materials List Available: Yes

Price Category: B

This farmhouse design squeezes space-efficient features into its compact design. Twin dormer windows flood the vaulted interior with natural light and accentuate the high ceilings.

Images provided by designer/architect.

Features:

- **Porch:** This cozy front porch opens into a vaulted great room and its adjoining dining room.

- **Great Room:** A warm hearth in this gathering place for the family adds to its coziness.

- **Kitchen:** This U-shaped kitchen has a breakfast bar open to the dining room and a sink overlooking a flower box. Nearby side-door access is found in the handy laundry room.

- **Bedrooms:** Vaulted bedrooms are positioned along the back of the plan. They contain wall closets and share a full bathroom with a soaking tub.

- **Future Expansion:** An open-rail staircase leads to the basement, which can be developed into living or sleeping space at a later time, if needed.

Copyright by designer/architect.

Rear Elevation

Right Side Elevation

Left Side Elevation

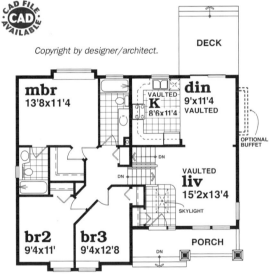

Plan #401041

Dimensions: 38' W x 31' D
Levels: 1
Square Footage: 1,108
Bedrooms: 3
Bathrooms: 2
Foundation: Basement
Materials List Available: Yes
Price Category: B

Craftsman styling and a welcoming porch create marvelous curb appeal for this design. A compact footprint allows economy in construction.

Features:

- **High Ceiling:** This volume ceiling in the living and dining rooms and the kitchen make the home live larger than its modest square footage suggests.

- **Kitchen:** This area features generous cabinet space and flows directly into the dining room to create a casual country feeling. (Note the optional buffet.)

- **Master Bedroom:** This room offers a walk-in closet, a full bath, and a bumped-out window overlooking the rear yard.

- **Expansion:** The lower level provides room for an additional bedroom, den, family room, and full bath.

Copyright by designer/architect.

Images provided by designer/architect.

front Elevation

Rear Elevation

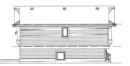

Left Side Elevation

Right Side Elevation

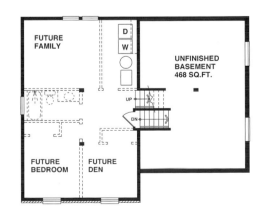

Optional Basement Level Floor Plan

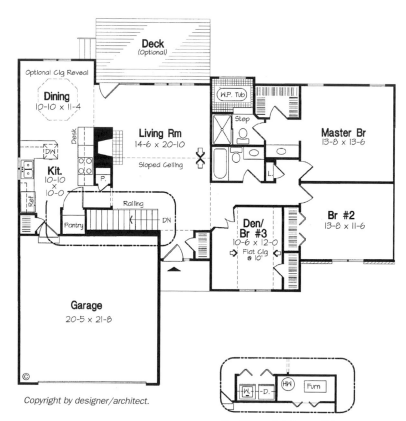

Plan #391069

Dimensions: 56' W x 48' D

Levels: 1

Square Footage: 1,492

Bedrooms: 3

Bathrooms: 2

Foundation: Crawl space, slab, or basement

Materials List Available: Yes

Price Category: B

Images provided by designer/architect.

This design opens wide from the living room to the kitchen and dining room. All on one level, even the bedrooms are easy to reach.

Features:

• Living Room: This special room features a fireplace and entry to the deck.

• Dining Room: This formal room shows off special ceiling effects.

• Bedrooms: Bedroom 3 is inspired by a decorative ceiling, and bedroom 2 has double closet doors. There's a nearby bath for convenience.

• Master Suite: This private area features a roomy walk-in closet and private bath.

Copyright by designer/architect.

Optional Floor Plan

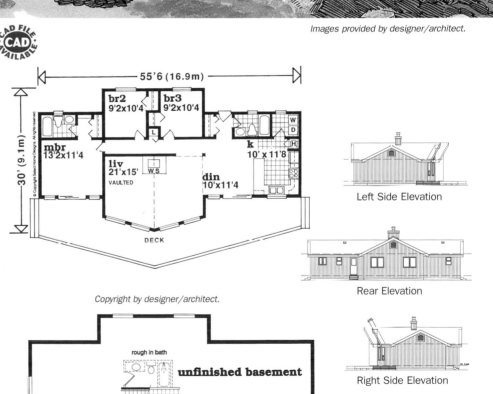

Plan #401020

Dimensions: 55'6" W x 30' D
Levels: 1
Square Footage: 1,230
Bedrooms: 3
Bathrooms: 2
Foundation: Basement or crawl space
Materials List Available: Yes
Price Category: B

This is a grand vacation or retirement home, designed for views and the outdoor lifestyle. The full-width deck complements the abundant windows in the rooms that face it.

Features:

- **Living Room:** This area, with a vaulted ceiling, a fireplace, and full-height windows overlooking the deck, is made for gathering.

- **Dining Room:** This room is open to the living room; it has sliding glass doors that lead to the outdoors.

- **Kitchen:** This room has a pass-through counter to the dining room and is U-shaped in design.

- **Bedrooms:** Two family bedrooms in the middle of the plan share a full bath.

- **Master Suite:** This area has a private bath and deck views.

Left Side Elevation

Rear Elevation

Right Side Elevation

Optional Basement Level Floor Plan

Plan #371005

Dimensions: 52'6" W x 45'8" D

Levels: 1½

Square Footage: 1,250

Bedrooms: 2

Bathrooms: 2

Foundation: Crawl space, slab, or basement

Materials List Available: No

Price Category: B

Images provided by designer/architect.

Copyright by designer/architect.

This quaint country home feels much larger because of the cathedral ceiling in the living room and an upstairs loft. This is the perfect vacation getaway or a home for a small family.

Features:

- **Front Porch:** This large front porch is perfect for relaxing and entertaining.

- **Living Room:** This room is an open area and is great for having guests over.

- **Loft:** This area overlooks the living room and has an optional bath.

- **Master Suite:** This area has a large walk-in closet and its own private bath.

CAD FILE AVAILABLE

PORCH

BED RM. 2
12'-6" X 12'-0"

SHR.

LIN.

W. D.

KITCH.
12'-0" X 11'-0"

DINING
10'-6" X 12'-0"

RAISED BAR

DESK

MASTER SUITE
12'-0" X 15'-0"

STOR.

OPEN ABOVE
LIVING RM.
15'-0" X 16'-0"

B. 1

STAIR UP

PORCH

WOOD RAIL

LOFT
18'-0" x 16'-0"

OPEN ABOVE LIVING RM.

OPTIONAL BATH

STAIR DOWN

Optional Bonus Area

Plan #401031

Dimensions: 42' W x 52' D

Levels: 1

Square Footage: 1,260

Bedrooms: 3

Bathrooms: 2

Foundation: Basement

Materials List Available: Yes

Price Category: B

Images provided by designer/architect.

This economical-to-build bungalow works well as a small family home or a retirement cottage. The covered porch leads to a vaulted living room with a fireplace.

Features:

- **Kitchen:** This L-shaped space with a walk-in pantry and an island with a utility sink. An attached breakfast nook has sliding glass doors to a rear patio.

- **Master Suite:** The master bedroom has a private full bathroom with bright skylight.

- **Bedrooms:** There are three bedrooms, each with a roomy wall closet, that share a main bathroom with skylight.

- **Garage:** A two-car garage sits at the front of the plan to protect the bedrooms from street noise.

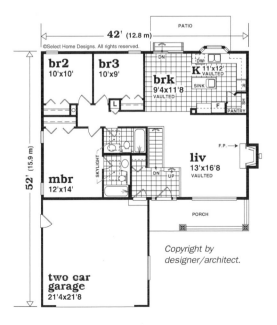

Copyright by designer/architect.

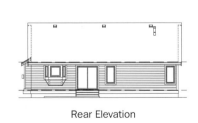

Rear Elevation

Right Side Elevation

Left Side Elevation

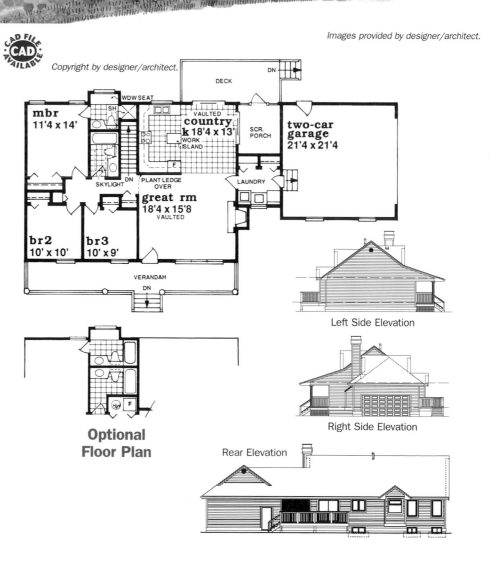

Plan #401024

Dimensions: 70' W x 36' D

Levels: 1

Square Footage: 1,298

Bedrooms: 3

Bathrooms: 2

Foundation: Basement

Materials List Available: Yes

Price Category: B

Images provided by designer/architect.

A front veranda, cedar lattice, and a solid-stone chimney enhance the appeal of this one-story country-style home.

Features:

• **Great Room:** The open plan begins with this great room, which includes a fireplace and a plant ledge over the wall separating the living space from the country kitchen.

• **Kitchen:** This U-shaped kitchen provides an island work counter and sliding glass doors to the rear deck and screened porch.

• **Master Suite:** This area has a wall closet and a private bath with window seat.

mbr 11'4 x 14'

country k 18'4 x 13'

two-car garage 21'4 x 21'4

great rm 18'4 x 15'8 VAULTED

br2 10' x 10'

br3 10' x 9'

VERANDAH

Optional Floor Plan

Left Side Elevation

Right Side Elevation

Rear Elevation

Plan #151220

Dimensions: 48' W x 56'2" D
Levels: 1
Square Footage: 1,325
Bedrooms: 3
Bathrooms: 2
Foundation: Crawl space or slab
CompleteCost List Available: Yes
Price Category: B

This charming home, great for a narrow lot, is perfect for first-time homeowners. Welcome friends and family on the front porch before entering the living room.

Features:

- **Living Room:** This large room has a raised ceiling and a clever bay window.

- **Kitchen:** This kitchen, with a raised bar for additional seating, is open to the dining room.

- **Master Suite:** This space features a large walk-in closet and a private bathroom.

- **Bedrooms:** Two secondary bedrooms have large closets and share a hall bathroom.

- **Garage:** This garage has room for two cars, plus there is a storage area.

Images provided by designer/architect.

Copyright by designer/architect.

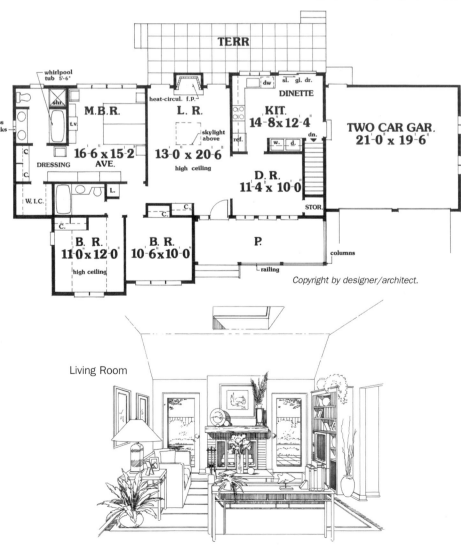

Plan #131012

Dimensions: 71'4" W x 35'10" D
Levels: 1
Square Footage: 1,366
Bedrooms: 3
Bathrooms: 2
Foundation: Basement, crawl space, or slab
Materials List Available: Yes
Price Category: C

Images provided by designer/architect.

You're sure to love this home, with its covered front porch and gabled roofline.

Features:

- **Entry:** The 11-ft. ceiling height makes an impressive entryway.

- **Living Room:** A pair of French doors frames the fireplace in this room, and a central sky light provides natural lighting during the day and drama at night.

- **Dining Room:** Open to the living room, this area also features an 11-ft.-high ceiling.

- **Kitchen:** A laundry closet, ample counter space, and dinette opening to the expansive backyard terrace add up to convenience in this room.

- **Master Suite:** Enjoy the dressing area, two closets, and bath with whirlpool tub and shower.

- **Additional Bedrooms:** An arched window and 11-ft. ceiling mark the larger of these two rooms.

Copyright by designer/architect.

Living Room

Plan #371006

Dimensions: 49'7" W x 48'6" D

Levels: 1

Square Footage: 1,374

Bedrooms: 3

Bathrooms: 2

Foundation: Crawl space, slab, or basement

Materials List Available: No

Price Category: B

Images provided by designer/architect.

This elegant brick-and-siding country home brings affordable living to a new level. The three bedrooms and two baths makes the most of the floor space.

Features:

- **Master Suite:** This large master suite has a large master bath with two walk-in closets.

- **Dining Room:** This formal room is located just off the entry.

- **Living Room:** This large but comfortable room has a cozy fireplace.

- **Kitchen:** This spacious kitchen with a breakfast nook has a view of the backyard.

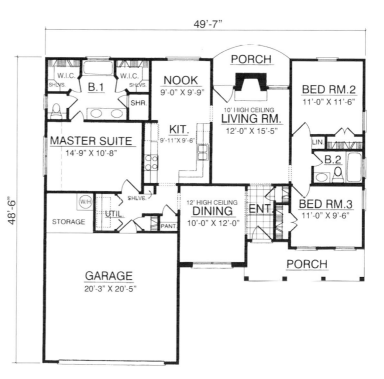

Copyright by designer/architect.

Plan #131014

Dimensions: 48' W x 43'4" D
Levels: 1
Square Footage: 1,380
Bedrooms: 3
Bathrooms: 2
Foundation: Crawl space, slab, or basement
Materials List Available: Yes
Price Category: C

The exterior of this home looks formal, thanks to its twin dormers, gables, and the bay windows that flank the columned porch, but the inside is contemporary in both design and features.

Features:

- Great Room: Centrally located, this great room has a 10-ft. ceiling. A fireplace, built-in cabinets, and windows that overlook the rear covered porch make it as practical as it is attractive.

- Dining Room: A bay window adds to the charm of this versatile room.

- Kitchen: This U-shaped room is designed to make cooking and cleaning jobs efficient.

- Master Suite: With a bay window, a walk-in closet, and a private bath with an oval tub, the master suite may be your favorite area.

- Additional Bedrooms: Located on the opposite side of the house from the master suite, these rooms share a full bath in the hall.

Living Room

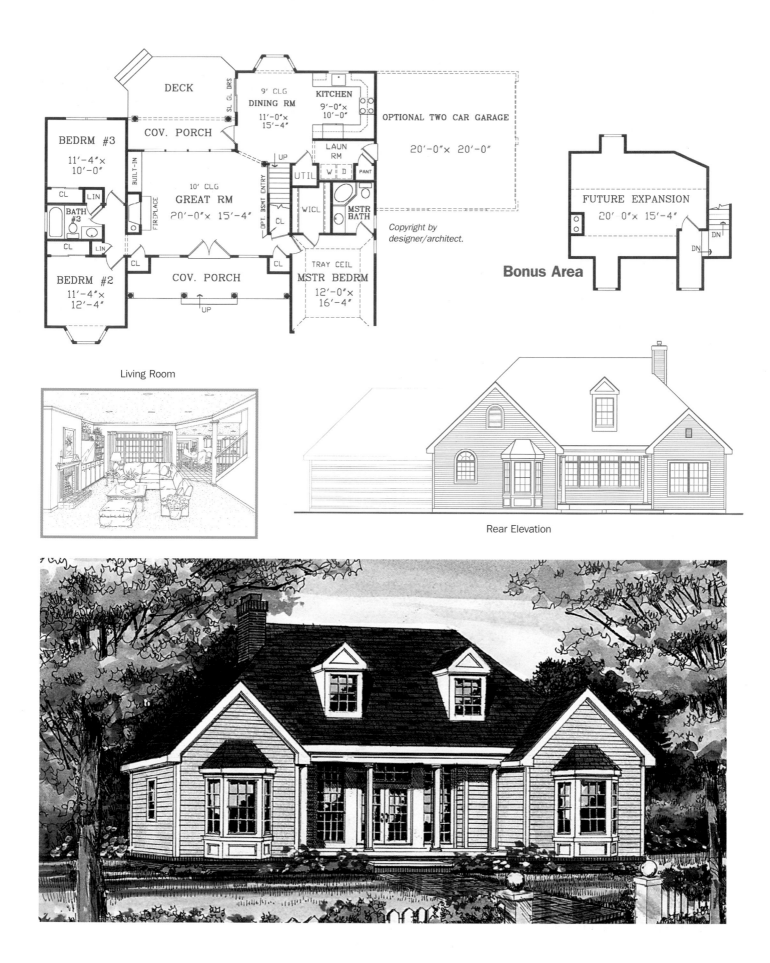

DECK

9' CLG
DINING RM
11'-0" x
15'-4"

KITCHEN
9'-0" x
10'-0"

OPTIONAL TWO CAR GARAGE

20'-0" x 20'-0"

BEDRM #3
11'-4" x
10'-0"

COV. PORCH

BUILT-IN

CL   LIN

BATH #3

CL   LIN

LAUN RM

UTIL   W D   PANT

WICL

MSTR BATH

FUTURE EXPANSION
20'-0" x 15'-4"

Bonus Area

SL. GL. DRS

UP

OPT. BSMT ENTRY

10' CLG
GREAT RM
20'-0" x 15'-4"

FIREPLACE

Copyright by
designer/architect.

DN

DN

BEDRM #2
11'-4" x
12'-4"

COV. PORCH

CL

CL

CL

TRAY CEIL
MSTR BEDRM
12'-0" x
16'-4"

UP

Living Room

Rear Elevation

Plan #371028

Dimensions: 50'2" W x 47' D

Levels: 1

Square Footage: 1,376

Bedrooms: 3

Bathrooms: 2

Foundation: Slab

Materials List Available: No

Price Category: B

An efficient and affordable floor plan comes to life in this traditional brick home. This is the perfect home for anyone just starting out or for the "empty-nester."

Features:

- **Living Room:** This open room boasts a media center and cozy fireplace.

- **Dining Room:** The living room leads to this spacious room with a beautiful bay window that looks out into the backyard.

- **Kitchen:** This kitchen has a raised bar and a pantry.

- **Bedrooms:** The two other bedrooms share a convenient bath.

Images provided by designer/architect.

Copyright by designer/architect.

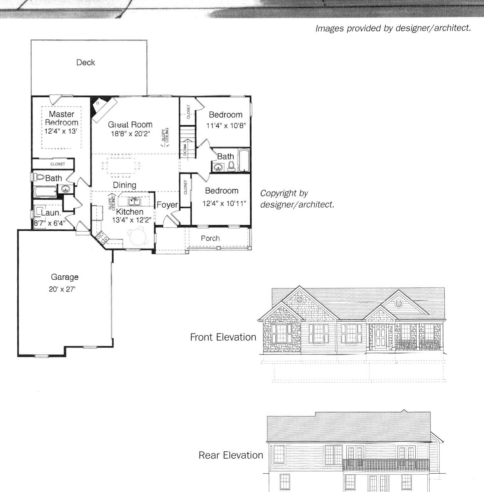

Plan #161081

Dimensions: 50' W x 55'8" D
Levels: 1
Square Footage: 1,390
Bedrooms: 3
Bathrooms: 2
Foundation: Walk-out Basement
Materials List Available: Yes
Price Category: B

Images provided by designer/architect.

The stone-and-siding facade, front porch, and multiple gables decorate the exterior of this charming one-floor plan.

Features:

- **Great Room:** The standard 8–ft. ceiling height vaults to an 11-ft. height through this room.

- **Kitchen:** This kitchen can accommodate a small dining area or can be designed to offer more cabinets and allow for a larger great room.

- **Master Suite:** This suite enjoys a raised center ceiling and a private bath.

- **Basement:** The home is designed with this unfinished walk-out basement, which can be finished to provide additional living space.

Copyright by designer/architect.

Front Elevation

Rear Elevation

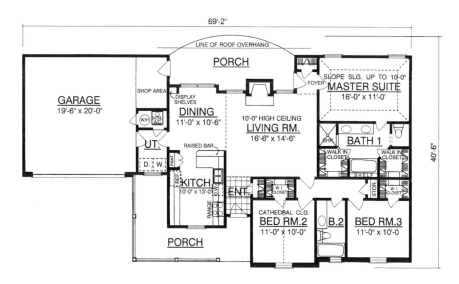

Images provided by designer/architect.

Plan #371029

Dimensions: 69'2" W x 40'6" D

Levels: 1

Square Footage: 1,394

Bedrooms: 3

Bathrooms: 2

Foundation: Crawl space

Materials List Available: No

Price Category: B

This charming country home brings affordability and luxury together.

Features:

- **Living Room:** This spacious room opens to the dining room for easy entertaining.

- **Dining Room:** This room has display shelves and a view of the backyard.

- **Kitchen:** This kitchen has a raised bar and a pantry.

- **Master Suite:** This large getaway boasts his and her walk-in closets, a soaking tub, and a shower.

- **Bedrooms:** The two other bedrooms have walk-in closets and share a convenient bathroom.

Copyright by designer/architect.

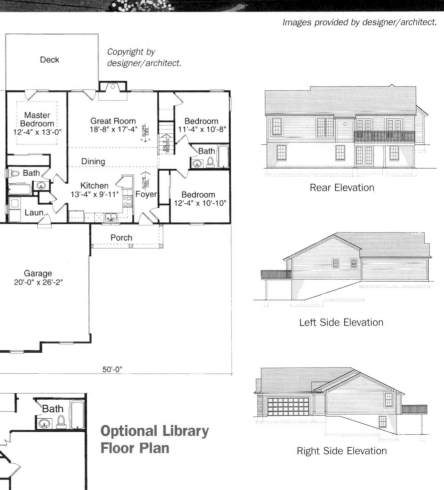

Plan #161004

Dimensions: 50' W x 54'8" D

Levels: 1

Square Footage: 1,315

Bedrooms: 3

Bathrooms: 2

Foundation: Basement

Materials List Available: Yes

Price Category: B

This multi-featured ranch has a covered porch, a ceiling that slopes to an 11-ft. height, an optional library, and a full basement to enhance your living enjoyment.

Features:

- **Great Room:** Experience the expansive entertainment area created by this open great room and the dining area. Enjoy the lovely fireplace, with full glass on both sides.

- **Kitchen:** This kitchen is designed for total convenience and easy work patterns with immediate access to the first-floor laundry area.

- **Master Bedroom:** This master bedroom, split from the other bedrooms, offers privacy and features tray ceiling design.

- **Basement:** Designed with the future in mind, this full basement has open stairs leading to it and can be updated to expand your living space.

Images provided by designer/architect.

Copyright by designer/architect.

Deck

Master Bedroom 12'-4" x 13'-0"

Great Room 18'-8" x 17'-4"

Bedroom 11'-4" x 10'-8"

Bath

Dining

Bath

Kitchen 13'-4" x 9'-11"

Foyer

Bedroom 12'-4" x 10'-10"

Laun.

54'-8"

Porch

Garage 20'-0" x 26'-2"

50'-0"

Bath

Optional Library Floor Plan

Rear Elevation

Left Side Elevation

Right Side Elevation

Plan #151010

Dimensions: 38'4" W x 68'6" D
Levels: 1
Square Footage: 1,379
Bedrooms: 3
Bathrooms: 2
Foundation: Crawl space, slab
CompleteCost List Available: Yes
Price Category: B

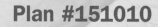

This French Country home has a spacious great room for friends and family to gather, but you can sneak away to the covered rear porch or patio off the master suite for cozy tête-à-têtes.

Features:

- Entry: Take advantage of the marvelous 10-ft. ceilings to hang groups of potted flowering plants.

- Great Room: This spacious room, with an optional 10-ft. boxed ceiling, is the place to curl up by the gas fireplace on a cold winter night.

- Kitchen: The kitchen includes a bar for casual meals, and is open to the breakfast room.

- Rear Porch: Enjoy leisurely meals on the covered rear porch that you can access from both the master suite and the breakfast room.

- Master Suite: The 10-ft. boxed ceiling in the bedroom and the master bath with a whirlpool tub and separate shower make this suite a luxurious place to end a long day.

Copyright by designer/architect.

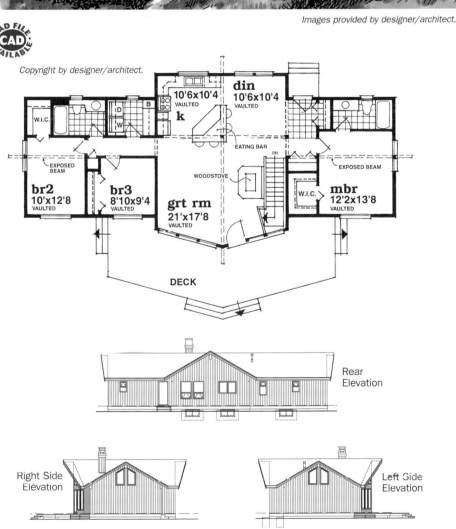

Plan #401033

Dimensions: 62' W x 29' D

Levels: 1

Square Footage: 1,405

Bedrooms: 3

Bathrooms: 2

Foundation: Basement

Materials List Available: Yes

Price Category: B

This three-bedroom leisure home is perfect for the family that spends casual time out of doors. An expansive wall of glass gives a spectacular view from the great room and accentuates the high vaulted ceilings throughout the design.

Features:

- **Great Room:** This room is warmed by a hearth and is open to the dining room and L-shaped kitchen.

- **Kitchen:** A triangular snack bar graces this kitchen and provides space for casual meals.

- **Bedrooms:** The bedrooms are split, with the master bedroom on the right side of the plan and family bedrooms on the left.

CAD FILE · CAD · AVAILABLE

Rear Elevation

Right Side Elevation

Left Side Elevation

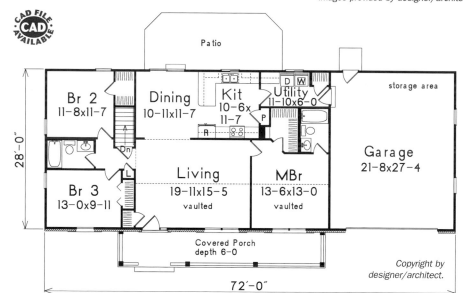

Plan #321002

Dimensions: 72' W x 28' D
Levels: 1
Square Footage: 1,400
Bedrooms: 3
Bathrooms: 2
Foundation: Basement, crawl space
Materials List Available: Yes
Price Category: B

Images provided by designer/architect.

If you're looking for a well-designed compact home with contemporary amenities, this could be the home of your dreams.

Features:

- **Porch:** Just the right size for some rockers and a swing, this porch could become your outdoor living area when the weather is fine.

- **Living Room:** A vaulted ceiling adds to the spacious feeling in this room, where friends and family are sure to gather.

- **Kitchen:** This space-saving design, in combination with the ample counter and cabinet space, makes cooking a pleasure.

- **Utility Room:** This large room is fitted with cabinets for extra storage space. You'll find storage space in the large garage, too.

- **Master Bedroom:** This room is somewhat secluded for privacy, making it an ideal place for some quiet time at the end of the day.

SMARTtip

Fabric Draping Ability

Test a fabric's draping ability by looking at a large piece in a fabric store. Gather at least two to three yards of material, holding one end in your hand. Check how it drapes. Does it fall into folds easily? Also look at the pattern when it is gathered. Does the design become lost in the folds? Ask a salesclerk or a friend to hold the fabric, and look at it from a few feet away.

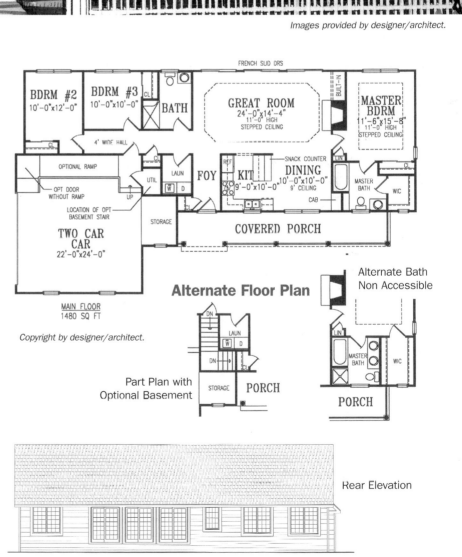

Plan #131017

Dimensions: 69'8" W x 39'4" D
Levels: 1
Square Footage: 1,480
Bedrooms: 3
Bathrooms: 2
Foundation: Crawl space, slab, or basement
Materials List Available: Yes
Price Category: C

Images provided by designer/architect.

This fully accessible home is designed for wheelchair access to every area, giving everyone true enjoyment and freedom of movement.

Features:

- **Great Room:** Facing towards the rear, this great room features a volume ceiling that adds to the spacious feeling of the room.

- **Kitchen:** Designed for total convenience and easy work patterns, this kitchen also offers a view out to the covered front porch.

- **Master Bedroom:** Enjoy the quiet in this room which is sure to become your favorite place to relax at the end of the day.

- **Additional Bedrooms:** Both rooms have easy access to a full bath and feature nicely sized closet spaces.

- **Garage:** Use the extra space in this attached garage for storage..

Copyright by designer/architect.

Alternate Floor Plan

Part Plan with Optional Basement

Alternate Bath Non Accessible

Rear Elevation

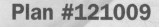

Plan #121009

Dimensions: 50' W x 58' D
Levels: 1
Square Footage: 1,422
Bedrooms: 3
Bathrooms: 2
Foundation: Basement
Materials List Available: Yes
Price Category: B

Images provided by designer/architect.

This amenity-filled home is perfect for the growing family or as a retirement retreat.

Features:

- Ceiling Height: 8 ft. unless otherwise noted.
- Great Room: This inviting space is the perfect place for gatherings of all sizes. It shares 12-ft. ceilings with the dining room and kitchen.

- Dining Room: In addition to the 12-ft. ceiling, arched openings, and built-in book cases make this an elegant place to dine.
- Private Porch: After dinner, step through a door in the dining room to enjoy a summer breeze in this inviting porch.
- Master Suite: The boxed ceiling lends drama to this suite and a walk-in closet adds convenience. Luxury comes from the whirlpool bath.
- Garage: You won't be short of parking and storage space in this two-bay garage. As a bonus there is space for a workbench.

SMARTtip
Window Cornices

You can transform plain rooms by making jogs in cornice molding that will hold shades, blinds, and other window treatments. You can create individual pockets over each window or continue the molding past narrow wall sections between windows to form a more expansive detail. Housings below the cornice can be painted or papered.

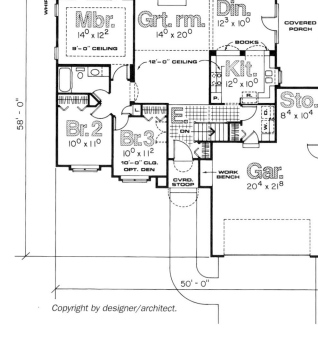

Copyright by designer/architect.

Plan #121056

Dimensions: 48' W x 50' D
Levels: 1
Square Footage: 1,479
Bedrooms: 2
Bathrooms: 2
Foundation: Basement
Materials List Available: Yes
Price Category: B

This home is ideal if the size of your live-in family is increasing with the addition of a baby, or if it's decreasing as children leave the nest.

Features:

- **Entry:** This entry gives you a long view into the great room that it opens into.

- **Great Room:** An 11-ft. ceiling and a fireplace framed by transom-topped windows make this room comfortable in every season and any time of day or night.

- **Den:** French doors open to this den, with its picturesque window. This room would also make a lovely third bedroom.

- **Kitchen:** This kitchen has an island that can double as a snack bar, a pantry, and a door into the backyard.

- **Master Suite:** A large walk-in closet gives a practical touch; you'll find a sunlit whirlpool tub, dual lavatories, and a separate shower in the bath.

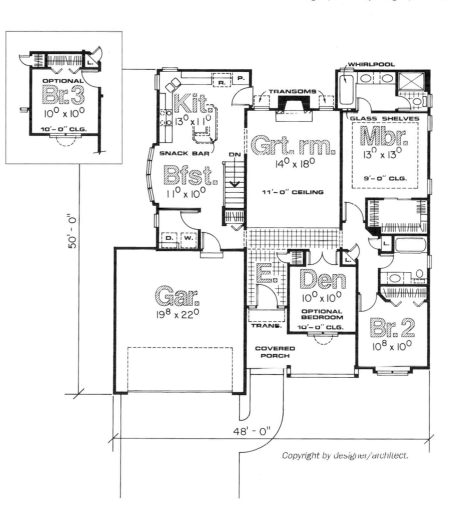

OPTIONAL
Br. 3
10⁰ x 10⁰
10'–0" CLG.

Kit.
13⁰ x 11⁰

SNACK BAR

Bfst.
11⁰ x 10⁰

D. W.

Grt. rm.
14⁰ x 18⁰
11'–0" CEILING

TRANSOMS

WHIRLPOOL

GLASS SHELVES

Mbr.
13⁰ x 13⁰
9'–0" CLG.

Gar.
19⁸ x 22⁰

Den
10⁰ x 10⁰
OPTIONAL BEDROOM
10'–0" CLG.

Br. 2
10⁸ x 10⁰

TRANS.

COVERED PORCH

50'–0"

48'–0"

Copyright by designer/architect.

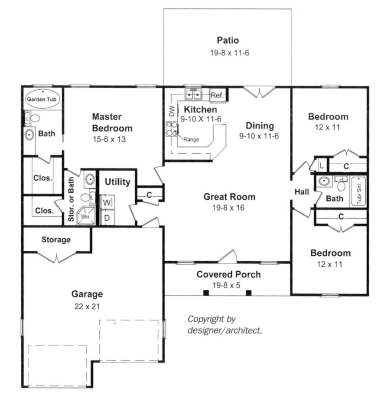

Plan #351019

Dimensions: 54' W x 47' D

Levels: 1

Square Footage: 1,427

Bedrooms: 3

Bathrooms: 3

Foundation: Crawl space or slab (basement for fee)

Materials List Available: Yes

Price Category: B

This fine three-bedroom home, with its open floor plan, may be just what you have been looking for.

Features:

- Great Room: This large room is open to the dining room.

- Kitchen: This fully equipped kitchen has a peninsula counter and is open into the dining room.

- Master Suite: This private area, located on the other side of the home from the secondary bedrooms, features large walk-in closets and bath areas.

- Bedrooms: Two secondary bedrooms have large closets and share a hall bathroom.

Images provided by designer/architect.

Copyright by designer/architect.

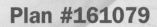

Plan #161079

Dimensions: 66'4" W x 44'10" D

Levels: 1

Square Footage: 1,498

Bedrooms: 3

Bathrooms: 2

Foundation: Basement

Materials List Available: Yes

Price Category: B

Images provided by designer/architect.

This three-bedroom one-story house enjoys step-saving convenience, plus a beautiful stone-and-siding facade with a covered porch.

Features:

- **Great Room:** This gathering area, with a gas fireplace and sloped ceiling, is visible from the foyer, breakfast room, and kitchen, creating a large open area.

- **Kitchen:** This large kitchen, with its snack bar, and the breakfast area both open generously to the great room for a continuous traffic flow.

- **Master Suite:** This suite enjoys a luxurious bath, large walk-in closet, and raised ceiling.

- **Basement:** This full basement shows a rough-in for a bathroom and offers space for a future living area.

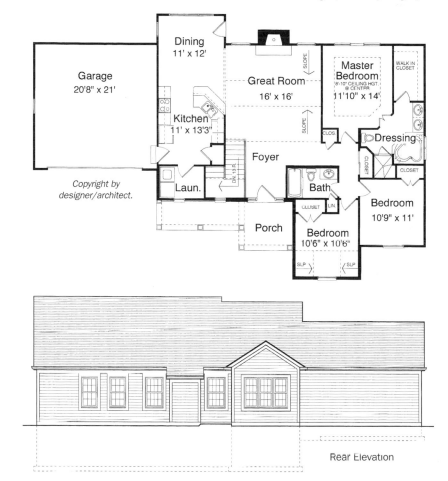

Copyright by designer/architect.

Rear Elevation

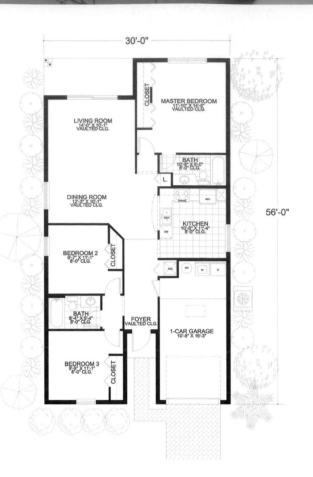

Plan #611005

Dimensions: 30' W x 56' D

Levels: 1

Square Footage: 1,281

Bedrooms: 3

Bathrooms: 2

Foundation: Slab

Materials List Available: No

Price Category: B

Images provided by designer/architect.

CAD FILE AVAILABLE

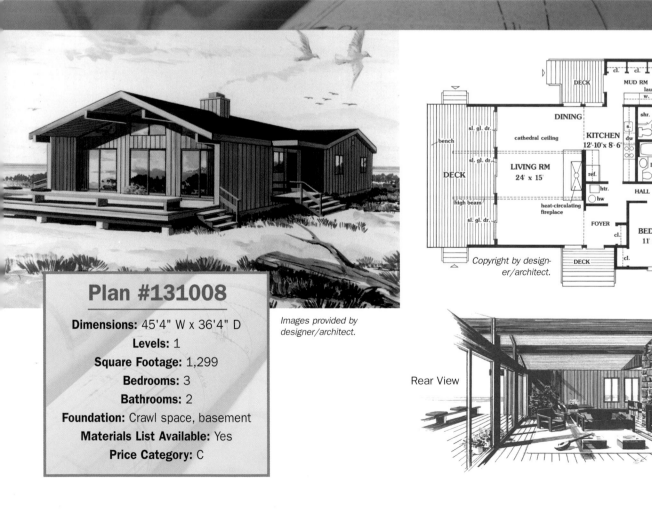

Plan #131008

Dimensions: 45'4" W x 36'4" D

Levels: 1

Square Footage: 1,299

Bedrooms: 3

Bathrooms: 2

Foundation: Crawl space, basement

Materials List Available: Yes

Price Category: C

Images provided by designer/architect.

Copyright by designer/architect.

Rear View

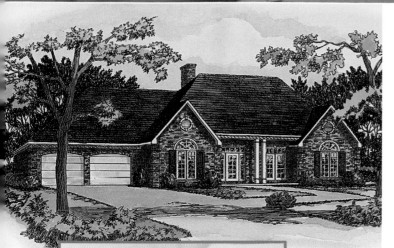

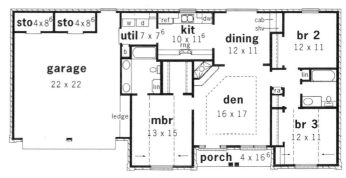

Copyright by designer/architect.

Plan #201023

Dimensions: 67'4" W x 32'10" D
Levels: 1
Square Footage: 1,390
Bedrooms: 3
Bathrooms: 2
Foundation: Crawl space, slab
Materials List Available: Yes
Price Category: B

Images provided by designer/architect.

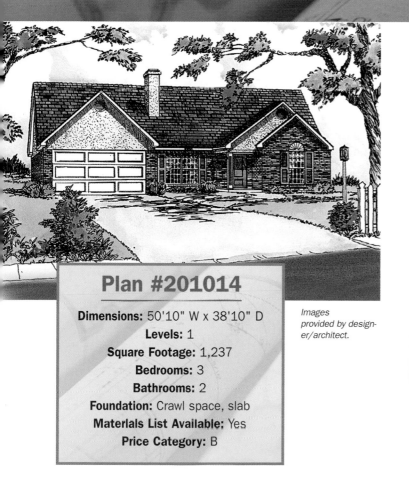

Plan #201014

Dimensions: 50'10" W x 38'10" D
Levels: 1
Square Footage: 1,237
Bedrooms: 3
Bathrooms: 2
Foundation: Crawl space, slab
Materials List Available: Yes
Price Category: B

Images provided by designer/architect.

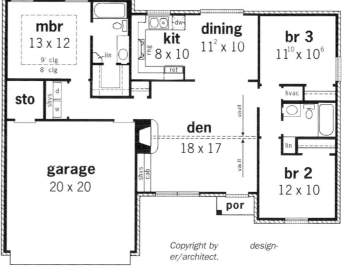

Copyright by designer/architect.

Images provided by designer/architect.

Copyright by designer/architect.

Plan #181147

Dimensions: 52' W x 40' D

Levels: 1

Square Footage: 1,360

Bedrooms: 2

Bathrooms: 2

Foundation: Full basement with walkout

Materials List Available: Yes

Price Category: B

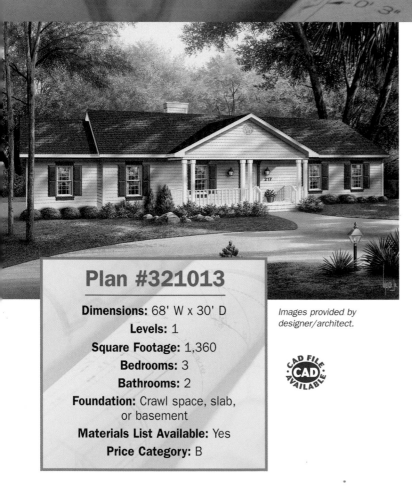

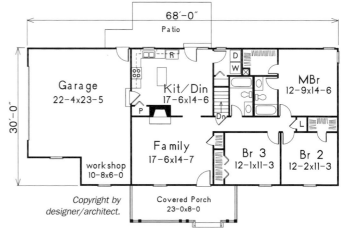

Copyright by designer/architect.

Plan #321013

Dimensions: 68' W x 30' D

Levels: 1

Square Footage: 1,360

Bedrooms: 3

Bathrooms: 2

Foundation: Crawl space, slab, or basement

Materials List Available: Yes

Price Category: B

Images provided by designer/architect.

SMARTtip

Glass Doors and Fire Safety

Professionals recommend keeping glass doors open while a fire is burning. When the doors are left completely open, the burning flame has a more realistic appearance and the glass doesn't become soiled by swirling ashes. When the doors are closed, heat from a large hot fire can break the glass.

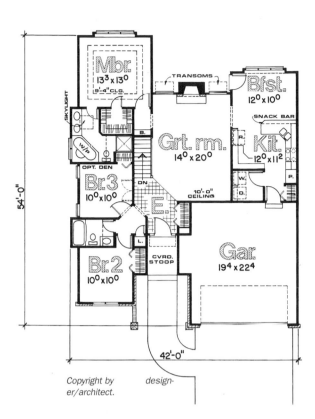

Plan #121002

Dimensions: 42' W x 54' D

Levels: 1

Square Footage: 1,347

Bedrooms: 3

Bathrooms: 2

Foundation: Basement

Materials List Available: Yes

Price Category: B

Images provided by designer/architect.

This home, as shown in the photograph, may differ from the actual blueprints. For more detailed information, please check the floor plans carefully.

Copyright by designer/architect.

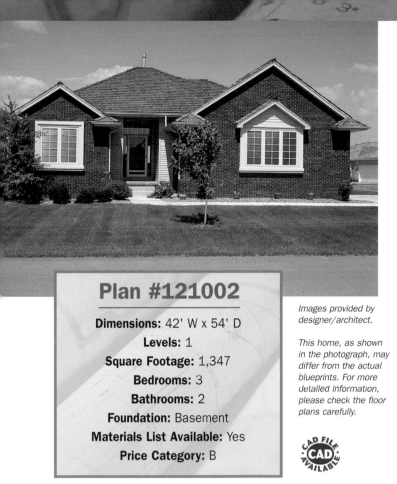

Plan #121012

Dimensions: 40' W x 48'8" D

Levels: 1

Square Footage: 1,195

Bedrooms: 3

Bathrooms: 2

Foundation: Basement

Materials List Available: Yes

Price Category: B

Images provided by designer/architect.

Copyright by designer/architect.

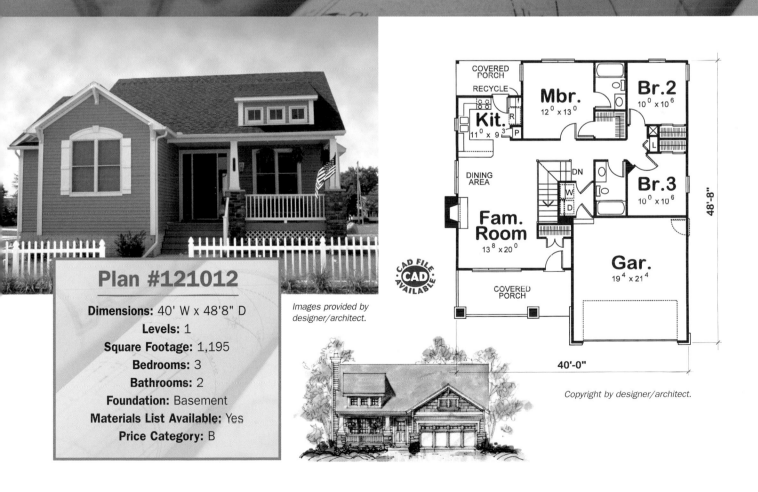

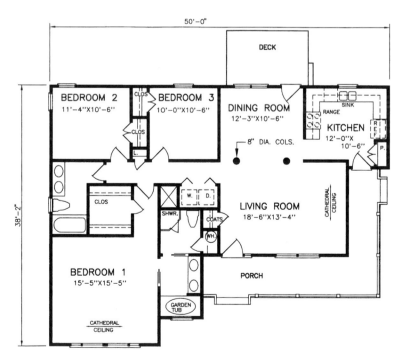

Plan #341034

Dimensions: 50' W x 38'2" D

Levels: 1

Square Footage: 1,445

Bedrooms: 3

Bathrooms: 2

Foundation: Crawl space; basement or slab for fee

Materials List Available: Yes

Price Category: B

Images provided by designer/architect.

This country charmer has a wraparound front porch.

Features:

- **Living Room:** This large gathering area welcomes you home and features a cathedral ceiling.

- **Kitchen:** This U-shaped kitchen has plenty of counter space and an exit onto the front porch.

- **Master Suite:** This suite features a walk-in closet and a private bathroom with double vanities.

- **Bedrooms:** Two secondary bedrooms have large closets and share a hall bathroom.

Copyright by designer/architect.

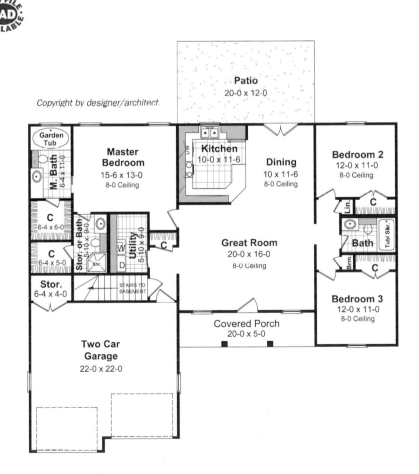

Plan #351020

Dimensions: 54' W x 48' D

Levels: 1

Square Footage: 1,488

Bedrooms: 3

Bathrooms: 2

Foundation: Crawl space, slab, or basement

Materials List Available: Yes

Price Category: B

Images provided by designer/architect.

This is a lot of house for its size and is an excellent example of the popular split bedroom layout.

Features:

- **Great Room:** This large room is open to the dining room.

- **Kitchen:** This fully equipped kitchen has a peninsula counter and is open into the dining room.

- **Master Suite:** This private area, located on the other side of the home from the secondary bedrooms, features large walk-in closets and bath areas.

- **Bedrooms:** The two secondary bedrooms have large closets and share a hall bathroom.

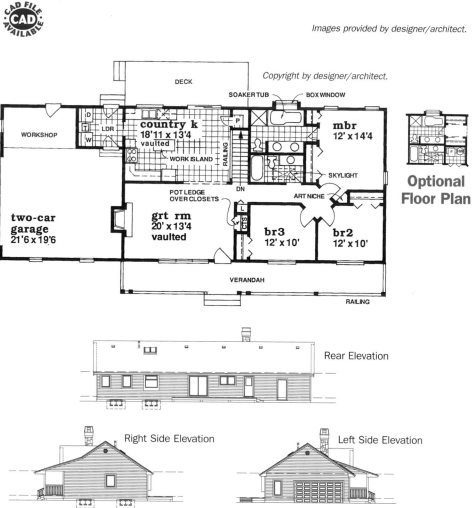

Plan #401025

Dimensions: 70' W x 34' D

Levels: 1

Square Footage: 1,408

Bedrooms: 3

Bathrooms: 2

Foundation: Basement, crawl space

Materials List Available: Yes

Price Category: B

An eyebrow dormer and a large veranda give guests a warm country greeting outside, while inside vaulted ceilings lend a sense of spaciousness to this three-bedroom home.

Features:

- Front Entry: A broad veranda shelters this area.

- Kitchen: This bright country kitchen boasts an abundance of counter space and cup boards, a walk-in pantry, and an island workstation.

- Built-in Amenities: A number of built-ins adorn the interior, including a pot shelf over the entry coat closet, an art niche, and a skylight.

- Master Suite: A box-bay window and a spa-style tub highlight this retreat.

- Garage: The two-car garage provides a work shop area.

Images provided by designer/architect.

Copyright by designer/architect.

Optional Floor Plan

Rear Elevation

Right Side Elevation

Left Side Elevation

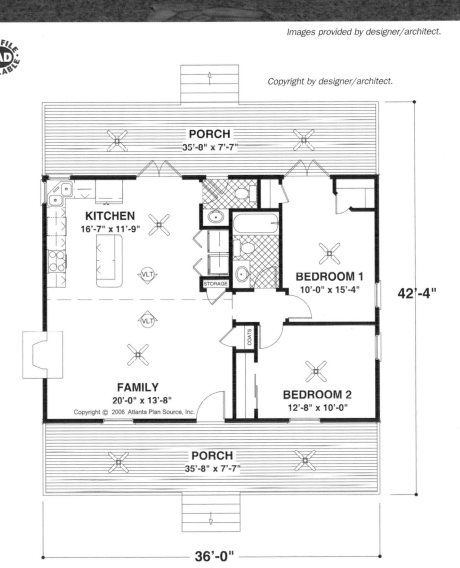

Plan #101147

Dimensions: 36' W x 42'4" D

Levels: 1

Square Footage: 953

Bedrooms: 2

Bathrooms: 1½

Foundation: Crawl space

Materials List Available: No

Price Category: B

Relax on the rocking chair porches of this home.

Features:

- Porches: A front and a rear porch are wonderful for entertaining with friends or family, or relaxing with a book.

- Family Room: This family room shares a vaulted ceiling with the kitchen, which has a sunny corner double sink, roomy center island/snack bar.

- Laundry Center: Conveiently located off the kitchen, this laundry area will ensure you won't have to run around with loads of clothing while doing other chores.

- Bedrooms: Two bedrooms share a full bath. Bedroom 1 opens out to the rear porch for added convenience.

PORCH
35'-0" x 7'-7"

KITCHEN
16'-7" x 11'-9"

STORAGE

BEDROOM 1
10'-0" x 15'-4"

COATS

FAMILY
20'-0" x 13'-8"

Copyright © 2006 Atlanta Plan Source, Inc.

BEDROOM 2
12'-8" x 10'-0"

PORCH
35'-8" x 7'-7"

42'-4"

36'-0"

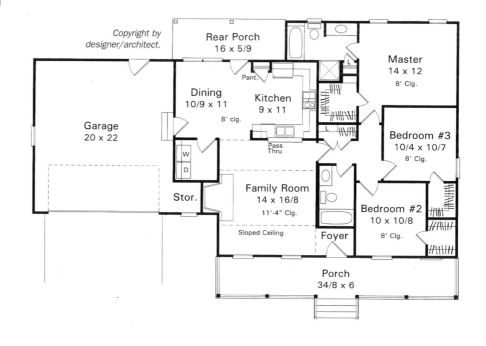

Plan #251001

Dimensions: 61'3" W x 40'6" D

Levels: 1

Square Footage: 1,253

Bedrooms: 3

Bathrooms: 2

Foundation: Crawl space, slab

Materials List Available: Yes

Price Category: B

• Master Bedroom: This master bedroom features a large walk-in closet. It has its own master bath with a single vanity, a tub, and a walk-in shower.

• Garage: This attached garage provides plenty of extra storage space, as well as parking for two cars.

This charming country home has a classic full front porch for enjoying summertime breezes.

Features:

• Ceiling Height: 8 ft.

• Foyer: Guests will walk through the front porch into this foyer, which opens to the family room.

• Screened Porch: A second porch is screened and is located at the rear of the home off the dining room, so your guests can step out for a bit of fresh air after dinner.

• Family Room: Family and friends will be drawn to this large open space, with its handsome fireplace and sloped ceiling.

• Kitchen: This open and airy kitchen is a pleasure in which to work. It has ample counter space and a pantry.

Plan #341019

Dimensions: 44' W x 32' D

Levels: 1

Square Footage: 1,258

Bedrooms: 3

Bathrooms: 2

Foundation: Crawl space; basement or slab for fee

Materials List Available: Yes

Price Category: B

This quaint country home has a something for everyone.

Features:

- **Kitchen:** This U-shaped kitchen has plenty of counter space and opens to the dining area.

- **Family Room:** This large gathering area welcomes you home and features a vaulted ceiling.

- **Master Suite:** This suite features a private bathroom with double vanities and a walk-in closet.

- **Bedrooms:** Two secondary bedrooms have large closets and share a hall bathroom.

Images provided by designer/architect.

CAD FILE AVAILABLE

Copyright by designer/architect.

SMARTtip

Resin Outdoor Furniture

Resin furniture is made of molded plastic. Most resin pieces are quite affordable, but lacquered resin with brass fittings is a high-end item. Resin doesn't corrode and cleans easily, but a scratched finish cannot be repaired. Lacquered resin can be touched up, however.

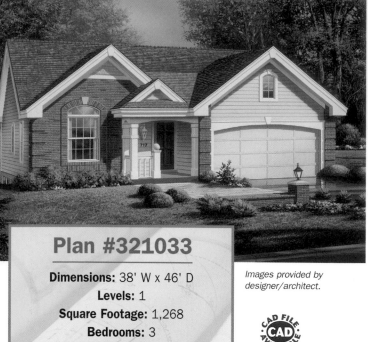

Plan #321033

Dimensions: 38' W x 46' D

Levels: 1

Square Footage: 1,268

Bedrooms: 3

Bathrooms: 2

Foundation: Basement

Materials List Available: Yes

Price Category: B

Images provided by designer/architect.

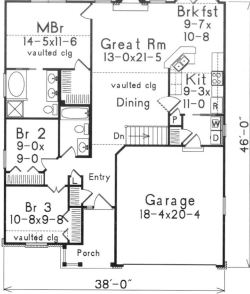

Copyright by designer/architect.

Plan #281011

Dimensions: 50' W x 54' D

Levels: 1

Square Footage: 1,314

Bedrooms: 3

Bathrooms: 2

Foundation: Basement

Materials List Available: Yes

Price Category: B

Images provided by designer/architect.

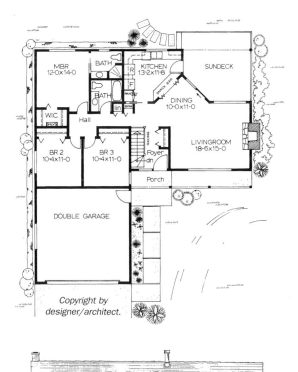

Copyright by designer/architect.

Rear Elevation

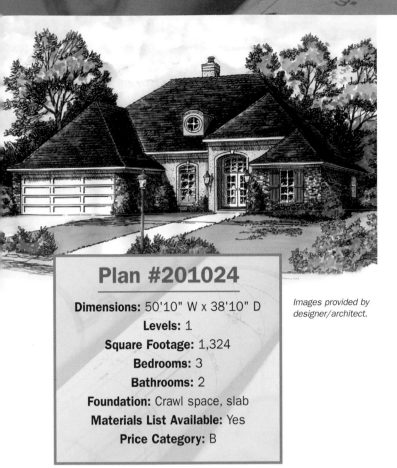

mbr
13 x 12

sto
6x6

garage
20 x 20

kit
8^2 x 11

dining
11^2 x 12

br 3
12 x 12^6

living
16^2 x 17

br 2
12 x 13

por

Images provided by designer/architect.

Copyright by designer/architect.

Plan #201024

Dimensions: 50'10" W x 38'10" D

Levels: 1

Square Footage: 1,324

Bedrooms: 3

Bathrooms: 2

Foundation: Crawl space, slab

Materials List Available: Yes

Price Category: B

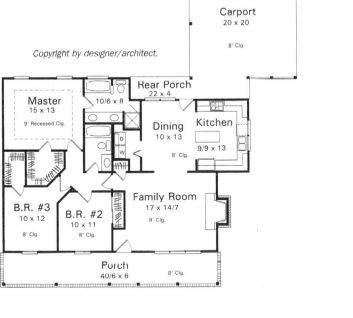

Storage
20 x 6   8' Clg.

Carport
20 x 20

8' Clg.

Copyright by designer/architect.

Master
15 x 13
9' Recessed Clg.

Rear Porch
22 x 4

Dining
10 x 13
8' Clg.

Kitchen
9/9 x 13

B.R. #3
10 x 12
8' Clg.

B.R. #2
10 x 11
8' Clg.

Family Room
17 x 14/7
9' Clg.

Porch
40/6 x 6   8' Clg.

Plan #251002

Dimensions: 55'6" W x 64'3" D

Levels: 1

Square Footage: 1,333

Bedrooms: 3

Bathrooms: 2

Foundation: Crawl space, slab

Materials List Available: Yes

Price Category: B

Images provided by designer/architect.

CAD FILE
CAD
AVAILABLE

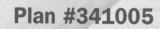

Plan #341005

Dimensions: 66' W x 30' D

Levels: 1

Square Footage: 1,334

Bedrooms: 3

Bathrooms: 2

Foundation: Crawl space; basement or slab for fee

Materials List Available: Yes

Price Category: B

Images provided by designer/architect.

CAD FILE AVAILABLE

This quaint country home has a welcoming front porch to greet your guests.

Features:

- Kitchen: This U-shaped kitchen has plenty of counter space and opens to the dining area. The raised bar leads to the living room.

- Living Room: This large gathering area welcomes you to the home, inviting you to sit by the cozy fireplace and relax.

- Master Suite: This suite features a walk-in closet and a private bathroom with double vanities.

- Bedrooms: Two secondary bedrooms have large closets and share a hall bathroom.

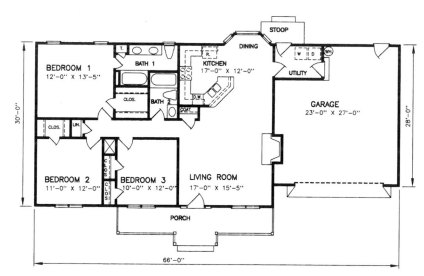

Copyright by designer/architect.

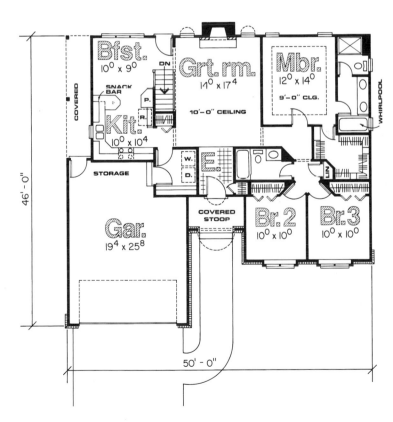

Images provided by designer/architect.

Plan #121060

Dimensions: 50' W x 46' D

Levels: 1

Square Footage: 1,339

Bedrooms: 3

Full Bathrooms: 2

Foundation: Basement

Materials List Available: Yes

Price Category: B

You'll love this compact design if you're looking for either a starter home or a luxurious place to spend your retirement years.

Features:

- Foyer: A covered stoop and arched entry open to this gracious foyer, where you'll love to greet guests.

- Great Room: From the foyer, you'll walk into this large area with its 10-ft. ceilings. A fireplace gives you a cozy spot on chilly days and cool evenings.

- Kitchen: This kitchen is truly step-saving and convenient. In addition to plenty of counter and storage space, it features a snack bar and an adjoining breakfast area.

- Master Suite: A 9-ft. ceiling gives a touch of elegance to the bedroom, and the walk-in closet adds practicality. In the bath, you'll find two vanities and a whirlpool tub.

- Garage: There's room for storage, a work bench, and three cars in this huge garage.

Copyright by designer/architect.

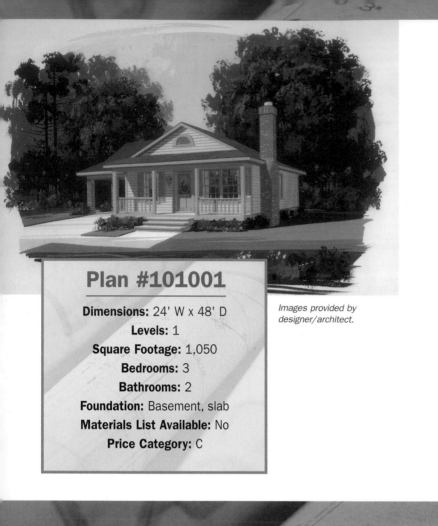

Plan #101001

Dimensions: 24' W x 48' D

Levels: 1

Square Footage: 1,050

Bedrooms: 3

Bathrooms: 2

Foundation: Basement, slab

Materials List Available: No

Price Category: C

Images provided by designer/architect.

Plan #321035

Dimensions: 55'8" W x 46' D

Levels: 1

Square Footage: 1,384

Bedrooms: 2

Bathrooms: 2

Foundation: Walk-out basement

Materials List Available: Yes

Price Category: B

Images provided by designer/architect.

Copyright by designer/architect.

CAD FILE AVAILABLE

Rear View

Optional Basement Level Floor Plan

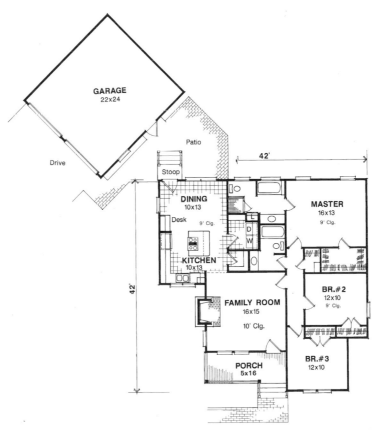

Plan #251003

Dimensions: 42' W x 42' D

Levels: 1

Square Footage: 1,393

Bedrooms: 3

Bathrooms: 2

Foundation: Crawl space or slab

Materials List Available: Yes

Price Category: B

Images provided by designer/architect.

Come home to this three-bedroom home with front porch and unattached garage.

Features:

- **Family Room:** This room feels large and warm, with its high ceiling and cozy fireplace.

- **Kitchen:** This island kitchen with dining area has plenty of cabinet space.

- **Master Bedroom:** This large master bedroom features a walk-in closet and a view of the backyard.

- **Master Bath:** Located in the rear of the home, this master bath features a soaking tub and a separate shower.

Copyright by designer/architect.

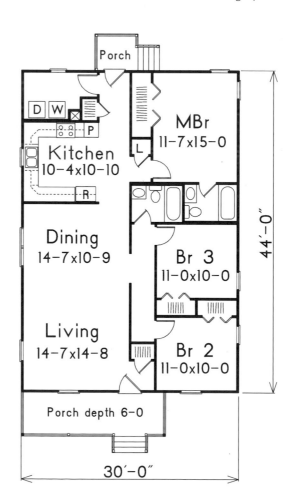

Plan #321121

Dimensions: 30' W x 44' D

Levels: 1

Square Footage: 1,320

Bedrooms: 3

Bathrooms: 2

Foundation: Crawl space

Materials List Available: Yes

Price Category: B

Images provided by designer/architect.

You'll love this adorable home, with all of its amenities in its small footprint.

Features:

• Front Porch: Relax with friends and family, or greet guests on this covered front porch.

• Living Room: You'll love to entertain in this living room, which is open to the dining room and close to the kitchen.

• Master Suite: Located in the back of the home for privacy, this master suite is perfect for unwinding at the end of a long day.

Porch

DW

P

L

MBr
11-7x15-0

Kitchen
10-4x10-10

R

Dining
14-7x10-9

Br 3
11-0x10-0

Living
14-7x14-8

Br 2
11-0x10-0

44'-0"

Porch depth 6-0

30'-0"

Copyright by designer/architect.

Plan #351012

Dimensions: 30' W x 32' D
Levels: 1
Square Footage: 600
Bedrooms: 1
Bathrooms: 1
Foundation: Crawl space, slab, or basement
Materials List Available: Yes
Price Category: A

This home is designed for the woods, the lake, or the beach for a weekend getaway. It is the perfect house to relax in all summer or winter long.

CAD FILE AVAILABLE

Images provided by designer/architect.

Features:

• Living Room: Just off the entry porch is this open living room with fireplace.

• Kitchen: This nice-size kitchen, with a raised bar into the living room, has plenty of cabinet space.

• Rear Porch: This rear porch is located just off the kitchen.

• Storage: A wonderful 12 x 30-ft. attic storage space, floored for all the "stuff" you need, is 8 ft. tall in the middle.

Rear Elevation

Covered Or Screened Porch 10 x 6
Rear Porch 20 x 6
C
C
TUB/SHOWER
Bath 5-6 x 9
KITCHEN 12-6 x 9-2
RANGE
W/D
P
Bedroom 12 x 12-6
RAISED BAR
Ref.
PULL-DOWN STAIRS
Bonus Room 12 x 7-4
C
Living Room 18 X 11
FIREPLACE
Front Porch 30 x 6

Optional Floor Plan for Basement

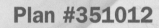

Covered Or Screened Porch 10 x 6
Rear Porch 20 x 6
TUB/SHOWER
Bath 5-6 x 9-2
KITCHEN 12-6 x 9-2
RANGE
W/C
P
Master Bedroom 12 x 13-8
RAISED BAR
Ref.
C
C
PULL-DOWN STAIRS
Down To Basement
Living Room 18 X 11
FIREPLACE
HANDRAIL
Front Porch 30 x 6

Copyright by designer/architect.

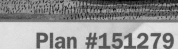

Plan #151279

Dimensions: 51'6" W x 49' D

Levels: 1

Square Footage: 1,485

Bedrooms: 3

Bathrooms: 2

Foundation: Basement, crawl space, slab, or walkout

CompleteCost List Available: Yes

Price Category: B

Welcome friends and neighbors on the cozy front porch of this home.

Features:

• **Great Room:** Leading your guests through the foyer, you'll enter a spacious great room with convenient access to the dining room.

• **Rear Grilling Porch:** Entertaining becomes simple for the grill masters on the convenient rear grilling porch with access to the great room.

• **Kitchen:** This fully functional kitchen is perfect for any chef. The adjoining breakfast room is a wonderful place to enjoy a meal or a cup of coffee.

• **Master Suite:** As the night falls and your guests leave, retreat to your master bath and relax in the whirlpool tub.

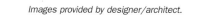
Images provided by designer/architect.

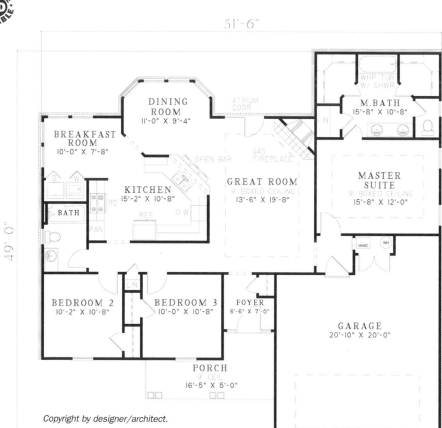

Copyright by designer/architect.

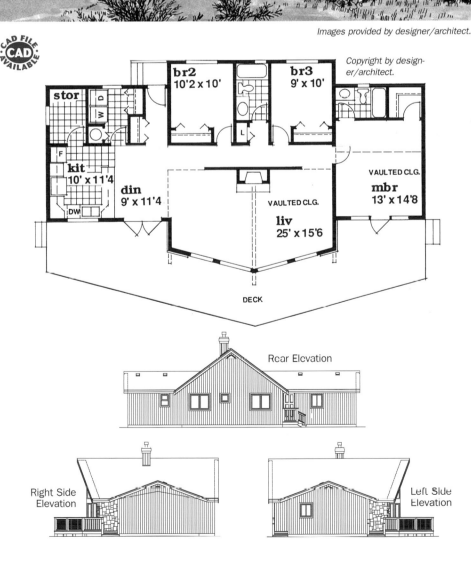

Plan #401022

Dimensions: 58'6" W x 41' D

Levels: 1

Square Footage: 1,495

Bedrooms: 3

Bathrooms: 2

Foundation: Basement

Materials List Available: Yes

Price Category: B

Images provided by designer/architect.

Copyright by designer/architect.

This three-bedroom cottage has just the right rustic mix of vertical wood siding and stone accents. Inside, the living is pure resort-style comfort.

Features:

- **High Ceilings:** Vaulted ceilings are featured throughout the living room and master bedroom.

- **Living Room:** This room has a fireplace and full-height windows overlooking the deck.

- **Dining Room:** This room features double-door access to the deck

- **Master Bedroom:** This principal sleeping area has a single door that opens to the deck.

- **Bedrooms:** Two family bedrooms share a bathroom that is situated between them.

Copyright by
designer/architect.

*Images provided by
designer/architect.*

Plan #171002

Dimensions: 67' W x 40' D

Levels: 1

Square Footage: 1,458

Bedrooms: 3

Bathrooms: 2

Foundation: Crawl space, slab

Materials List Available: Yes

Price Category: B

SMARTtip

Accent Landscape Lighting

Accent highlights elements in your landscape. It creates ambiance and helps integrate the garden with the deck. Conventional low-voltage floodlights are excellent for creating effects such as wall grazing, silhouetting, and uplighting.

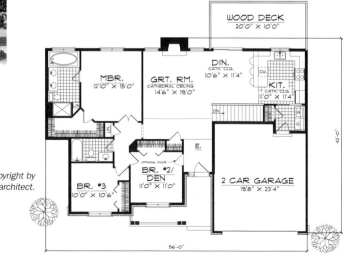

Rear Elevation

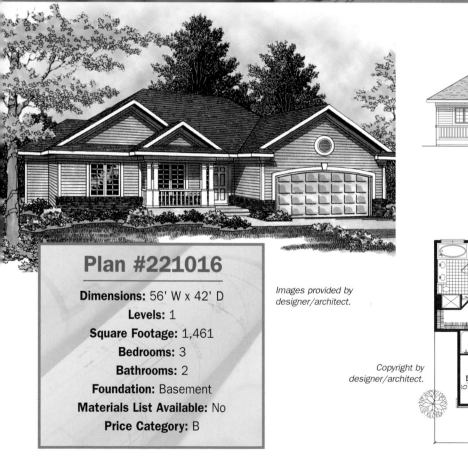

Plan #221016

Dimensions: 56' W x 42' D

Levels: 1

Square Footage: 1,461

Bedrooms: 3

Bathrooms: 2

Foundation: Basement

Materials List Available: No

Price Category: B

*Images provided by
designer/architect.*

Copyright by
designer/architect.

Flooring

Selecting a flooring material is one of the most important decisions you will make when decorating a room. The right material can enhance the color scheme and the overall look of the room, and flooring provides a unique tactile component to the design.

If you are are acting as your own designer, one of the first things you should do is learn about the various types of flooring—from wood to stone to vinyl—on today's market. The choices are myriad and innovations in technology have widened the range of finishes.

Choices in Wood

In bygone eras, a wood floor was simply one that was created by laying wide wood planks side by side. Later, as the milling of lumber improved, homeowners were able to choose narrower planks that look more refined than rustic. Parquet floors were created by woodcrafters with a flair for the dramatic and an appreciation of the artistic richness of wood grains set in nonlinear patterns.

Today's manufacturers have made it possible to have it all. The wood floor, factory- or custom-stained to suit a particular style or mood in a room, is still a traditional favorite. It's readily available in strips of 1 to 2¼ inches wide, or in country-style planks of 3 to 8 inches wide. The formal, sophisticated look of a parquet floor is unparalleled for richness of visual texture.

Types of Wood Flooring

Wood varieties available as a surface material are vast, and cost varies widely, depending on the type and grade of wood and on the choice of design.

Softwoods, like pine and fir, are often used to make simple tongue-and-groove floorboards. These floors are less expensive than hardwoods but also less durable. The hardwoods—maple, birch, oak, ash—are far less likely to mar with normal use. A hardwood floor is not indestructible; however, it will stand up to demanding use.

Both hardwoods and softwoods are graded according to their color, grain, and imperfections. The top of the line is known as clear, followed by select, No. 1 common, and No. 2 common. In addition to budget considerations, the decision whether to pay top dollar for clear wood or to economize with a lesser grade depends on use factors and on the design objectives. For example, if you plan to install a wood floor in a small room and then cover most of it with an area rug, the No. 2 common grade may be a good choice; lesser grades are also fine for informal rooms where a few defects just enhance a lived-in look. If your design calls for larger areas of rich wood grain that will be exposed, with scatter rugs used for color accents, a clear or select grade will make an attractive choice.

Finishing Options

Color stains—reds, blues, and greens—may work in settings where a casual or rustic feeling is desired. This, however, is a departure from the traditional use of

Wood flooring, below, fits well in both formal and informal spaces.

Laminate flooring, opposite, can mimic the look of real wood or natural stone.

Laminate Flooring

Laminate flooring is the great pretender among flooring materials. When your creative side tells you to install wood but your practical side knows it just won't hold up in the traffic-heavy location for which you're considering it, a wood floor look-alike might be just the thing. Faux wood and faux stone laminate floors provide you with the look you want, tempered with physical wear and care properties that you and your family can live with. Laminate is particularly suited to rooms where floors are likely to see heavy duty—kitchens, family rooms, hallways, and children's bedrooms and playrooms—anywhere stain and scratch resistance and easy cleanup count. Prolonged exposure to moisture will damage some laminate products, but many can now be used in wet areas. Manufacturers of laminate offer warranties against staining, scratching, cracking, and peeling for up to 25 years.

Laminate is made from paper impregnated with melamine, an organic resin, and bonded to a core of particleboard, fiberboard, or other wood by-products. It can be laid over virtually any subflooring surface, including wood and concrete. It can also be applied on top of an existing wood, ceramic, or vinyl tile, as well as vinyl or other sheet flooring. You can even install it over certain types of carpeting, but check the manufacturer's guidelines before doing so.

Installation and Care

The installation of laminate flooring is a reasonably quick and relatively easy do-it-yourself project. It requires sheets of a special foam underlayment followed by the careful placement, cutting, and gluing of the laminate.

Laminate is available in sheets that are ideal when your design calls for a uniform look, such as monotone stone, or a linear design that mimics strip or plank wood flooring. Laminate planks, squares, and blocks offer added design flexibility: with them, you can design your own tile patterns, lay strips of wood-look planks with alternating "stain" finishes, or border your floor with a contrasting color.

---

wood. Wood is not typically used to deliver color impact; instead it blends with and subtly enhances its surroundings. Natural wood stains range from light ash tones to deep, coffee-like colors. Generally, lighter stains make a room feel less formal, and darker, richer stains suggest a stately atmosphere. As with lighter colors, lighter stains create a feeling of openness; darker stains foster a more intimate feeling and can reduce the visual vastness of a large space.

Installation

If the design plan calls for the laying of unfinished wood strips, factor the cost of hiring a skilled professional into your budget. Many manufacturers offer products with installation kits that make wood flooring a do-it-yourself option for those whose skills are good but don't necessarily approach a professional carpenter's level. Some make strips or planks already finished and sealed. Most parquet tiles come finished and sealed as well.

Vinyl Sheet & Tile Flooring

Like laminate, resilient flooring is also available in design-friendly sheet or tile form. Resilient floors can be made from a variety of materials, including linoleum, asphalt, cork, or rubber. However, the most commonly used material in manufacturing today's resilient floors for homes is vinyl.

Price, durability, and easy maintenance make resilient flooring an attractive and popular choice. Do-it-yourself installation, an option even for those who are not particularly skilled, can mean further savings.

Sheet versus Tiles

Resilient flooring comes in an enormous array of colors and patterns, plus many of the flooring styles have a textured surface. With the tiles, you can combine color and pattern in limitless ways. Even the sheet form of resilient flooring can be customized with inlay strips.

Cushioned sheet vinyl offers the most resilience. It provides excellent stain resistance; it's comfortable and quiet underfoot and easy to maintain, with no-wax and never-wax finishes often available. These features make the floor especially attractive for areas with lots of kid traffic. Beware though: only the more expensive grades show an acceptable degree of resistance to nicking and denting. In rooms where furniture is often moved around, this could be a problem. Although the range of colors, patterns, and surface textures is wide, sheet floor-

Vinyl sheet flooring, left, is a good choice for high-traffic areas, such as kitchens, family rooms, and playrooms. Most products have a no-wax finish that is easy to maintain.

Vinyl flooring, above, comes in a variety of styles and colors. Tiles and sheet flooring can look like ceramic tiles and natural stone.

Ceramic tile, opposite, offers a number of possibilities—from simple patterns to more elaborate designs that feature borders and inlays.

ing is not as flexible as vinyl tile when it comes to customizing your look.

Regular sheet vinyl is less expensive than the cushioned types, but it carries the same disadvantages and is slightly less resilient. Except for the availability of no-wax finishes, a vinyl tile floor is as stain resistant and as easy to maintain as the sheet-vinyl products. Increased design possibilities are the trade-off.

Here, as with other flooring materials, one possible way out of the choice maze is to take the unconventional step of mixing flooring materials. For example, use a durable cushioned sheet vinyl in more trafficked areas, but frame it with a pretty vinyl tile or laminate border.

Ceramic Choices

Ceramic tile—actually fired clay—is an excellent choice for areas subject to a lot of traffic and in rooms where resistance to moisture and stains is needed. These features, combined with easy cleanup, have made ceramic tile a centuries-old tradition for flooring, walls, and ceilings in bathrooms and kitchens. Color, texture, and pattern choices available today make ceramic tile the most versatile flooring option in terms of design possibilities.

Tile Options

Some handcrafted ceramic tiles are very costly, but manufacturers have created a market full of design and style options.

Tiles come in a variety of sizes, beginning with 1-inch-square mosaic tiles up to large 16 x 16-inch squares. Other shapes, such as triangles, diamonds, and rectangles, are also available. Tile textures range from shiny to matte-finished and from glass-smooth to ripple-surfaced. Tiles are available either glazed or unglazed. Glazed tiles have a hard, often colored, surface that is applied during the firing process; the resulting finish can range from glossy to matte. Unglazed tiles, such as terra-cotta or quarry tiles, have a matte finish, are porous, and need to be sealed to prevent staining.

Consider using accent borders to create unique designs, such as a faux area rug, that visually separate sections of a room or separate one room from another. When added in a random pattern, embossed accent tiles add interest, variety, and elegance to an expanse of single-colored tiles.

Alas, no surfacing material is perfect. Ceramic tile offers long-lasting beauty, design versatility, and simplicity of maintenance, but it also has some hard-to-live-with features. Tile is cold underfoot, noisy when someone walks across it in hard-soled shoes, and not at all resilient—always expect the worst when something breakable falls on a tile floor. If you have infants and toddlers around, it may be best to wait a few years for your tiled floor.

Natural Stone

Like ceramic tile, stone and marble are classified as "non-resilients." Like tile, these materials offer richness of color, durability, moisture and stain resistance, and ease of maintenance. They also share with tile the drawbacks of being cold to the touch, noisy to walk on, and unforgivingly hard.

Stone and marble floors are clearly, unmistakably natural. As remarkably good as some faux surfaces look, no product manufactured today actually matches the rustic irregularity and random color variation of natural stone.

Picking a Flooring Material

Now that you've got the facts about each floor surface option, picking the right one for your design will be much less confusing. The following steps can make it downright simple.

Step 1: Make a "Use/Abuse" Analysis. Begin by asking yourself the most important question: How will this room used? Your answer should tell you just what kind of traffic the future floor surface will endure. With a relatively expensive investment like a floor, it's best not to guess. Instead, use this system to arrive at an accurate use/abuse analysis.

On a piece of paper, make columns headed "Who" and "Activities," and then list who in the family will use the room and what activities will occur there. Will the kids play with toys on the floor? Will they do arts and crafts projects with paint, glue, and glitter? Will the family gather on Saturday afternoons and snack while watching a football game on television? Is it a formal living room where you will entertain your friends and business clients? Is it a busy kitchen? Does the hallway extend from your front entrance or from a busier back door where the kids will drop off their hockey skates?

The answers to these questions will help you to determine how durable and resilient a flooring surface needs to be, whether warmth and softness are requirements, and how much maintenance will be necessary to keep the surface clean.

Step 2: Determine Your Design Objectives. Your choices are limited by the other elements in the room. Your color choices can enhance the color palette you are planning. Because you will be starting from scratch—including walls, furniture, and accessories—you have more flexibility, although your job is a bit more complex and involves more decisions.

Once you've determined your design objectives, compare your use/abuse analysis

High-traffic areas, below left, require flooring that can stand up to abuse.

Laminate flooring, below right, is a good choice for a variety of rooms.

to the types of flooring that meet both your style and use needs. From the list of options that are left, you can narrow down your choices even more.

Step 3: Draw and Use a Floor Plan.

After you have completed the use/abuse analysis and the list of design objectives, draw up a floor plan—a separate one for experimenting with your flooring ideas. Follow these guidelines: measure the length and width of the room, and plot it on graph paper, using a scale of 1 inch to 1 foot. If your room is larger than 8 x 10 feet, you can tape two pieces of 8½- x 11-inch graph paper together. Measure and mark the locations of entryways and any permanent features in the room, such as cabinets, fixtures, or appliances.

Make several photocopies of your floor plan. Reserve one copy as a template. Use the other copies for previewing pattern ideas for flooring that comes in tiles (ceramic, vinyl, or carpeting tiles). Buy

multicolored pencils, and fill in your grid. You'll be able to determine not only how the pattern will look but also how many tiles of various colors you'll need to buy to complete the project. Don't forget to include such items as borders and inlays.

Step 4: Convert Your Overall Budget to Cost per Square Foot.

After you've completed the use/abuse analysis, determined your design objectives, and created a floor plan, the next step is determining cost.

Most flooring is priced in terms of square feet. To determine how many square feet are in your room, round the measurements up to the next foot. Then simply multiply the length by the width. For example, for a room measuring 10 feet 4 inches x 12 feet 6 inches, round the figures to 11 x 13 feet. Multiply 11 x 13 feet (that's 143 square feet). You will end up with extra flooring, but it is better to have more than less.

Some flooring—like carpeting—is priced in terms of square yards. To determine the number of square yards in your room, divide the number of square feet by nine. In our example, there are just under 16 square yards in 143 square feet.

Let's say you have a budget of $850 to purchase tile for your 10-foot-4-inch x 12-foot-6-inch room. For the sake of the illustration, let's assume your subflooring is adequate, you have the tools, and the cost of adhesive and grout for your room is about $75. That leaves you with $775. To determine how much you can spend per tile, divide the remainder by the number of square feet in the room. In our example, $775 divided by 143 square feet equals about $5.40 per square foot of tile.

Light colors, below left, make a room feel more open than darker colors.

Consider the rest of the room, below, when selecting flooring.

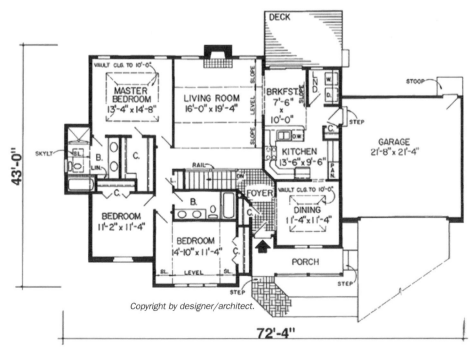

Plan #391034

Dimensions: 72'4" W x 43' D

Levels: 1

Square Footage: 1,737

Bedrooms: 3

Bathrooms: 2

Foundation: Crawl space, slab, or basement

Materials List Available: Yes

Price Category: C

Images provided by designer/architect.

- Kitchen: This close-knit kitchen with pantry embraces a cheerful breakfast nook with sliding doors to the deck.
- Master Suite: This suite is a visual treat, with its own vaulted ceiling as well as a skylight over the master bathtub and shower area.

- Bedrooms: The two secondary bedrooms are pampered with good closeting, proximity to a shared bath with double sink vanities, and wonderful windows that enhance the spacious atmosphere.

This lovely home brings together traditional single-level architectural elements, current features, and just the right amount of living space.

Features:

- Entry: A demure covered porch and well-mannered foyer deliver all the important rooms.

- Dining Room: This formal room features exquisite vaulted ceilings.

Rear Elevation

Copyright by designer/architect.

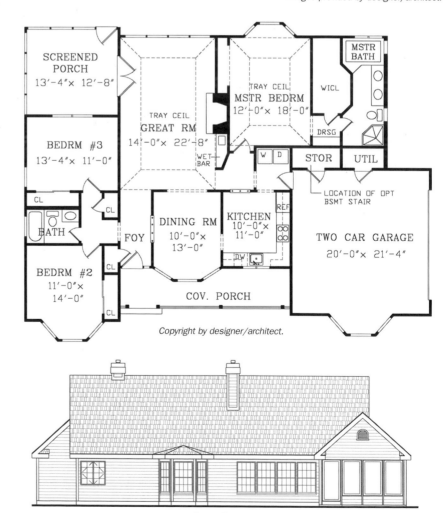

Plan #131007

Dimensions: 59'10" W x 47'8" D
Levels: 1
Square Footage: 1,595
Bedrooms: 3
Bathrooms: 2
Foundation: Crawl space, slab, basement, or walkout
Materials List Available: Yes
Price Category: D

Images provided by designer/architect.

Imagine living in this home, with its traditional country comfort and individual brand of charm.

Features:

- **Exterior elements:** The mixture of a front porch with a cameo front door, decorative posts, bay windows, and dormers will delight you.

- **Great Room:** A tray ceiling gives distinction to this large room, and a wet bar eases entertaining.

- **Screened Porch:** At dusk and dawn, this porch is sure to be your favorite outdoor spot.

- **Kitchen:** Eat any meal in this large kitchen for a touch of homey charm.

- **Dining Room:** Perfect for hosting a formal dinner, this bayed dining room can increase your enjoyment of simple family meals.

- **Master Bedroom:** For the sake of privacy, this room is somewhat secluded. Decorate to emphasize the elegant tray ceiling.

Copyright by designer/architect.

Rear Elevation

Alternate Front View

Foyer / Dining Room

Great Room

Add the Extras

Simple or plain, it's the little conveniences and miscellaneous touches that push the dining experience to perfection. Here are some extra things to think about.

- You can never have too many serving trays when you entertain outside. For carrying food or drinks from the kitchen or the grill, trays are indispensable.

- A serving cart on wheels makes a perfect movable outdoor bar and provides an additional serving surface. Look for one at yard sales or buy one new.

- Chances are you won't have a sideboard, but a few small tables to hold excess items are great substitutes for one. They're also easier to position in the different places where you need them.

- For cooler weather or even a summer's evening with a bit of nip in the air, nothing beats an outdoor fireplace for comfort. You could build one into the house, but various types of stand-alone units are sold in home centers. To add a Southwest ambiance, consider a chiminea, a clay fireplace. Try burning some piñon pine, and you'll feel as if you're in Santa Fe. Be sure to follow manufacturers' instructions when using these fireplaces. You might also have to store them during the winter.

- Pots of fragrant plants—lavender, scented geraniums, flowering tobacco, or jasmine—provide a sensual aroma. Flowers such as roses climbing up an arbor or trellis are beautiful, evoke a romantic feeling, and lend a delicate scent to the atmosphere as well.

Nothing adds romance and intrigue to an evening soiree as candlelight does. Include just a few candles for an intimate dinner. Use more for a larger gathering, placing one or more on each table. Scatter luminaries around the yard. As the beautiful evening dusk begins, light candles, a few at a time, so your eyes can adjust to the dimming light. Not only do the candles illuminate the night in a magical way but they can also keep bugs at bay.

Plan #391019

Dimensions: 56' W x 32' D
Levels: 1
Square Footage: 1,792
Bedrooms: 3
Bathrooms: 1¾
Foundation: Basement
Materials List Available: Yes
Price Category: C

Images provided by designer/architect.

This southern-style cottage with sociable porch fits in almost anywhere, from a leafy lane to hillside or curbside and renders a lot of living space and hospitality.

Features:

• Family Room: This room features a central stone fireplace, plus two walls of windows to usher in the light. Sloping ceilings and decorative beams boost its rustic charm. An enormously generous space, it opens wide to the corner kitchen.

• Dining Room: This room has its own level of sophistication, including entry outside to the deck.

• Utility Areas: The family-sized pantry and laundry area are set off by themselves to avoid interference with everyday living.

• Master Suite: A leisurely hall leads to the master bedroom and private full bath, wide walk-in closets, and a trio of windows.

• Bedrooms: Across the hall the two secondary bedrooms share a roomy bath and a view of the front porch.

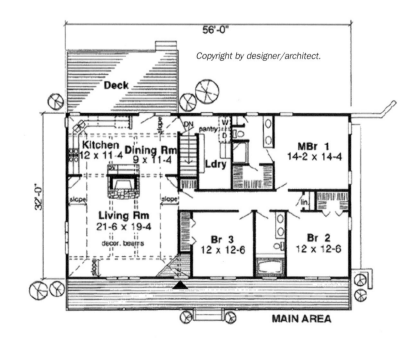

Copyright by designer/architect.

56'-0"

Deck

Kitchen
12 x 11-4

Dining Rm
9 x 11-4

pantry

Ldry

MBr 1
14-2 x 14-4

Living Rm
21-6 x 19-4

decor. beams

Br 3
12 x 12-6

Br 2
12 x 12-6

32'-0"

MAIN AREA

Images provided by designer/architect.

Plan #391039

Dimensions: 50' W x 45'4" D

Levels: 1

Square Footage: 1,539

Bedrooms: 3

Bathrooms: 2

Foundation: Crawl space, slab, or basement

Materials List Available: Yes

Price Category: C

A gabled roofline and easy-going front porch charm the exterior. Practical and pretty touches dramatize the interior.

Features:

- **Foyer:** This entry hall has a large walk-in closet.

- **Kitchen:** This kitchen's creative horizontal shape invites plenty of amenities. There is abundant cabinet space and a close-at-hand laundry facility.

- **Dining Room:** The kitchen's breakfast bar looks cheerfully into this formal room.

- **Master Bedroom:** A tray ceiling adds to the appeal of this room. The bump-out window seat invites breaks for daydreaming; a large walk-in closet handles wardrobes for two.

- **Master Bath:** This lavish master bathroom features a window over the tub.

- **Bedrooms:** The two additional bedrooms have their own unique styling, including excellent closet space and charming windows.

Copyright by designer/architect.

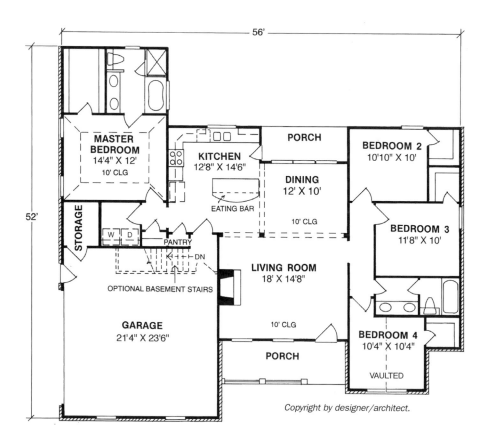

Plan #121177

Dimensions: 56' W x 52' D
Levels: 1
Square Footage: 1,539
Bedrooms: 4
Bathrooms: 2
Foundation: Slab; basement for fee
Materials List Available: Yes
Price Category: C

The open floor plan layout of this home makes it wonderful for entertaining

Features:

- Living Room: This spacious area is open to both the dining room and the kitchen. You and your guests will love to relax in front of the fireplace in this room.

- Kitchen: This kitchen is spacious enough to accommodate multiple helping hands.

- Master Suite: You'll love this master suite, complete with its large walk-in closet, dual sink vanity, and tub.

- Bedrooms: Family bedrooms share a full bath that includes a soaking tub. Each bed room has its own walk-in closet

MASTER BEDROOM 14'4" X 12' 10' CLG

KITCHEN 12'8" X 14'6"

PORCH

BEDROOM 2 10'10" X 10'

DINING 12' X 10'

EATING BAR

10' CLG

STORAGE

W | D

PANTRY

DN

OPTIONAL BASEMENT STAIRS

LIVING ROOM 18' X 14'8"

BEDROOM 3 11'8" X 10'

GARAGE 21'4" X 23'6"

10' CLG

PORCH

BEDROOM 4 10'4" X 10'4"

VAULTED

56'

52'

Images provided by designer/architect.

Plan #371050

Dimensions: 50' W x 49'6" D

Levels: 1

Square Footage: 1,542

Bedrooms: 3

Bathrooms: 2

Foundation: Slab

Materials List Available: No

Price Category: C

Simple elegance defines this traditional brick home, which with three bedrooms invites years of growth.

Features:

- **Family Room:** This large gathering room has a high ceiling and a cozy fireplace.

- **Dining Room:** The family room flows into this elegant dining area with a bay window.

- **Kitchen:** This gourmet kitchen with a raised bar looks into the family and dining rooms.

- **Master Suite:** This large suite has a step-up ceiling. The large master bath features two vanities, a soaking tub, a glass shower enclosure, and two walk-in closets.

- **Bedrooms:** The two large additional bedrooms share a convenient bathroom.

Copyright by designer/architect.

Plan #391021

Dimensions: 54' W x 48'4" D

Levels: 1

Square Footage: 1,568

Bedrooms: 3

Bathrooms: 2

Foundation: Crawl space, slab, or basement

Materials List Available: Yes

Price Category: C

Images provided by designer/architect.

A peaked porch roof and luminous Palladian window play up the exterior appeal of this ranch home, while other architectural components dramatize the interior.

Features:

- Living Room: There is a soaring ceiling in this living room, where a corner fireplace and built-in bookshelves provide cozy comfort.

- Dining Room: Open to the living room, this room features sliders to the wood deck, which makes it conducive to both casual and formal entertaining.

- Kitchen: This well-planned kitchen seems to have it all—a built-in pantry, a double sink, and a breakfast bar that feeds into the dining room. The bar provides additional serving space when needed.

- Master Suite: This private retreat is situated far from the public areas. A large walk-in closet with a private bath and double vanity add to the suite's intimate appeal.

- Bedrooms: The two additional bedrooms boast large closets and bright windows. The generous hall bathroom is located conveniently nearby.

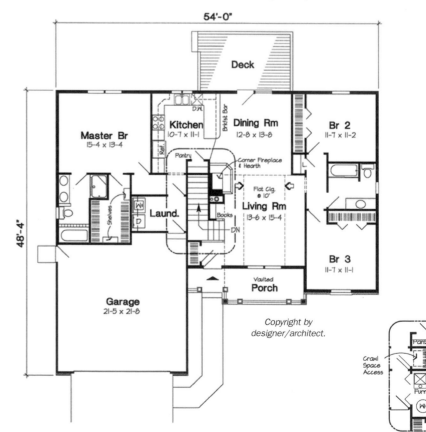

Copyright by designer/architect.

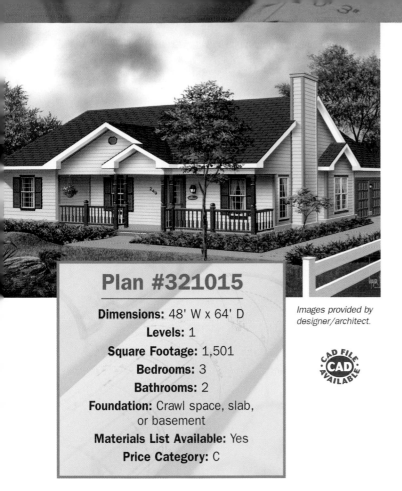

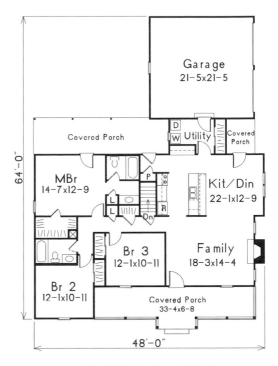

Plan #321015

Dimensions: 48' W x 64' D

Levels: 1

Square Footage: 1,501

Bedrooms: 3

Bathrooms: 2

Foundation: Crawl space, slab, or basement

Materials List Available: Yes

Price Category: C

CAD FILE AVAILABLE

Copyright by designer/architect.

Plan #151003

Dimensions: 51'6" W x 52'4" D

Levels: 1

Square Footage: 1,680

Bedrooms: 3

Bathrooms: 2

Foundation: Crawl space, slab, or basement

CompleteCost List Available: Yes

Price Category: C

CAD FILE AVAILABLE

Copyright by designer/architect.

Images provided by designer/architect.

Copyright by designer/architect.

Plan #221008

Dimensions: 60'4" W x 46' D

Levels: 1

Square Footage: 1,540

Bedrooms: 3

Bathrooms: 2

Foundation: Basement

Materials List Available: No

Price Category: C

Rear Elevation

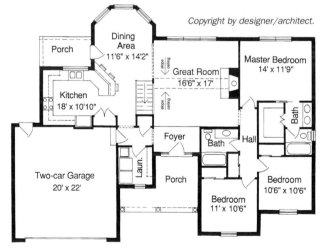

Copyright by designer/architect.

Images provided by designer/architect.

Plan #161003

Dimensions: 60' W x 47' D

Levels: 1

Square Footage: 1,508

Bedrooms: 3

Bathrooms: 2

Foundation: Basement

Materials List Available: Yes

Price Category: C

Rear Elevation

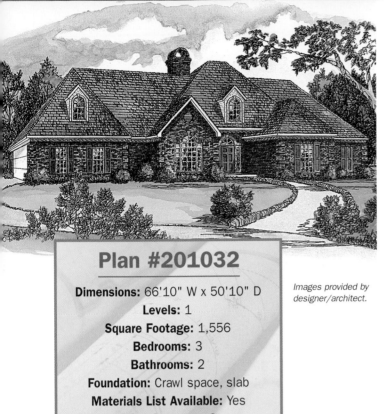

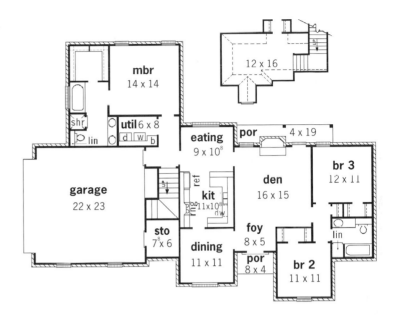

Plan #201032

Dimensions: 66'10" W x 50'10" D

Levels: 1

Square Footage: 1,556

Bedrooms: 3

Bathrooms: 2

Foundation: Crawl space, slab

Materials List Available: Yes

Price Category: C

Images provided by designer/architect.

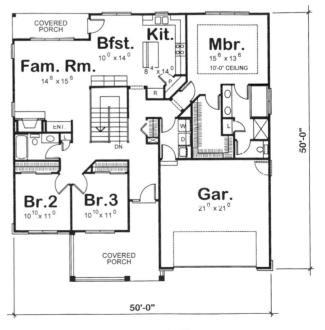

Plan #121011

Dimensions: 50' W x 50' D

Levels: 1

Square Footage: 1,724

Bedrooms: 3

Bathrooms: 2

Foundation: Slab, basement

Materials List Available: Yes

Price Category: C

Images provided by designer/architect.

This home, as shown in the photograph, may differ from the actual blueprints. For more detailed information, please check the floor plans carefully.

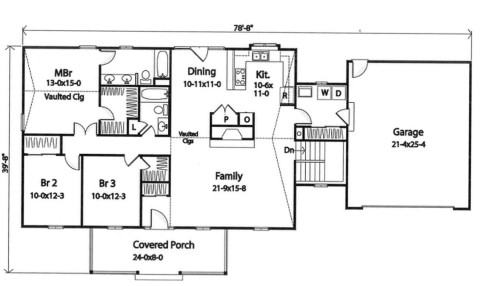

Plan #631065

Dimensions: 78'8" W x 39'8" D

Levels: 1

Square Footage: 1,682

Bedrooms: 3

Bathrooms: 2

Foundation: Basement

Materials List Available: Yes

Price Category: C

Images provided by designer/architect.

Dramatic ceilings create openness in this traditional ranch home.

Features:

- Laundry/Mud Room: A coat closet in the laundry/mud room helps organize household items.

- Kitchen: The kitchen features a step-saving U-shape and pantry for efficiency.

- Master Suite: The secluded master bedroom boasts vaulted ceilings, a walk-in closet, and private bath.

Copyright by designer/architect.

Plan #151009

Dimensions: 44' W x 86'2" D
Levels: 1
Square Footage: 1,601
Bedrooms: 3
Bathrooms: 2
Foundation: Crawl space, slab
CompleteCost List Available: Yes
Price Category: C

This can be the perfect home for a site with views you can enjoy in all seasons and at all times.

Features:

- **Porches:** Enjoy the front porch with its 10-ft. ceiling and the more private back porch where you can set up a grill or just get away from it all.

- **Foyer:** With a 10-ft. ceiling, this foyer opens to the great room for a warm welcome.

- **Great Room:** Your family will love the media center and the easy access to the rear porch.

- **Kitchen:** This well-designed kitchen is open to the dining room and the breakfast nook, which also opens to the rear porch.

- **Master Suite:** The bedroom has a 10-ft. boxed ceiling and a door to the rear. The bath includes a corner whirlpool tub with glass block windows.

- **Bedrooms:** Bedroom 2 has a vaulted ceiling, while bedroom 3 features a built-in desk.

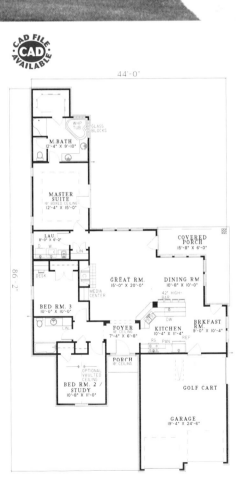

SMARTtip
Fertilizing Your Grass

Fertilizers contain nutrients balanced for different kinds of growth. The ratio of nutrients is indicated on the package by three numbers (for example, 10-10-10). The first specifies nitrogen content; the second, phosphorus; and the third, potash.

Nitrogen helps grass blades to grow and improves the quality and thickness of the turf. Fertilizers contain up to 30 percent nitrogen.

Phosphorus helps grass to develop a healthy root system. It also speeds up the maturation process of the plant.

Potash helps grass stay healthy by providing amino acids and proteins to the plants.

Plan #271060

Dimensions: 72' W x 64'8" D
Levels: 1
Square Footage: 1,726
Bedrooms: 2
Bathrooms: 2½
Foundation: Walkout basement
Materials List Available: No
Price Category: C

Comfortable living spaces such as a cozy study and a warm hearth room make this design one you'll love to come home to.

Features:

• **Great Room:** A spacious great room with a vaulted ceiling and wall of windows dazzles the main floor, and shares a two-way fireplace with the hearth room.

• **Hearth Room:** Strategically located, the hearth room adjoins both the dining room and kitchen -- let a crackling ire warm the ambience of any of your evening meals.

• **Master Suite:** The master suite basks in seclusion on the opposite corner of the home, and boasts a pampering whirlpool tub and a sizable walk-in closet.

Images provided by designer/architect.

Images provided by designer/architect.

Copyright by designer/architect.

Optional Lower Level Floor Plan

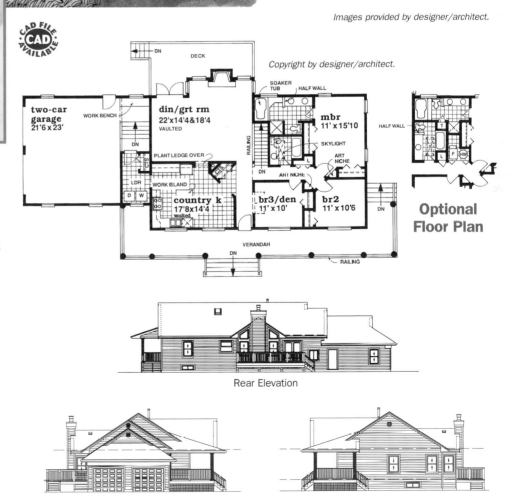

Plan #401026

Dimensions: 83' W x 40'6" D
Levels: 1
Square Footage: 1,578
Bedrooms: 3
Bathrooms: 2
Foundation: Basement
Materials List Available: Yes
Price Category: C

With a graceful pediment above and a sturdy, colonnaded veranda below, this quaint home was made for country living.

Features:

- **Foyer:** The veranda wraps slightly around on two sides of the facade and permits access to this central foyer with a den (or third bedroom) on the right and the country kitchen on the left.

- **Kitchen:** This functional kitchen features an island workspace and a plant ledge over the entry to the great room.

- **Great Room:** A fireplace warms this room and is flanked by windows overlooking the rear deck.

- **Dining Area:** This casually defined dining space has double-door access to the same deck as that off the great room.

Images provided by designer/architect.

Copyright by designer/architect.

Optional Floor Plan

Rear Elevation

Left Side Elevation

Right Side Elevation

Images provided by designer/architect.

Plan #351023

Dimensions: 61'8" W x 45'8" D

Levels: 1

Square Footage: 1,600

Bedrooms: 3

Bathrooms: 2

Foundation: Crawl space, slab, or basement

Materials List Available: Yes

Price Category: C

This beautiful three-bedroom home has everything your family needs to live the comfortable life.

Features:

- **Great Room:** Just off the foyer is this large room. It features a cozy fireplace and access to the rear covered porch.

- **Dining Room:** This formal room has large windows with a view of the backyard.

- **Kitchen:** This kitchen has an abundance of cabinets and counter space. It is open to the dining room.

- **Master Suite:** This isolated suite, with its jetted tub, separate shower, large closet, and dual vanities, is a perfect retreat.

- **Bedrooms:** The two secondary bedrooms have large closets and share a hall bathroom.

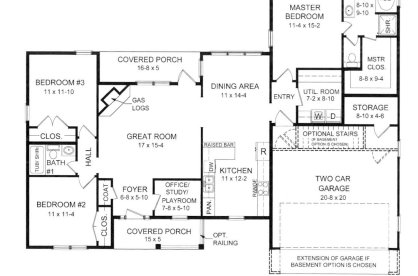

Copyright by designer/architect.

Plan #131001

Dimensions: 72'4" W x 32'4" D
Levels: 1
Square Footage: 1,615
Bedrooms: 3
Bathrooms: 2
Foundation: Crawl space, slab, basement, or walkout
Materials List Available: Yes
Price Category: D

Cathedral ceilings and illuminating skylights add drama and beauty to this practical ranch house.

Features:

Ceiling Height: 8 ft.

- **Front Porch:** Watch the rain in comfort from the covered front porch.

- **Foyer:** The stone-tiled foyer flows into the living areas.

- **Living Room:** Oriented towards the front of the house, the living room opens to the dining room and shares a lovely three-sided fireplace with the family room.

- **Family Room:** Conveniently located to share the fireplace with the living room, this room is bright and cheery thanks to its skylights as well as the sliding glass doors that open onto the rear patio.

- **Kitchen:** An island makes this sunny room both efficient and attractive.

- **Breakfast Nook:** Located just off the kitchen, this area can serve double-duty as a spot for kitchen visitors to sit.

- **Dining Room:** The open design between the dining and living rooms adds to the spacious feeling that the cathedral ceiling creates in this area.

- **Laundry Room:** This area opens from the kitchen for convenience.

- **Master Suite:** A walk-in closet makes this room practical, but the master bathroom with a skylight, dual-sink vanity, soaking tub, and separate shower makes it luxurious.

- **Bedrooms:** The two additional bedrooms share a bathroom.

Images provided by designer/architect.

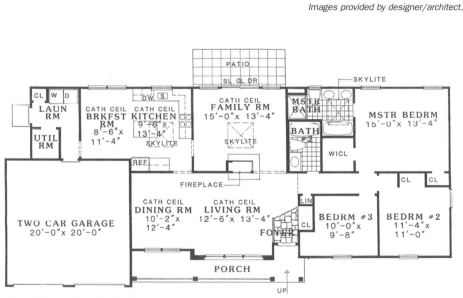

Copyright by designer/architect.

Plan #161007

Dimensions: 66'4" W x 43'10" D

Levels: 1

Square Footage: 1,611

Bedrooms: 3

Bathrooms: 2

Foundation: Basement, optional crawl space for no additional charge

Materials List Available: Yes

Price Category: C

A lovely front porch and an entry with sidelights invite you to experience the impressive amenities offered in this exceptional ranch home.

Features:

- **Great Room:** Grand openings, featuring columns from the foyer to this great room and continuing to the bayed dining area, convey an open, spacious feel. The fireplace and matching windows on the rear wall of the great room enhance this effect.

- **Kitchen:** This well-designed kitchen offers convenient access to the laundry and garage. It also features an angled counter with ample space and an abundance of cabinets.

- **Master Suite:** This deluxe master suite contains many exciting amenities, including a lavishly appointed dressing room and a large walk-in closet.

- **Porch:** Sliding doors lead to this delightful screened porch for relaxing summer interludes.

Images provided by designer/architect.

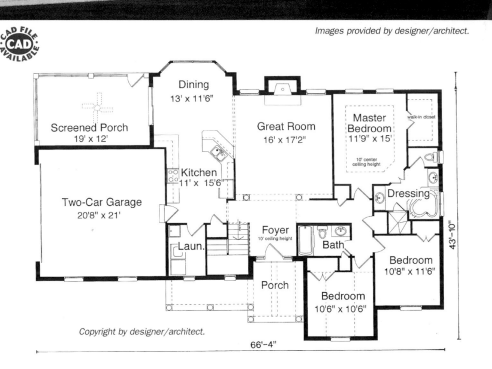

Copyright by designer/architect.

Rear Elevation

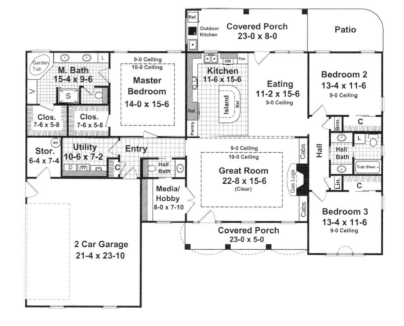

Images provided by designer/architect.

Copyright by designer/architect.

Plan #351102

Dimensions: 67' W x 56' D

Levels: 1

Square Footage: 2,000

Bedrooms: 3

Bathrooms: 2½

Foundation: Basement, crawl space or slab

Materials List Available: Yes

Price Category: F

This inviting home has European Country styling with upscale features.

Features:

• **Porches:** The front and rear covered porches add plenty of usable outdoor living space, and include that much-requested outdoor kitchen.

• **Great Room:** This expansive great room includes a beautiful trayed ceiling and features built-in cabinets and a gas fireplace.

• **Kitchen:** The spacious kitchen features an oversized island with a large eating bar and breakast area.

• **Master Suite:** This room has a raised ceiling and opens into the well-equipped bath with dual lavatories, oversized corner jet tub, and large his and her walk-in closets.

Plan #391025

Dimensions: 54' W x 48'4" D

Levels: 1

Square Footage: 1,625

Bedrooms: 3

Bathrooms: 2

Foundation: Crawl space, slab, or basement

Materials List Available: Yes

Price Category: C

Images provided by designer/architect.

This lovely home, ideal for starters or empty nesters, conveys rustic charm while maintaining clean contemporary lines.

Features:

- **Kitchen:** This functional U-shaped kitchen features an adjacent utility area that can serve as a pantry and direct access to the garage for unloading groceries after a shopping trip.

- **Fireplace:** This cozy two-sided fireplace joins the living room and dining room, which is open to the adjacent kitchen.

- **Den:** The roomy den (or guest bedroom) features a beautiful Palladian window.

- **Master Suite:** With plenty of elbowroom, this master suite has a large walk-in closet and bathroom with double sinks, a whirlpool tub, and separate shower.

54'-0"

48'-4"

open shelves

Dining Rm
11-9 x 12-11
9' clg.
brkfst bar

two-sided fireplace

Living Rm
13-8 x 17-8
9' clg.

9' clg.

railing

DN

Master Br
15-9 x 11-11
10'-5" clg.

whirlpool

Kitchen
11-9 x 12-9
9' clg.

DW
Ref.

utility/
pantry

8' clg.

Foy.

Den/Guest
11-11 x 12-11

Br 2
12-8 x 10-11

planter

Garage
20-5 x 21-5

**Main Level
Floor Plan**

Optional Floor Plan
Copyright by designer/architect.

Living Rm
13-8 x 17-8
9'-0" clg.

linen

storage

crawl
access

util/
pantry

w/h
furn.

Foy.

Alternate Foundation Plan

Plan #351006

Dimensions: 64' W x 39' D

Levels: 1

Square Footage: 1,638

Bedrooms: 3

Bathrooms: 2

Foundation: Crawl space, slab, or basement

Materials List Available: Yes

Price Category: C

Images provided by designer/architect.

This arched window and three-bedroom brick home offers traditional styling featuring an open floor plan.

Features:

- **Great Room:** This room, with its 10-ft.-high ceiling, features a fireplace and two large glass doors that provide access to the rear covered porch.

- **Dining Room:** Located just off the entry, this room has a view of the front yard.

- **Kitchen:** This kitchen has a raised bar and is open to the breakfast area.

- **Master Suite:** This private area, located on the opposite side of the home from the secondary bedrooms, features a master bath and walk-in closet.

- **Bedrooms:** Two bedrooms with large closets share a hallway bathroom.

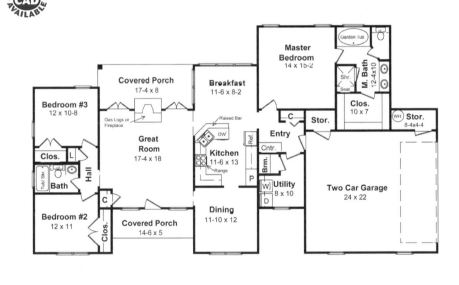

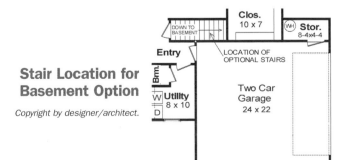

Stair Location for Basement Option

Copyright by designer/architect.

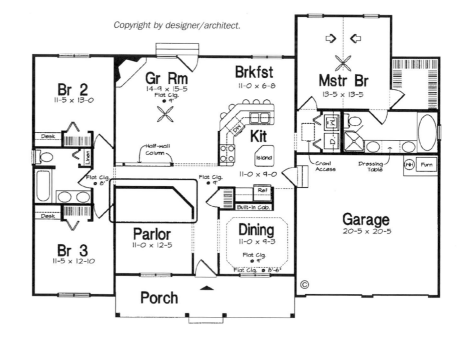

Plan #391038

Dimensions: 59' W x 44' D

Levels: 1

Square Footage: 1,642

Bedrooms: 3

Bathrooms: 2

Foundation: Crawl space, slab, or basement

Materials List Available: Yes

Price Category: C

Images provided by designer/architect.

This home features triple arches trimming a restful exterior front porch, great arched windows with shutters, and a complex classic roofline that steals the eye.

Features:

- **Dining Room:** A formal parlor sits across the hall from this spectacular room with decorative tray ceiling and built-in cabinetry.

- **Kitchen:** This kitchen is the heart of the home, with an island and peninsula counter/snack bar that opens into the great room.

- **Great Room:** This expansive room boasts a big, open layout with a corner fireplace.

- **Master Suite:** This super-private suite has a large walk-in closet and a sunny bath with a tub beneath a window.

- **Bedrooms:** These two additional bedrooms flank a full bathroom.

- **Garage:** This two-car garage makes all the difference for families with more than one automobile.

Copyright by designer/architect.

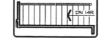

Optional Basement Stairs

Plan #321001

Dimensions: 83' W x 42' D

Levels: 1

Square Footage: 1,721

Bedrooms: 3

Bathrooms: 2

Foundation: Crawl space, slab, or basement

Materials List Available: Yes

Price Category: C

Rear View

You'll love the atrium that creates a warm, naturally lit space inside this gracious home, as well as the roof dormers that give it wonderful curb appeal from the outside.

Features:

- Great Room: Bathed in light from the atrium window wall, this room, with its vaulted ceiling, will be the hub of your family life.

- Dining Room: This room also has a vaulted ceiling and is lit by the atrium, but you can draw drapes at night to create a cozy, warm feeling.

- Kitchen: Designed for functionality, this step-saving kitchen is easy to organize and makes cooking a pleasure.

- Breakfast Room: For convenience, this room is located between the kitchen and the rear covered porch.

- Master Suite: Retire with pleasure to this lovely retreat, with its luxurious bath.

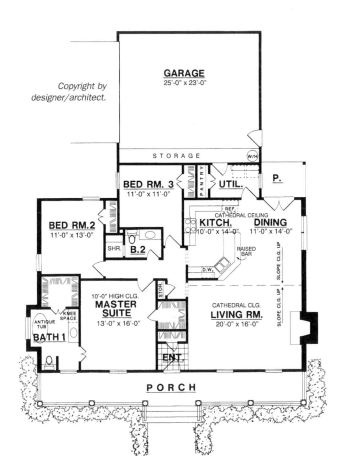

Plan #371053

Dimensions: 51'2" W x 66'7" D

Levels: 1

Square Footage: 1,654

Bedrooms: 3

Bathrooms: 2

Foundation: Slab

Materials List Available: No

Price Category: C

Images provided by designer/architect.

A cozy country porch and large inviting windows are the perfect way to say, "I'm home." This country charmer has everything you need.

Features:

- **Kitchen:** This large kitchen boasts a cathedral ceiling and a raised bar.

- **Dining Room:** This room has a cathedral ceiling and is open to the living room and kitchen.

- **Living Room:** The fireplace and cathedral ceiling give this room an inviting feeling.

- **Master Suite:** This private retreat features two walk-in closets. The old-fashioned bath with an antique tub is perfect for relaxing.

Copyright by designer/architect.

GARAGE
25'-0" x 23'-0"

STORAGE

BED RM. 3
11'-0" x 11'-0"

UTIL.

P.

PANTRY

W/H

REF.
CATHEDRAL CEILING

BED RM.2
11'-0" x 13'-0"

KITCH.
10'-0" x 14'-0"

DINING
11'-0" x 14'-0"

SHR.

B.2

RAISED BAR

D.W.

SLOPE CLG. UP

SLOPE CLG. UP

10'-0" HIGH CLG.
MASTER SUITE
13'-0" x 16'-0"

STOR.

CATHEDRAL CLG.
LIVING RM.
20'-0" x 16'-0"

KNEE SPACE

ANTIQUE TUB

BATH 1

ENT.

SLOPE CLG. UP

PORCH

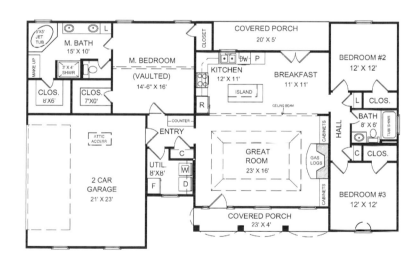

Plan #351033

Dimensions: 62'2" W x 45'8" D

Levels: 1

Square Footage: 1,654

Bedrooms: 3

Bathrooms: 2

Foundation: Crawl space, slab, or basement

Materials List Available: Yes

Price Category: C

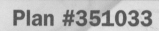

This gorgeous three-bedroom brick home would be the perfect place to raise your family.

Features:

- **Great Room:** This terrific room has a gas fireplace with built-in cabinets on either side.

- **Kitchen:** This island kitchen with breakfast area is open to the great room.

- **Master Suite:** This private room features a vaulted ceiling and a large walk-in closet. The bath area has a walk-in closet, jetted tub, and double vanities.

- **Bedrooms:** The two additional bedrooms share a bathroom located in the hall.

Copyright by designer/architect.

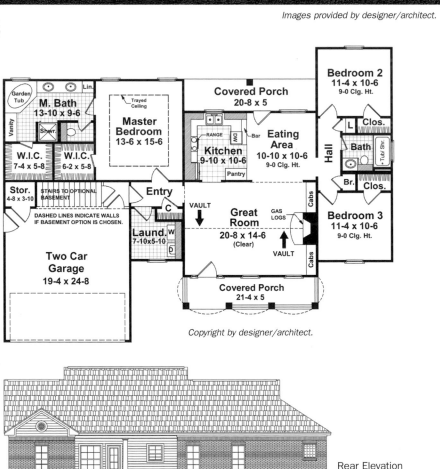

Plan #351079

Dimensions: 62' W x 48' D

Levels: 1

Square Footage: 1,509

Bedrooms: 3

Bathrooms: 2

Foundation: Basement, crawl space, or slab

Materials List Available: Yes

Price Category: E

You'll love the special features of this home, which has been designed for efficiency and comfort.

Features:

- Foyer: This raised foyer offers a view through the great room and beyond it to the covered deck.

- Great Room: Elegant windows allow versatility — decorate casually or more formally.

- Kitchen: You'll find ample counter space and cabinets in this spacious room, which adjoins the dining room and opens onto the rear yard.

- Library: Curl up on the window seat that wraps around the tower in this quiet spot.

- Laundry Room: A tub makes this large room practical for crafts as well as laundry.

Images provided by designer/architect.

Copyright by designer/architect.

Rear Elevation

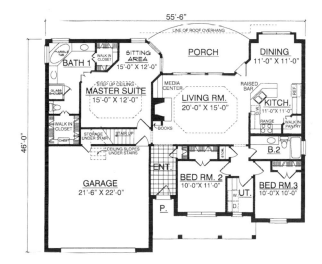

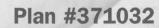

Plan #371032

Dimensions: 55'6" W x 46' D

Levels: 1

Square Footage: 1,659

Bedrooms: 3

Bathrooms: 2

Foundation: Slab

Materials List Available: No

Price Category: C

This charming country home has an impressive look that is all its own. This is the perfect home for any size family.

Features:

- **Living Room:** This massive room boasts a stepped ceiling, built in bookshelves and a media center.

- **Kitchen:** This large kitchen with walk-in pantry opens into the dining room.

- **Master Suite:** This area also has a high stepped ceiling and a sitting area with a view of the backyard. The large master bath has two walk-in closets and a marble tub.

- **Bonus Room:** Located above the garage, this area can be a playroom.

Images provided by designer/architect.

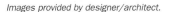

Copyright by designer/architect.

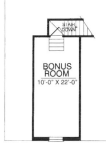

Bonus Area Floor Plan

Plan #401045

Dimensions: 78'6" W x 48' D

Levels: 1

Square Footage: 1,652

Bedrooms: 3

Bathrooms: 2

Foundation: Basement

Materials List Available: Yes

Price Category: C

Images provided by designer/architect.

• Master Suite: This fine area also has doors to the rear porch and is graced by a walk-in closet, plus a full bathroom with a garden tub and dual vanity.

• Garage: This two-car garage contains space for a freezer and extra storage cabinets that are built in.

This long, low ranch home has outdoor living on two porches—one to the front and one to the rear.

Features:

• High Ceilings: Vaulted ceilings in the great room, kitchen, and master bedroom add a dimension of extra space.

• Great Room: A fireplace warms this room, which opens to the country kitchen.

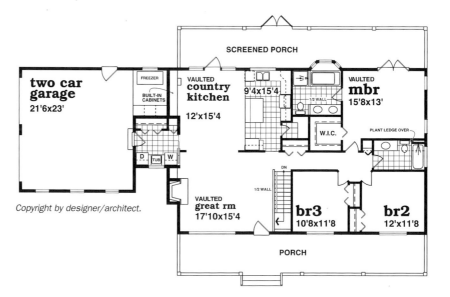

Copyright by designer/architect.

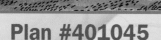

Rear Elevation

Left Side Elevation

Right Side Elevation

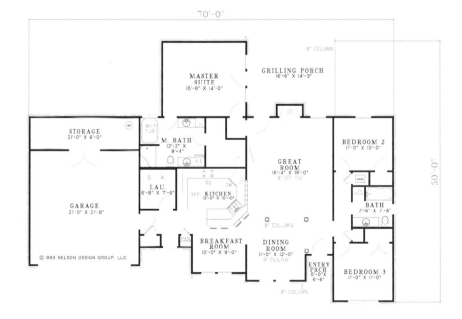

Plan #151210

Dimensions: 70' W x 50' D
Levels: 1
Square Footage: 1,716
Bedrooms: 3
Bathrooms: 2
Foundation: Crawl space or slab
CompleteCost List Available: Yes
Price Category: C

Images provided by designer/architect.

Copyright by designer/architect.

This traditional three-bedroom brick home will be the envy of the neighborhood.

Features:

- **Great Room:** This large gathering room, with a cozy fireplace, has access to the rear porch.

- **Dining Room:** This room with a view of the front yard is located just of the entry.

- **Kitchen:** This kitchen boasts an abundant amount of cabinets, and counter space is open to the breakfast area and the great room.

- **Master Suite:** This suite features a private bathroom with double vanities and a whirlpool tub.

- **Bedrooms:** Two secondary bedrooms have large closets and share a hall bathroom.

Images provided by designer/architect.

Plan #371071

Dimensions: 73' W x 47'4" D

Levels: 1

Square Footage: 1,729

Bedrooms: 3

Bathrooms: 2

Foundation: Crawl space, slab

Materials List Available: No

Price Category: C

This beautiful brick-and-stone country home will be the envy of the neighborhood.

Features:

- **Front Porch:** This charming yet functional porch welcomes you home.

- **Family Room:** This large room, with its cathedral ceiling and cozy fireplace, is ideal for entertaining.

- **Kitchen:** This gourmet kitchen has all the necessities you will ever need, including a raised bar area.

- **Master Suite:** This master bedroom features a stepped ceiling. The luxurious bath boasts a marble tub and two walk-in closets.

Copyright by designer/architect.

Plan #351010

Dimensions: 61'8"W x 45'8" D

Levels: 1

Square Footage: 1,502

Bedrooms: 3

Bathrooms: 2

Foundation: Crawl space, slab, or basement

Materials List Available: Yes

Price Category: C

Images provided by designer/architect.

This uniquely designed house has both beauty and great function. It is simple to build and, through its use of contrasting building materials, color, overlapping planes, shades, and shadows, displays tremendous curb appeal.

Features:

- **Great Room:** This room has a corner fireplace and access to the rear covered porch.

- **Kitchen:** This kitchen boasts a raised bar and is open to the dining area.

- **Master Suite:** Located on the opposite side of the home from the secondary bedrooms, this suite features a private bath with a walk-in closet.

- **Bedrooms:** Two bedrooms share a common bathroom and have large closets.

Copyright by designer/architect.

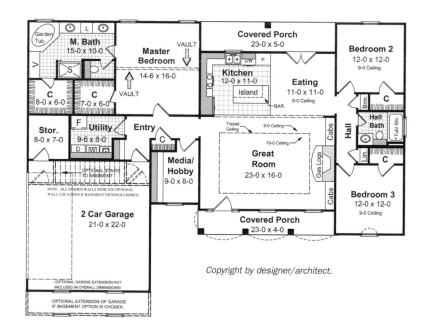

Plan #351003

Dimensions: 64' W x 45'10" D

Levels: 1

Square Footage: 1,751

Bedrooms: 3

Bathrooms: 2

Foundation: Crawl space, slab, or basement

Materials List Available: Yes

Price Category: D

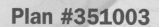

Images provided by designer/architect.

This beautiful three-bedroom brick house with a covered porch is perfect for today's family.

Features:

- **Great Room:** This gathering room features a tray ceiling, a gas fireplace, and built-in cabinets.

- **Kitchen:** This island kitchen with a raised bar is open to the great room and eating area.

- **Master Suite:** This primary bedroom features a vaulted ceiling and large walk-in closet. The bath boasts a double vanity, corner tub, and walk-in closet.

- **Bedrooms:** Two additional bedrooms are located on the other side of the home from the master suite and share a common bathroom.

Copyright by designer/architect.

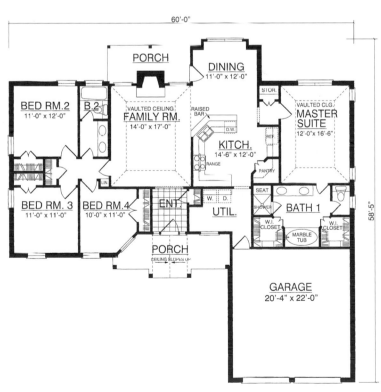

Plan #371036

Dimensions: 60' W x 58'5" D

Levels: 1

Square Footage: 1,764

Bedrooms: 4

Bathrooms: 2

Foundation: Slab

Materials List Available: No

Price Category: C

This quaint traditional brick house is the perfect place to call home.

Features:

- Family Room: This large room boasts a vaulted ceiling and cozy fireplace.

- Dining Room: This area has access to the rear porch and is open to the kitchen.

- Kitchen: This spacious kitchen has a raised bar and views into the family room.

- Master Suite: This private area also has a vaulted ceiling. The luxurious master bath boasts his and her vanities, a marble tub, a large shower area, and two walk-in closets.

- Bedrooms: The three additional bedrooms are on the opposite side of the house from the master suite and share a convenient second bath.

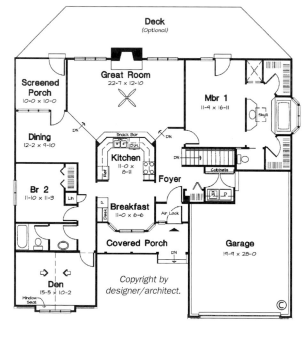

Plan #391028

Dimensions: 54' W x 50' D
Levels: 1
Square Footage: 1,771
Bedrooms: 2
Bathrooms: 2
Foundation: Crawl space, slab
Materials List Available: Yes
Price Category: C

Images provided by designer/architect.

Here's a "real-life" rancher, where there's plenty of room for stretching out and growing your family in contemporary comfort.

Features:

- **Dining Area:** This dining area, a demure space for formal affairs, owns an entrance to the back deck and flows easily into the great room.

- **Kitchen:** This creative U-shaped kitchen serves up a snack bar that reaches into the enormous sunken great room with fireplace.

- **Master Suite:** This expansive suite with dual walk-in closets and private entrance to the deck lives luxuriously on the other side of this home. The master bath flaunts a platform tub set beneath a grand geometric window.

- **Bedroom:** A stylish secondary bedroom, with nearby full bathroom, and cheerful den with a window seat are arranged on one side of the house.

Optional Floor Plan

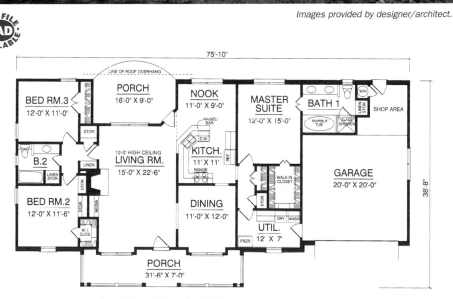

Plan #371072

Dimensions: 75'10" W x 38'8" D

Levels: 1

Square Footage: 1,772

Bedrooms: 3

Bathrooms: 2

Foundation: Crawl space, slab

Materials List Available: No

Price Category: C

This home, with its enclosed covered porch, defines country charm.

Features:

- **Living Room:** This large room has a 10-foot-high ceiling and large windows looking out onto a covered back porch. The cozy fireplace and built-in media center will be great for relaxing.

- **Kitchen:** This large country kitchen with breakfast nook features a raised bar.

- **Dining Room:** This beautiful room has large windows located in a boxed-out extension.

- **Master Suite:** This secluded suite has a large walk-in closet and a luxurious master bath.

Images provided by designer/architect.

Copyright by designer/architect.

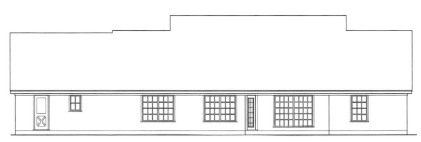

Rear Elevation

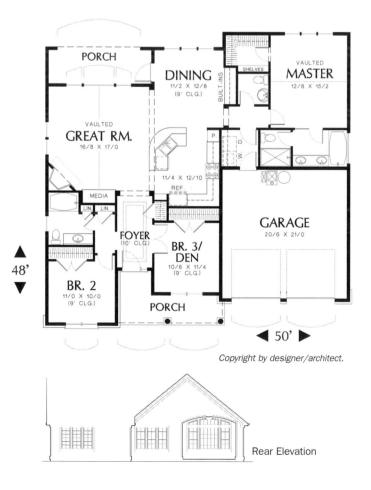

Plan #441003

Dimensions: 50' W x 48' D
Levels: 1
Square Footage: 1,580
Bedrooms: 3
Bathrooms: 2½
Foundation: Crawl space;
slab or basement available for fee
Materials List Available: No
Price Category: C

Images provided by designer/architect.

Craftsman styling with modern floor planning—that's the advantage of this cozy design. Covered porches at front and back enhance both the look and the livability of the plan.

Features:

- **Great Room:** This vaulted entertaining area boasts a corner fireplace and a built-in media center. The area is open to the kitchen and the dining area.

- **Kitchen:** This large, open island kitchen will please the chef in the family. The raised bar is open to the dining area and the great room.

- **Master Suite:** Look for luxurious amenities such as double sinks and a separate tub and shower in the master bath. The master bedroom has a vaulted ceiling and a walk-in closet with built-in shelves.

- **Bedrooms:** Two secondary bedrooms are located away from the master suite. Each has a large closet and access to a common bathroom.

Copyright by designer/architect.

Rear Elevation

Plan #151007

Dimensions: 54'2" W x 56'2" D

Levels: 1

Square Footage: 1,787

Bedrooms: 3

Bathrooms: 2

Foundation: Crawl space, slab, basement, or walkout

CompleteCost List Available: Yes

Price Category: C

This home, as shown in the photograph, may differ from the actual blueprints. For more detailed information, please check the floor plans carefully.

Images provided by designer/architect.

This compact, well-designed home is graced with amenities usually reserved for larger houses.

Features:

- Foyer: A 10-ft. ceiling creates unity between the foyer and the dining room just beyond it.

- Dining Room: 8-in. boxed columns welcome you to this dining room, with its 10-ft. ceilings.

- Great Room: The 9-ft. boxed ceiling suits the spacious design. Enjoy the fireplace in the winter and the rear-grilling porch in the summer.

- Breakfast Room: This bright room is a lovely spot for any time of day.

- Master Suite: Double vanities and a large walk-in closet add practicality to this quiet room with a 9-ft. pan ceiling. The master bath includes whirlpool tub with glass block and a separate shower.

- Bedrooms: Bedroom 2 features a bay window, and both rooms are convenient to the bathroom.

Copyright by designer/architect.

Plan #351146

Dimensions: 61' W x 47'4" D

Levels: 1

Square Footage: 1,509

Bedrooms: 3

Bathrooms: 2

Foundation: Basement, crawl space, or slab

Materials List Available: Yes

Price Category: C

Images provided by designer/architect.

Copyright by designer/architect.

Plan #151280

Dimensions: 51'6" W x 49'10" D

Levels: 1

Square Footage: 1,525

Bedrooms: 3

Bathrooms: 2

Foundation: Basement, crawl space, slab, or walkout

CompleteCost List Available: Yes

Price Category: C

Images provided by designer/architect.

Copyright by designer/architect.

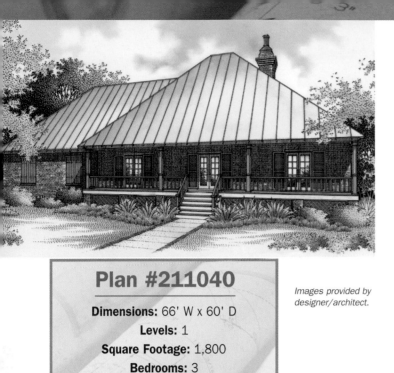

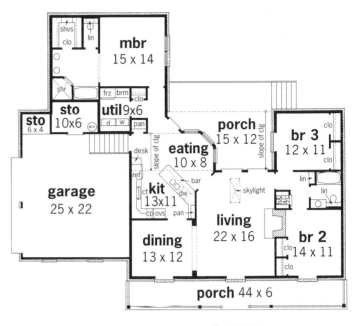

Images provided by designer/architect.

Plan #211040

Dimensions: 66' W x 60' D

Levels: 1

Square Footage: 1,800

Bedrooms: 3

Bathrooms: 2

Foundation: Slab

Materials List Available: Yes

Price Category: D

Copyright by designer/architect.

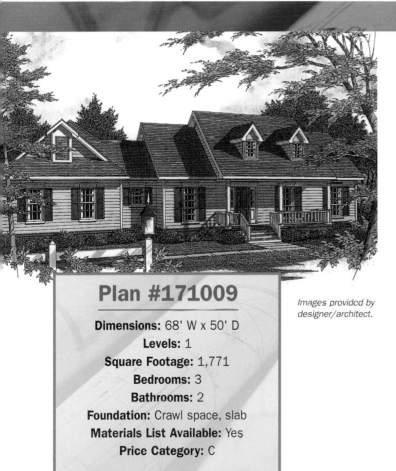

Images provided by designer/architect.

Plan #171009

Dimensions: 68' W x 50' D

Levels: 1

Square Footage: 1,771

Bedrooms: 3

Bathrooms: 2

Foundation: Crawl space, slab

Materials List Available: Yes

Price Category: C

Copyright by designer/architect.

SMARTtip

Deck Awnings

Awnings come in bright colors. As light filters through, it will cast a hue to anything under the deck. Warm colors, such as red or pink, will create a rosy glow; cool colors, such blues or greens, will enhance the shade.

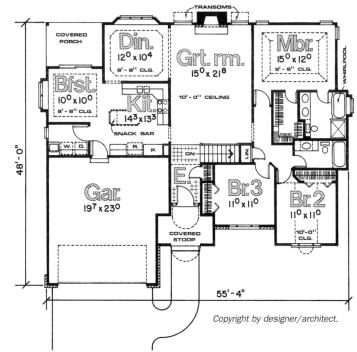

Plan #121004

Dimensions: 55'4" W x 48' D
Levels: 1
Square Footage: 1,666
Bedrooms: 3
Bathrooms: 2
Foundation: Basement
Materials List Available: Yes
Price Category: C

An efficient floor plan and plenty of amenities create a luxurious lifestyle.

Features:

- Ceiling Height: 8 ft. except as noted.

- Entry: Enjoy summer breezes on the porch; then step inside the entry where sidelights and an arched transom create a bright, cheery welcome.

- Great Room: The 10-ft. ceiling and the transom-topped windows flooding the room with light provide a sense of spaciousness. The fireplace adds warmth and style.

- Dining Room: You'll usher your guests into this room located just off the great room.

- Breakfast Area: Also located off the great room, the breakfast area offers another dining option.

- Master Suite: The master bedroom is highlighted by a tray ceiling and a large walk-in closet. Luxuriate in the private bath with its sunlit whirlpool, separate shower, and double vanity.

Images provided by designer/architect.

Copyright by designer/architect.

SMARTtip

Carpeting

Install the best underlayment padding available, as well as the highest grade of carpeting you can afford. This will guarantee a feeling of softness beneath your feet and protect your investment for years to come by reducing wear and tear on the carpet.

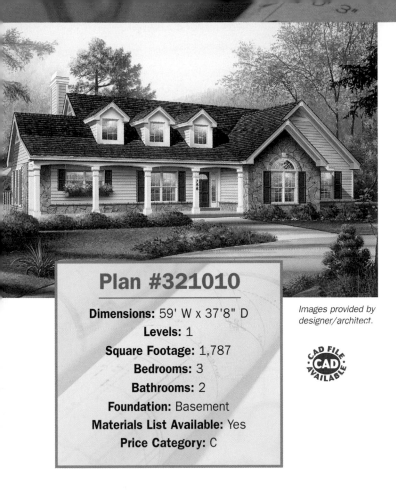

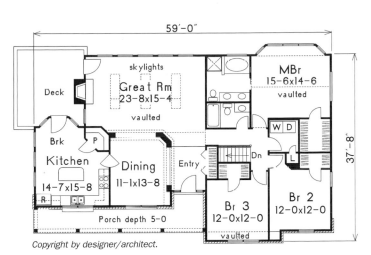

Copyright by designer/architect.

Plan #321010

Dimensions: 59' W x 37'8" D

Levels: 1

Square Footage: 1,787

Bedrooms: 3

Bathrooms: 2

Foundation: Basement

Materials List Available: Yes

Price Category: C

Images provided by designer/architect.

CAD FILE AVAILABLE
CAD

SMARTtip

Country Décor in Your Bathroom

Collections are often part of a country decor, even in the bathroom. All you need is three or more of anything that have size, shape, or color in common. You can mass them on walls, on shelves, on the windowsills, or even along the edge of the tub.

Plan #151173

Dimensions: 58' W x 53'6" D

Levels: 1

Square Footage: 1,739

Bedrooms: 3

Bathrooms: 2

Foundation: Crawl space, slab, basement, or walk-out

CompleteCost List Available: Yes

Price Category: C

Images provided by designer/architect.

CAD FILE AVAILABLE
CAD

Copyright by designer/architect.

Plan #211086

Dimensions: 71' W x 50' D

Levels: 1

Square Footage: 1,704

Bedrooms: 3

Bathrooms: 2½

Foundation: Crawl space

Materials List Available: Yes

Price Category: C

Images provided by designer/architect.

Copyright by designer/architect.

CAD FILE AVAILABLE

Bonus Area

bonus rm 20 x 14

Plan #481150

Dimensions: 60' W x 61' D

Levels: 1

Square Footage: 1,792

Bedrooms: 3

Bathrooms: 2

Foundation: Basement or crawl space

Materials List Available: No

Price Category: C

Images provided by designer/architect.

CAD FILE AVAILABLE

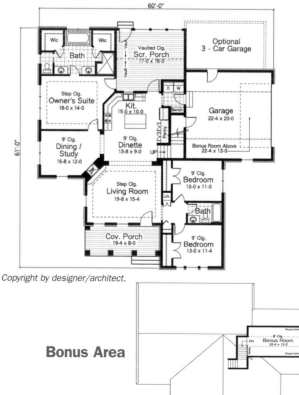

Copyright by designer/architect.

Bonus Area

Plan #391004

Dimensions: 66' W x 52' D

Levels: 1

Square Footage: 1,750

Bedrooms: 2

Bathrooms: 2

Foundation: Crawl space, slab, or basement

Materials List Available: Yes

Price Category: C

This creatively compact ranch is made especially for effortless everyday living.

Features:

- Kitchen: This centralized U-shaped kitchen and look-alike breakfast nook with professional pantry have a wonderful view of the porch.

- Laundry Room: Laundry facilities are cleverly placed within reach while neatly out of the way.

- Great Room: Step into this lavish-looking sunken great room for fire-side gatherings, and move easily into the nearby formal dining area where a screened porch allows you to entertain guests after dinner.

- Master Suite: Flanking one side of the house, this master suite is serenely private and amenity-filled. Its features include full bath, a wall of walk-in closets and a dressing area.

- Bedroom: This second spacious bedroom enjoys great closeting, (with double-doors), a full bath and a close-at-hand den (or bedroom #3).

- Garage: This three-car garage goes beyond vehicle protection, providing plenty of storage and work space.

Crawl Space/Slab Option

Rear View

Images provided by designer/architect.

Plan #151037

Dimensions: 50' W x 56' D

Levels: 1

Square Footage: 1,538

Bedrooms: 3

Bathrooms: 2

Foundation: Crawl space, slab, or basement

CompleteCost List Available: Yes

Price Category: C

You'll love this traditional-looking home, with its covered porch and interesting front windows.

Features:

- Ceiling Height: 8 ft.

- Great Room: This large room has a boxed window that emphasizes its dimensions and a fireplace where everyone will gather on chilly evenings. A door opens to the backyard.

- Dining Room: A bay window overlooking the front porch makes this room easy to decorate.

- Kitchen: This well-planned kitchen features ample counter space, a full pantry, and an eating bar that it shares with the dining room.

- Master Suite: A pan ceiling in this lovely room gives an elegant touch. The huge private bath includes two walk-in closets, a whirlpool tub, a dual-sink vanity, and a skylight in the ceiling.

- Additional Bedrooms: On the opposite side of the house, these bedrooms share a large bath, and both feature excellent closet space.

Copyright by designer/architect.

Plan #151037

Dimensions: 50' W x 56' D

Levels: 1

Square Footage: 1,538

Bedrooms: 3

Bathrooms: 2

Foundation: Crawl space, slab, or basement

CompleteCost List Available: Yes

Price Category: C

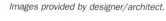
Images provided by designer/architect.

You'll love this traditional-looking home, with its covered porch and interesting front windows.

Features:

- Ceiling Height: 8 ft.

- Great Room: This large room has a boxed window that emphasizes its dimensions and a fireplace where everyone will gather on chilly evenings. A door opens to the backyard.

- Dining Room: A bay window overlooking the front porch makes this room easy to decorate.

- Kitchen: This well-planned kitchen features ample counter space, a full pantry, and an eating bar that it shares with the dining room.

- Master Suite: A pan ceiling in this lovely room gives an elegant touch. The huge private bath includes two walk-in closets, a whirlpool tub, a dual-sink vanity, and a skylight in the ceiling.

- Additional Bedrooms: On the opposite side of the house, these bedrooms share a large bath, and both feature excellent closet space.

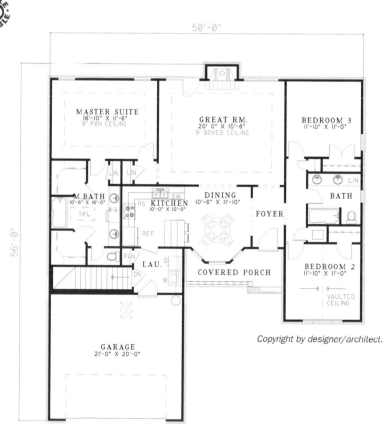

Copyright by designer/architect.

Plan #391004

Dimensions: 66' W x 52' D

Levels: 1

Square Footage: 1,750

Bedrooms: 2

Bathrooms: 2

Foundation: Crawl space, slab, or basement

Materials List Available: Yes

Price Category: C

This creatively compact ranch is made especially for effortless everyday living.

Features:

• Kitchen: This centralized U-shaped kitchen and look-alike breakfast nook with professional pantry have a wonderful view of the porch.

• Laundry Room: Laundry facilities are cleverly placed within reach while neatly out of the way.

• Great Room: Step into this lavish-looking sunken great room for fire-side gatherings, and move easily into the nearby formal dining area where a screened porch allows you to entertain guests after dinner.

• Master Suite: Flanking one side of the house, this master suite is serenely private and amenity-filled. Its features include full bath, a wall of walk-in closets and a dressing area.

• Bedroom: This second spacious bedroom enjoys great closeting, (with double-doors), a full bath and a close-at-hand den (or bedroom #3).

• Garage: This three-car garage goes beyond vehicle protection, providing plenty of storage and work space.

Images provided by designer/architect
This home, as shown in the photograph, may differ from the actual blueprints. For more detailed information, please check the floor plans carefully.

Crawl Space/Slab Option

Copyright by designer/architect.

Rear View

Plan #211086

Dimensions: 71' W x 50' D

Levels: 1

Square Footage: 1,704

Bedrooms: 3

Bathrooms: 2½

Foundation: Crawl space

Materials List Available: Yes

Price Category: C

Images provided by designer/architect.

Copyright by designer/architect.

Bonus Area

Plan #481150

Dimensions: 60' W x 61' D

Levels: 1

Square Footage: 1,792

Bedrooms: 3

Bathrooms: 2

Foundation: Basement or crawl space

Materials List Available: No

Price Category: C

Images provided by designer/architect.

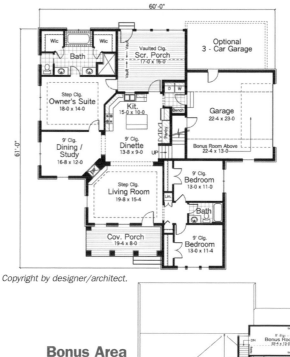

Copyright by designer/architect.

Bonus Area

Plan #321010

Dimensions: 59' W x 37'8" D
Levels: 1
Square Footage: 1,787
Bedrooms: 3
Bathrooms: 2
Foundation: Basement
Materials List Available: Yes
Price Category: C

Images provided by designer/architect.

CAD FILE AVAILABLE

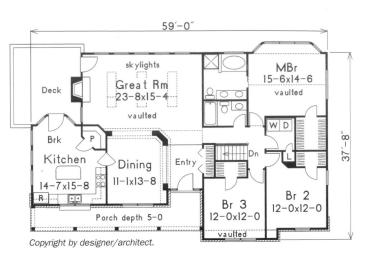

Copyright by designer/architect.

SMARTtip

Country Décor in Your Bathroom

Collections are often part of a country decor, even in the bathroom. All you need is three or more of anything that have size, shape, or color in common. You can mass them on walls, on shelves, on the windowsills, or even along the edge of the tub.

Plan #151173

Dimensions: 58' W x 53'6" D
Levels: 1
Square Footage: 1,739
Bedrooms: 3
Bathrooms: 2
Foundation: Crawl space, slab, basement, or walk-out
CompleteCost List Available: Yes
Price Category: C

Images provided by designer/architect.

CAD FILE AVAILABLE

Copyright by designer/architect.

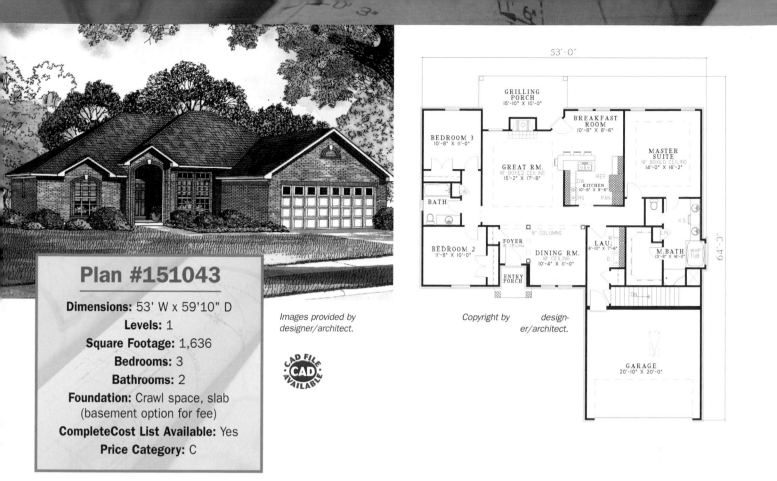

Plan #151043

Dimensions: 53' W x 59'10" D

Levels: 1

Square Footage: 1,636

Bedrooms: 3

Bathrooms: 2

Foundation: Crawl space, slab (basement option for fee)

CompleteCost List Available: Yes

Price Category: C

Images provided by designer/architect.

Copyright by designer/architect.

CAD FILE AVAILABLE

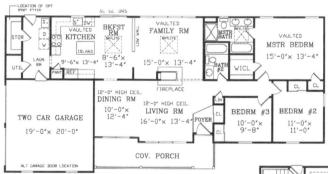

Plan #131010

Dimensions: 70' W x 34'4" D

Levels: 1

Square Footage: 1,667

Bedrooms: 3

Bathrooms: 2

Foundation: Crawl space, slab, or basement

Materials List Available: Yes

Price Category: D

Images provided by designer/architect.

Copyright by designer/architect.

Optional Laundry Room with Basement Floor Plan

Family Room / Kitchen Living Room

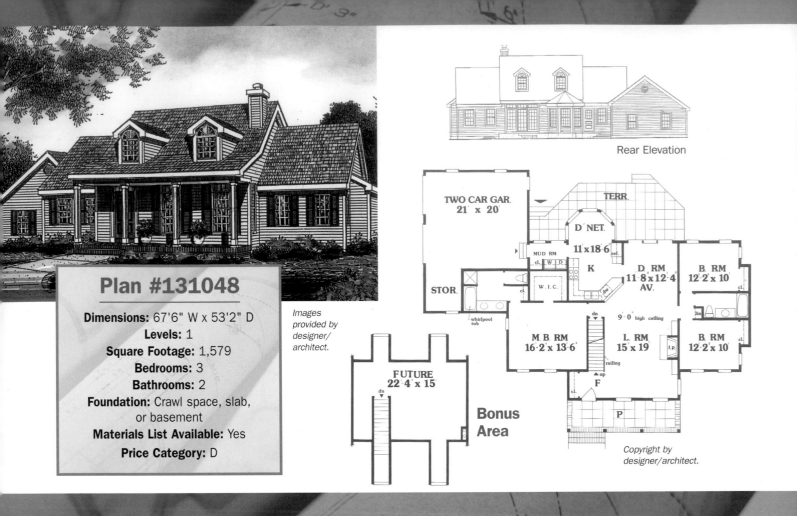

Plan #131048

Dimensions: 67'6" W x 53'2" D

Levels: 1

Square Footage: 1,579

Bedrooms: 3

Bathrooms: 2

Foundation: Crawl space, slab, or basement

Materials List Available: Yes

Price Category: D

Images provided by designer/architect.

Rear Elevation

TWO CAR GAR. 21' x 20'

TERR.

STOR.

D'NET. 11' x 18-6

MUD RM

K

D. RM 11-8 x 12-4 AV.

B. RM 12-2' x 10'

W.I.C.

whirlpool tub

M. B. RM 16-2' x 13-6

9'-0 high ceiling

L. RM 15' x 19

B. RM 12-2' x 10'

dn railing

up

F

P

FUTURE 22-4' x 15

Bonus Area

Copyright by designer/architect.

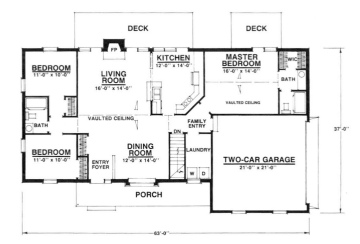

Plan #291002

Dimensions: 63' W x 37' D

Levels: 1

Square Footage: 1,550

Bedrooms: 3

Bathrooms: 2

Foundation: Basement

Materials List Available: No

Price Category: C

Images provided by designer/architect.

DECK

DECK

BEDROOM 11'-0'' x 10'-0''

BATH

LIVING ROOM 16'-0'' x 14'-0''

VAULTED CEILING

KITCHEN 12'-0'' x 14'-0''

MASTER BEDROOM 16'-0'' x 14'-0''

WIC

BATH

VAULTED CEILING

BEDROOM 11'-0'' x 10'-0''

ENTRY FOYER

DINING ROOM 12'-0'' x 14'-0''

DN

FAMILY ENTRY

LAUNDRY

W D

TWO-CAR GARAGE 21'-0'' x 21'-0''

PORCH

37'-0''

63'-0''

Copyright by designer/architect.

Rear View

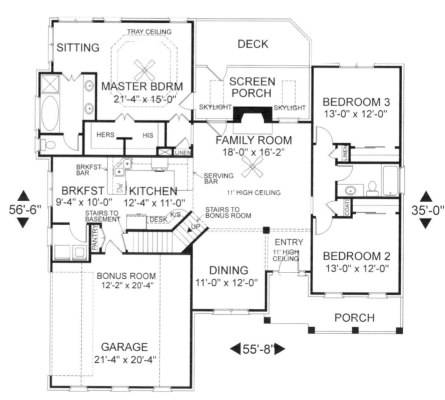

Plan #101004

Dimensions: 55'8" W x 56'6" D
Levels: 1
Square Footage: 1,787
Bedrooms: 3
Bathrooms: 2
Foundation: Crawl space, slab, or basement
Materials List Available: Yes
Price Category: D

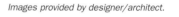

Images provided by designer/architect.

This carefully designed ranch provides the feel and features of a much larger home.

Features:

- Ceiling Height: 9 ft. unless otherwise noted.

- Entry: Guests will step up onto the inviting front porch and into this entry, with its impressive 11-ft. ceiling.

- Dining Room: Open to the entry and to its left is this elegant dining room, perfect for entertaining or informal family gatherings.

- Family Room: This family gathering place features an 11-ft. ceiling to enhance its sense of spaciousness.

- Kitchen: This intelligently designed kitchen has an open plan. A breakfast bar and a serving bar are features that add to its convenience.

- Master Suite: This suite is loaded with amenities, including a double-step tray ceiling, direct access to the screened porch, a sitting room, deluxe bath, and his and her walk-in closets.

Copyright by designer/architect.

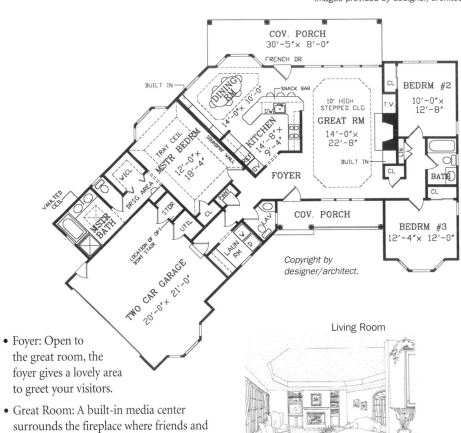

Plan #131002

Dimensions: 70'1" W x 60'7" D
Levels: 1
Square Footage: 1,709
Bedrooms: 3
Bathrooms: 2½
Foundation: Crawl space, slab, or basement
Materials List Available: Yes
Price Category: D

Images provided by designer/architect.

Copyright by designer/architect.

Rear View

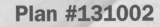

Living Room

You'll love the way this angled ranch brings out the best in a corner lot or on a slope.

Features:

- Ceiling Height: 8 ft.

- Front Porch: Hang baskets of plants from the roof of this porch, which is just the right size for a couple of rockers and a side table.

- Dining Room: Well-placed windows flood this room with sunlight during the day and a built-in cabinet gives ample storage space for all your china, linens, and collectables.

- Foyer: Open to the great room, the foyer gives a lovely area to greet your visitors.

- Great Room: A built-in media center surrounds the fireplace where friends and family are sure to gather.

- Master Suite: You'll love the privacy of this somewhat isolated but easily accessed room. Decorate to show off the large bay window and tray ceiling, and enjoy the luxury of a separate toilet room.

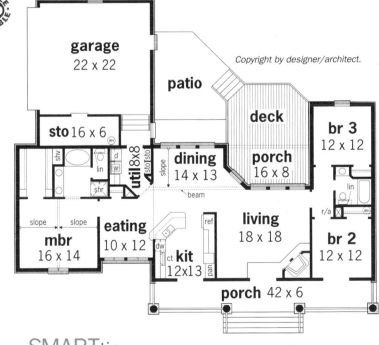

Plan #211029

Dimensions: 68' W x 60' D
Levels: 1
Square Footage: 1,672
Bedrooms: 3
Bathrooms: 2
Foundation: Crawl space
Materials List Available: Yes
Price Category: C

A large front porch adds charm to this three-bedroom home.

Features:

- **Living Room:** This large room features a corner fireplace.

- **Kitchen:** This efficient kitchen has lots of cabinet space and an adjoining eating area.

- **Master Suite:** This large bedroom boasts a spacious walk-in closet and a sloped ceiling. The bath features a double vanity and a separate shower area.

- **Bedrooms:** Two additional bedrooms share a common bathroom.

Images provided by designer/architect.

Copyright by designer/architect.

SMARTtip

Ponds

If a pond or small body of water already exists on your property, arrange your garden elements to take advantage of it. Build a bridge over it to connect it to other areas of the garden. If there's a dock already in place, make use of it for an instant midday picnic for one.

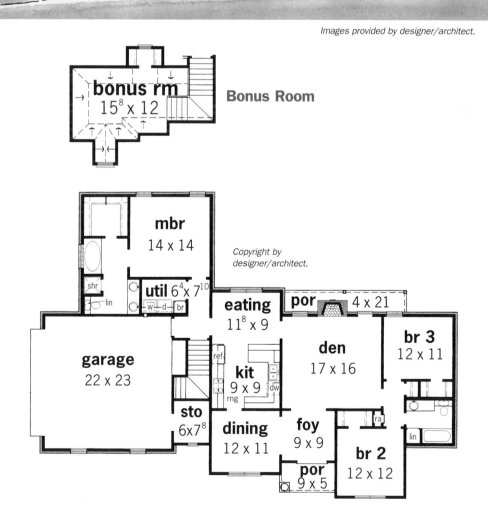

Plan #201087

Dimensions: 69'10" W x 51'5" D

Levels: 1

Square Footage: 1,672

Bedrooms: 3

Bathrooms: 2

Foundation: Crawl space, slab

Materials List Available: Yes

Price Category: C

This stucco-and-brick home will be the landmark home in your neighborhood.

Features:

- Dining Room: Once inside, you will find a large foyer that leads into this elegant room.

- Den: This family area has a cozy fireplace and a view of the backyard.

- Kitchen: This U-shaped kitchen has plenty of counter space and opens to the eating area.

- Master Suite: This suite features a private bathroom with a large walk-in closet and double vanities.

- Bedrooms: Two secondary bedrooms have large closets and share a hall bathroom.

Images provided by designer/architect.

Bonus Room

bonus rm
15^8 x 12

Copyright by designer/architect.

mbr
14 x 14

util 6^4 x 7^{10}

garage
22 x 23

eating
11^8 x 9

por
4 x 21

den
17 x 16

br 3
12 x 11

kit
9 x 9

sto
6x7^8

dining
12 x 11

foy
9 x 9

br 2
12 x 12

por
9 x 5

Plan #131020

Dimensions: 67'2" W x 48'10" D

Levels: 1

Square Footage: 1,735

Bedrooms: 3

Bathrooms: 2

Foundation: Crawl space, slab, or basement

Materials List Available: Yes

Price Category: C

Images provided by designer/architect.

This gorgeous ranch is designed for entertaining but is also comfortable for family living.

Features:

- Living Room: A 9-ft. stepped ceiling highlights the spaciousness of this room, which gives a view of one of the two covered porches.

- Dining Room: Also with a 9-ft. stepped ceiling and a view of the porch, this room features a bay window.

- Family Room: An 11-ft. vaulted ceiling and gliding French doors to the porch define this central gathering area.

- Kitchen: Enjoy the skylight, a fireplace that's shared with the family room, a central island cooktop, and a snack bar in this room.

- Master Suite: The tray ceiling is 9 ft. 9 in. high, and this area includes a sitting area and a bath with a whirlpool tub and dual-sink vanity.

Copyright by designer/architect.

Photos provided by designer/architect.

Kitchen

Foyer/Dining Room

Plan #211002

Dimensions: 68' W x 62' D
Levels: 1
Square Footage: 1,792
Bedrooms: 3
Bathrooms: 2
Foundation: Crawl space
Materials List Available: Yes
Price Category: C

Arched windows on the front of this home give it a European style that you're sure to love.

SMARTtip

Water Features

Water features create the ambiance of a soothing oasis on a deck. A water-filled urn becomes a mirror that reflects the sky— making a small deck look larger. Fish flashing in an ornamental pool add color and act as a focal point for a deck with no view.

A water fountain introduces a pleasant rhythmical sound that helps drown out the background noises of traffic and nearby neighbors.

Images provided by designer/architect.

Features:

- Living Room: The 12-ft. ceiling in this large, open room enhances its spacious feeling. A fireplace adds warmth on chilly days and cool evenings.

- Dining Room: Decorate to accentuate the 12-ft. ceiling and formal feeling of this room.

- Kitchen: Designed for comfort and efficiency, this room also has a 12-ft. ceiling. The cozy breakfast bar is a natural gathering spot for friends and family.

- Master Suite: A split design guarantees privacy here. A sloped cathedral ceiling adds elegance, and a walk-in closet makes it practical. The bath has two vanities, a tub, and a walk-in shower.

- Garage: Park two cars here, and use the balance of this 520 sq. ft. area as a handy storage area.

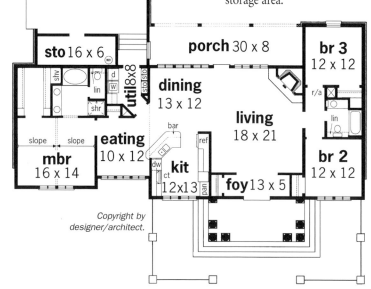

Copyright by designer/architect.

Plan #131047

Dimensions: 69'10" W x 51'8" D
Levels: 1
Square Footage: 1,793
Bedrooms: 3
Bathrooms: 2
Foundation: Crawl space, slab, or basement
Materials List Available: Yes
Price Category: D

Images provided by designer/architect.

The country charm of this well-designed home is mixed with the convenience and luxury normally reserved for more contemporary plans.

Features:

- Great Room: The spaciousness of this great room is enhanced by the 11-ft. stepped ceiling. A fireplace makes it cozy on cool evenings or on chilly winter days, and two sets of French sliding glass doors open to the back porch.

- Kitchen: In addition to the convenient layout of this design, you'll also love its bright, airy position. It includes an old-fashioned pantry,

a sink under a window, and a sunny breakfast area that opens to the wraparound porch.

- Master Suite: You'll find 11-ft. ceilings in both the master bedroom and the bayed sitting area that the suite includes. In the bath, the circular spa tub is surrounded by a glass-block wall.

- Bonus Space: A permanent staircase leads to an unfinished bonus space on the upper level.

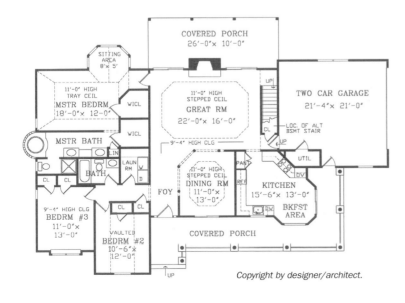

Copyright by designer/architect.

Rear Elevation

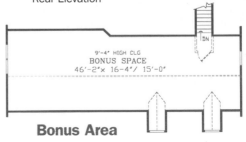

Bonus Area

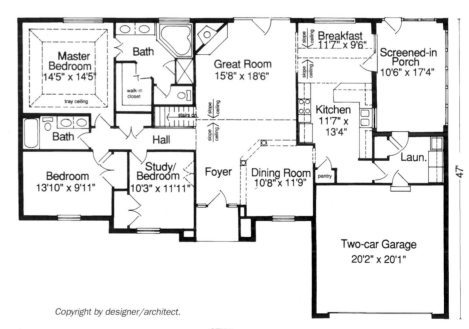

Plan #161001

Dimensions: 67'2" W x 47' D

Levels: 1

Square Footage: 1,782

Bedrooms: 3

Bathrooms: 2

Foundation: Basement

Materials List Available: Yes

Price Category: C

An all-brick exterior displays the solid strength that characterizes this gracious home.

Features:

- **Gathering Area:** A feeling of spaciousness permeates this gathering area, created by the foyer, great room, and dining room. Multiple windows provide natural light that dances along a sloped ceiling, spilling onto decorative columns and a fireplace.

- **Breakfast Area:** A continuation of the sloped ceiling leads to this breakfast area, where French doors open to a screened porch.

- **Kitchen:** An abundance of cabinets and counter space are the hallmarks of this large kitchen, with its easy access to a spacious laundry room and storage area.

- **Master Suite:** A tray ceiling and spacious walk-in closet in the master bedroom, along with a whirlpool tub and double-bowl vanity in the bathroom, enable you to pamper yourself.

Images provided by designer/architect.

Copyright by designer/architect.

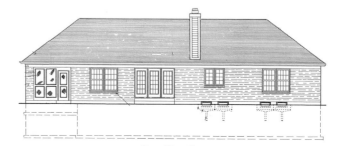

Rear Elevation

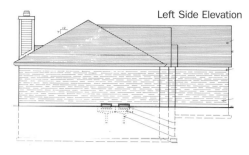

Left Side Elevation

Front View

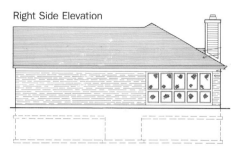

Right Side Elevation

Great Room / Foyer

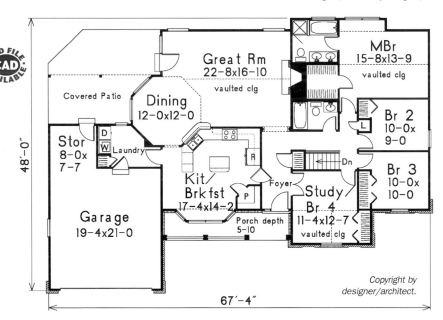

Plan #321003

Dimensions: 67'4" W x 48' D

Levels: 1

Square Footage: 1,791

Bedrooms: 4

Bathrooms: 2

Foundation: Basement

Materials List Available: Yes

Price Category: C

Images provided by designer/architect.

CAD FILE AVAILABLE

Great Rm
22-8x16-10
vaulted clg

MBr
15-8x13-9
vaulted clg

Covered Patio

Dining
12-0x12-0

Stor
8-0x
7-7

D W Laundry

Br 2
10-0x
9-0

Kit/
Brkfst
17-4x14-2

Foyer

Study/
Br. 4
11-4x12-7
vaulted clg

Br 3
10-0x
10-0

Garage
19-4x21-0

Porch depth
5-10

48'-0"

67'-4"

Copyright by designer/architect.

The traditional good looks of the exterior of this home are complemented by the stunning contemporary design of the interior.

Features:

- **Great Room:** With a vaulted ceiling to highlight its spacious dimensions, this room is certain to be the central gathering spot for friends and family.

- **Dining Room:** Also with a vaulted ceiling, this room has an octagonal shape for added interest. Windows here and in the great room look out to the covered patio.

- **Kitchen:** A center island gives a convenient work space in this well-designed kitchen, which features a pass-through to the dining room for easy serving, and large, walk-in pantry for storage.

- **Breakfast Room:** A bay window lets sunshine pour in to start your morning with a smile.

- **Master Bedroom:** A vaulted ceiling and a sitting area make you feel truly pampered in this room.

SMARTtip

Bay & Bow Windows

Occasionally too little room exists between the window frame (if there is one) and the ceiling. In this situation you might be able to use ceiling-mounted hardware. Alternatively, a cornice across the top and a rod mounted inside the cornice will give you the dual benefit of visually lowering the top of the window and concealing the hardware.

Plan #321008

Dimensions: 57' W x 52'2" D
Levels: 1
Square Footage: 1,761
Bedrooms: 4
Bathrooms: 2
Foundation: Basement
Materials List Available: Yes
Price Category: C

One look at the roof dormers and planter boxes that grace the outside of this ranch, and you'll know that the interior is planned for comfortable family living.

Features:

- **Great Room:** A vaulted ceiling in this room points up its generous dimensions. Put a grouping of chairs near the fireplace to take advantage of the cozy spot it creates in chilly weather.

- **Kitchen:** Open to the great room, this kitchen has been planned for convenience. It features a pass-through to the dining area for easy serving when you've got a crowd to feed.

- **Master Bedroom:** A vaulted ceiling here makes you feel especially pampered, and the walk-in closet and amenity-filled bath add to that feeling.

- **Additional Bedrooms:** Great closet space characterizes all the rooms in this home, making it easy for children of any age to keep it organized and tidy.

Images provided by designer/architect.

Copyright by designer/architect.

Floor plan rooms:

- MBr 14-6x13-0 vaulted clg
- Brk fst 11-8x10-8
- Great Rm 16-0x17-10 vaulted clg
- Kit 11-5x12-9
- Br 2 11-0x10-0
- Dining 12-4x10-0
- Br 3 11-0x10-0
- Br 4 12-0x10-0 vaulted clg
- Covered Porch
- Garage 20-4x20-10
- Patio

57'-0"
52'-2"

SMARTtip

Hanging Wallpaper

Use liner paper to smooth out a damaged wall and to provide uniform support for expensive paper.

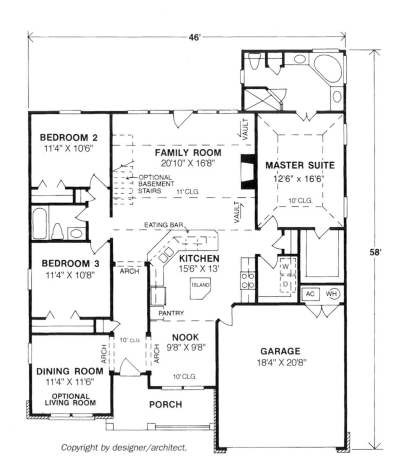

Plan #121006

Dimensions: 46' W x 58' D

Levels: 1

Square Footage: 1,762

Bedrooms: 3

Bathrooms: 2

Foundation: Crawl space, slab, or basement

Materials List Available: Yes

Price Category: C

Images provided by designer/architect.

The entry has a trio of arched openings that leads you to other areas of this amenity-packed home.

Features:

- Ceiling Height: 8 ft. except as noted.

- Eating Bar: Conveniently located between the kitchen and family room, this is sure to be a favorite spot for informal entertaining and family gatherings.

- Family room: A wall of windows, a fireplace, and a vaulted ceiling stretching to 11 ft. work together to make this a bright and warm room.

- Kitchen: There's no shortage of counter space in this well-planned kitchen that features a center island in addition to the eating bar.

- Master Suite: Luxuriate at the end of the day in this large bedroom with its decorative tray ceiling and walk-in closet. Enjoy the pampering bath with its sunlit corner whirlpool flanked by vanities.

- Garage: Two bays provide room for cars and plenty of storage as well.

Copyright by designer/architect.

Plan #241005

Dimensions: 53' W x 55'9" D
Levels: 1
Square Footage: 1,670
Bedrooms: 3
Bathrooms: 2
Foundation: Crawl space or slab
(basement for fee)
Materials List Available: No
Price Category: C

This charming starter home, in split-bedroom format, combines big-house features in a compact design.

Features:

- **Great Room:** With easy access to the formal dining room, kitchen, and breakfast area, this great room features a cozy fireplace.

- **Kitchen:** This big kitchen, with easy access to a walk-in pantry, features an island for added work space and a lovely plant shelf that separates it from the great room.

- **Master Suite:** Separated for privacy, this master suite offers a roomy bath with whirlpool tub, dual vanities, a separate shower, and a large walk-in closet.

- **Additional Rooms:** Additional rooms include a laundry/utility room—with space for a washer, dryer, and freezer—a large area above the garage, well-suited for a media or game room, and two secondary bedrooms.

Images provided by designer/architect.

Copyright by designer/architect.

SMARTtip

Window Scarf

The best way to wrap a window scarf around a pole is as follows:

- Lay out the material on a large, clean surface. Gather the fabric at the top of each jabot, and use elastic to hold it together.

- Swing one jabot into place over the pole and, starting from there, wind the swag portion as many times as you need around the pole until you reach the elastic at the second jabot, which should have landed at the opposite pole end.

- Readjust wraps along the pole. Generally, wrapped swags just touch or slightly overlap.

- For a dramatic effect, stuff the wrapped swags with tissue paper or thin foam, depending on the translucence and weight of fabric.

- Release elastics at tops of jabots.

Plan #161005

Dimensions: 60' W x 48'10" D

Levels: 1

Square Footage: 1,593

Bedrooms: 3

Bathrooms: 2

Foundation: Basement

Materials List Available: Yes

Price Category: C

Rear Elevation

This delightful ranch home includes many thoughtful conveniences and a full basement to expand your living enjoyment.

Features:

- **Great Room:** Take pleasure in welcoming guests through a spacious foyer into the warm and friendly confines of this great room with corner fireplace, sloped ceiling, and view to the rear yard.

- **Kitchen:** Experience the convenience of enjoying meals while seated at the large island that separates the dining area from this well-designed kitchen. Also included is an over-sized pantry with an abundance of storage.

- **Master Suite:** This master suite features a compartmented bath, large walk-in closet, and master bedroom that has a tray ceiling with 9-ft. center height.

- **Porch:** Retreat to this delightful rear porch to enjoy a relaxing evening.

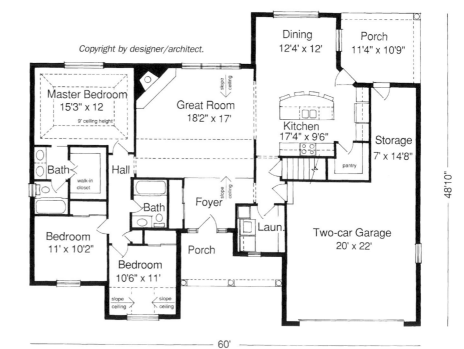

Copyright by designer/architect.

Plan #161010

Dimensions: 50'8" W x 54'2" D
Levels: 1
Square Footage: 1,544
Bedrooms: 3
Bathrooms: 2
Foundation: Basement
Materials List Available: Yes
Price Category: C

Images provided by designer/architect.

This one-story home's many distinctive and elegant features—including arched openings and sloped ceilings—will surprise and excite you at every turn.

Features:

- **Great Room:** Decorative columns frame the entrance from the foyer to this great room and are repeated at the opening to the formal dining area.

- **Kitchen:** Designed for quick meals or to accommodate an oversized crowd, this kitchen features a curved countertop with seating that functions as a delightful bar.

- **Master Bedroom:** This master bedroom is split to afford you more privacy and features a compartmented bath that forms a separate vanity area.

- **Additional Bedrooms:** Take advantage of the double doors off the foyer to allow one bedroom to function as a library.

Right Side Elevation

Left Side Elevation

Rear Elevation

Covered Porch
16' x 10'

Dining
14'2" x 11'8"

Master Bedroom
12' x 14'

Great Room
16'4" x 18'

Kitchen
14'2" x 8'10"

WALK-IN CLOSET

Bath

Laun.

Hall

Bath

CURVED CEILING

Two-Car Garage
20' x 20'

Foyer

Library/ Bedroom
10'9" x 11'

Bedroom
10' x 11'6"

Porch

54'2"

50'8"

Copyright by designer/architect.

Plan #241006

Dimensions: 51' W x 63' D

Levels: 1

Square Footage: 1,744

Bedrooms: 3

Bathrooms: 2

Foundation: Crawl space, slab

Materials List Available: No

Price Category: C

Images provided by designer/architect.

Copyright by designer/architect.

Plan #221011

Dimensions: 59' W x 58' D

Levels: 1

Square Footage: 1,756

Bedrooms: 3

Bathrooms: 2

Foundation: Basement

Materials List Available: No

Price Category: C

Images provided by designer/architect.

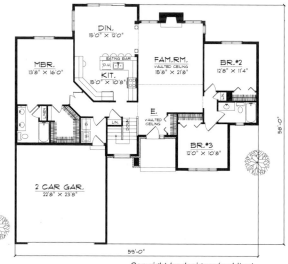

Copyright by designer/architect.

Rear Elevation

Images provided by designer/architect.

Copyright by designer/architect.

Plan #311013

Dimensions: 66' W x 49'11" D

Levels: 1

Square Footage: 1,698

Bedrooms: 3

Bathrooms: 2

Foundation: Crawl space, slab, or basement

Materials List Available: Yes

Price Category: C

Porch 32-4x10-10

Master Bedroom 15-3x13-6

M.Bath 9-0x16-2

Breakfast 10-0x9-8

Greatroom 17-9x16-6

Bedroom 11-3x11-0

Kitchen 10-0x13-5

Storage 3-6x21-0

Garage 20-8x21-0

Bath

Foyer

Dining 13-6x11-0

Bedroom 11-5x11-6

Stoop

Storage 13-6x4-9

Basement Stair Location

Kitchen

Garage

Dining

Stor.

Plan #171006

Dimensions: 68' W x 50' D

Levels: 1

Square Footage: 1,648

Bedrooms: 3

Bathrooms: 2½

Foundation: Crawl space, slab

Materials List Available: Yes

Price Category: C

Images provided by designer/architect.

BATH 10 X 10

MASTER SUITE 15 X 16

PORCH 42 X 6

CLOSET

BEDRM 11 X 12

GARAGE 21 X 22

1/8 BATH

DINING 10 X 11

GREAT RM 16 X 24

BATH

UTILITY

A/C

KITCHEN 11 X 14

BEDRM 12 X 12

PORCH 28 X 6

Copyright by designer/architect.

SMARTtip

Window Shades

While decorative hems add interest to roller shades, they also increase the cost. If you're handy with a glue gun, choose one of the trims available at fabric and craft stores, and consider attaching it yourself. Give your shades fancy pulls for an inexpensive dash of pizzazz.

Images provided by designer/architect.

CAD FILE AVAILABLE

Copyright by designer/architect.

Plan #351002

Dimensions: 64' W x 45'10" D

Levels: 1

Square Footage: 1,751

Bedrooms: 3

Bathrooms: 2

Foundation: Crawl space, slab, or basement

Materials List Available: Yes

Price Category: C

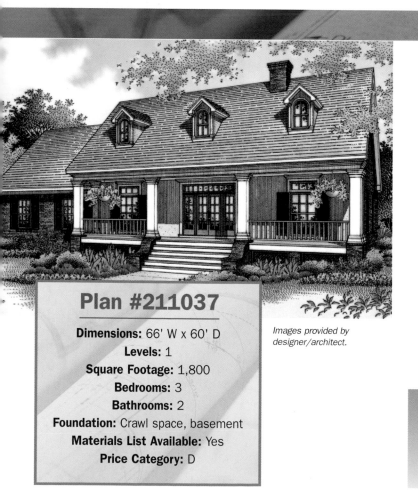

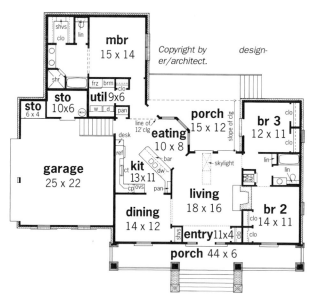

Images provided by designer/architect.

Copyright by designer/architect.

Plan #211037

Dimensions: 66' W x 60' D

Levels: 1

Square Footage: 1,800

Bedrooms: 3

Bathrooms: 2

Foundation: Crawl space, basement

Materials List Available: Yes

Price Category: D

SMARTtip
Reflected Light in the Bathroom
The addition of a large mirror can bring reflected light into a small bathroom, adding the illusion of space without the expense of renovation.

Plan #101003

Dimensions: 50' W x 55' D
Levels: 1
Square Footage: 1,593
Bedrooms: 3
Bathrooms: 2
Foundation: Crawl space, slab, or basement
Materials List Available: Yes
Price Category: D

Images provided by designer/architect.

The brick-and-siding exterior is accented with multilevel wood trim and copper roofing returns.

Features:

- Ceiling Height: 9 ft. unless otherwise noted.
- Covered Porch: The inviting covered porch is the perfect place for a swing or old-fashioned rockers. Rediscover the old-fashioned pleasure of relaxing on the porch.

- Kitchen: This large, carefully designed kitchen makes cooking a pleasure.
- Laundry Room: In addition to housing the washer and dryer, this laundry room provides a place to sort and fold.
- Family Room: The 12-ft. ceiling gives this family gathering place a sense of spaciousness.
- Dining Room: The tray ceiling makes this room a dramatic and elegant place in which to entertain.
- Master Suite: This luxurious retreat features a sitting area and a 6-ft x 10-ft. walk-in closet. The bathroom has a garden tub, shower, and enormous 8-ft. double vanity.

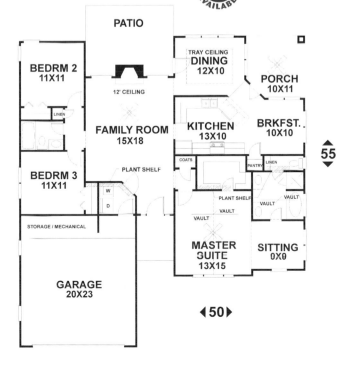

CAD FILE AVAILABLE — CAD

PATIO

BEDRM 2
11X11

LINEN

TRAY CEILING
DINING
12X10

PORCH
10X11

12' CEILING

FAMILY ROOM
15X18

KITCHEN
13X10

BRKFST.
10X10

55

PLANT SHELF

COATS

PANTRY LINEN

BEDRM 3
11X11

W
D

PLANT SHELF

VAULT

VAULT VAULT

VAULT

STORAGE / MECHANICAL

VAULT

GARAGE
20X23

MASTER SUITE
13X15

SITTING
0X0

◄ 50 ►

Plan #131005

Dimensions: 70' W x 37'4" D
Levels: 1
Square Footage: 1,595
Bedrooms: 3
Bathrooms: 2
Foundation: Crawl space, slab, or basement
Materials List Available: Yes
Price Category: D

SMARTtip

Create a Courtyard

Create a private walled-garden retreat with fences covered by climbing vines. Add height with trellises, and divide spaces with clipped boxwood hedges. Include an (almost) instant patio by digging away an area of sod and then covering it with a layer of sand and landscaping mesh to discourage weeds. Then cover it with pea gravel, and add a garden bench, statuary, and perhaps an antique or two. The result? European ambiance for even the most nondescript suburban yard.

With the finest features of an open design in the main living areas, this home gives privacy where you need it. Best of all, it's wheelchair accessible.

Features:

- **Foyer:** A high ceiling gives this area real presence and serves to blend it seamlessly with the great room and the dining room.

- **Great Room:** The open design allows you to use this room as an extension of the dining room or, if you wish, furnish it to create a private reading nook or visually separate media center.

- **Breakfast Room:** Both this room and the adjacent well-appointed kitchen flow into the rest of the living area. However, access to the rear porch, where you can sit out and enjoy the weather while you eat, distinguishes this room.

- **Master Suite:** Located in the same wing as the other bedrooms, this suite has a separate entrance and features a vaulted ceiling, three closets, and a compartmented bath.

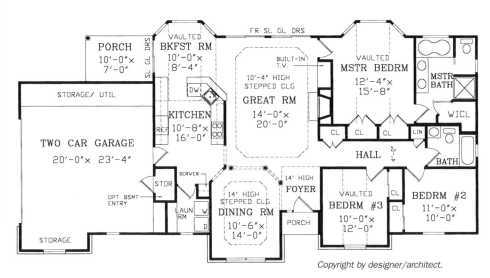

Copyright by designer/architect.

Foyer

Dining Room

Great Room

Living Room

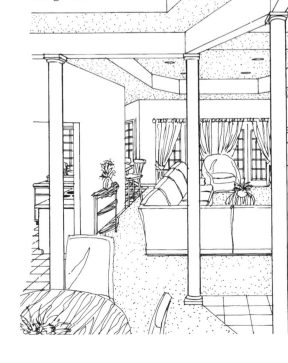

SMARTtip

Natural Trellis

Create a natural rustic trellis that might even, if growing conditions are right, produce its own pretty blooms. Cut and place saplings in the ground as uprights. Then weave old grapevines with smaller saplings for the lattice.

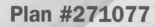

Plan #271077

Dimensions: 69'6" W x 53' D

Levels: 1

Square Footage: 1,786

Bedrooms: 1

Bathrooms: 1½

Foundation: Basement or daylight basement

Materials List Available: No

Price Category: C

Images provided by designer/architect.

This wonderful home has an optional finished basement plan to add three more bedrooms—ideal for a growing family.

Features:

- Great Room: This large gathering room has a fireplace with built-in cabinets on either side.

- Kitchen: This island kitchen, with dinette area, is open to the great room.

- Master Bedroom: This luxurious room provides a view of the backyard.

- Master Bath: This private bathroom has a walk-in closet and double vanities.

Copyright by designer/architect.

Optional Basement Level Floor Plan

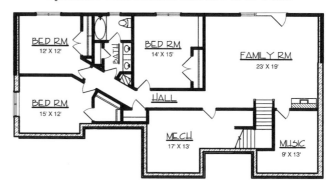

Plan #161013

Dimensions: 59'4" W x 46'4" D
Levels: 1
Square Footage: 1,509
Bedrooms: 3
Bathrooms: 2
Foundation: Basement
Materials List Available: Yes
Price Category: C

The unique roofline and stone accents make this home stand apart from the rest.

Features:

- Foyer: Just off the front porch, this entry opens to the great room.

- Great Room: This room warms up with a fireplace and is open to the dining area.

- Kitchen: This kitchen features a peninsula with a raised bar, creating more seating space for the adjacent dining room.

- Master Suite: This suite features a private bathroom with a walk-in closet and double vanities.

- Bedrooms: Two secondary bedrooms have large closets and share a hall bathroom.

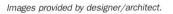
Images provided by designer/architect.

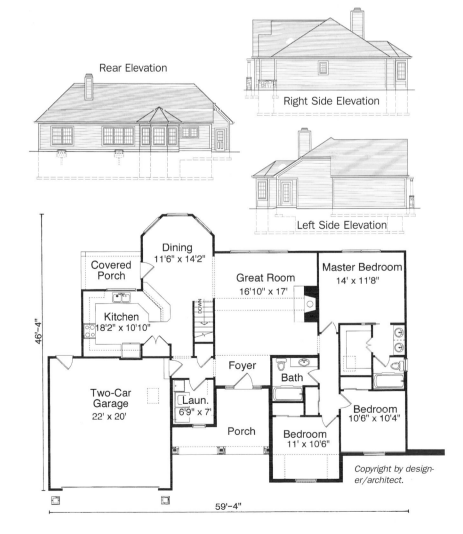

Rear Elevation

Right Side Elevation

Left Side Elevation

Dining 11'6" x 14'2"

Covered Porch

Kitchen 18'2" x 10'10"

Great Room 16'10" x 17'

Master Bedroom 14' x 11'8"

Two-Car Garage 22' x 20'

Laun. 6'9" x 7'

Foyer

Bath

Porch

Bedroom 11' x 10'6"

Bedroom 10'6" x 10'4"

46'-4"

59'-4"

Copyright by designer/architect.

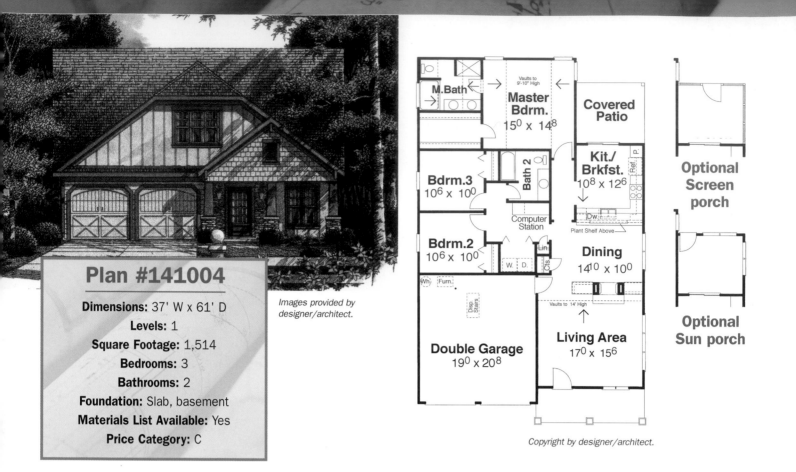

M.Bath

Master Bdrm.
15⁰ x 14⁸

Vaults to 9'-10" High

Covered Patio

Bdrm.3
10⁶ x 10⁰

Bath 2

Kit./ Brkfst.
10⁸ x 12⁶

Ref.

Optional Screen porch

Computer Station

Plant Shelf Above

Bdrm.2
10⁶ x 10⁰

Lin.

Dining
14¹⁰ x 10⁰

Dw

W. D.

Clts.

Optional Sun porch

Wh Furn.

Disp Stairs

Double Garage
19⁰ x 20⁸

Vaults to 14' High

Living Area
17⁰ x 15⁶

Images provided by designer/architect.

Plan #141004

Dimensions: 37' W x 61' D

Levels: 1

Square Footage: 1,514

Bedrooms: 3

Bathrooms: 2

Foundation: Slab, basement

Materials List Available: Yes

Price Category: C

Copyright by designer/architect.

Plan #161161

Dimensions: 55'6" W x 47'6" D

Levels: 1

Square Footage: 1,569

Bedrooms: 3

Bathrooms: 2

Foundation: Basement; crawl space, slab, or walkout for fee

Materials List Available: Yes

Price Category: C

Images provided by designer/architect.

CAD FILE AVAILABLE

Patio

Master Bedroom
12'-0" x 14'-1"
SLOPE CLG TO 9'-9½"

Laun.

Great Room
15'-2" x 18'-2"
SLOPE CLG TO 10'-5½"

Dining
12'-3" x 13'-3"
SLOPE CLG TO 9'-7½"

Bath

WALK-IN CLOSET

Bath

Hall

Kitchen
12'-3" x 11'-10"

Bedroom
10'-10" x 14'-4"

Bedroom/ Study
10'-6" x 11'-0"

Foyer

Garage
19'-8" x 21'-6"

Porch

Copyright by designer/architect.

Plan #131040

Dimensions: 50' W x 37' D

Levels: 1

Square Footage: 1,630

Bedrooms: 3

Bathrooms: 2

Foundation: Crawl space, slab, or basement

Materials List Available: Yes

Price Category: D

Images provided by designer/architect.

Optional Lower Level Floor Plan

Plan #121008

Dimensions: 62' W x 56' D

Levels: 1

Square Footage: 1,651

Bedrooms: 2

Bathrooms: 2

Foundation: Basement

Materials List Available: Yes

Price Category: C

Images provided by designer/architect.

CAD FILE AVAILABLE

Optional Bedroom

Copyright by designer/architect.

Images provided by designer/architect.

Copyright by designer/architect.

60'-9"

Rear Elevation

Plan #161009

Dimensions: 60'9" W x 49' D

Levels: 1

Square Footage: 1,651

Bedrooms: 3

Bathrooms: 2

Foundation: Basement

Materials List Available: Yes

Price Category: C

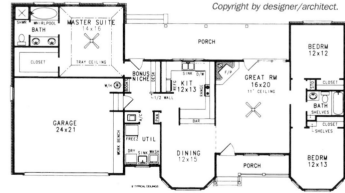

Copyright by designer/architect.

Plan #171008

Dimensions: 72' W x 40' D

Levels: 1

Square Footage: 1,652

Bedrooms: 3

Bathrooms: 2

Foundation: Crawl space, slab

Materials List Available: Yes

Price Category: C

Images provided by designer/architect.

SMARTtip

Lighting for Decorative Shadows

Use lighting to create decorative shadows. For interesting, undefined shadows, set lights at ground level aiming upward in front of a shrub or tree that is close to a wall. For silhouetting, place lights directly behind a plant or garden statue that is near a wall. In both cases, using a wide beam will increase the effect.

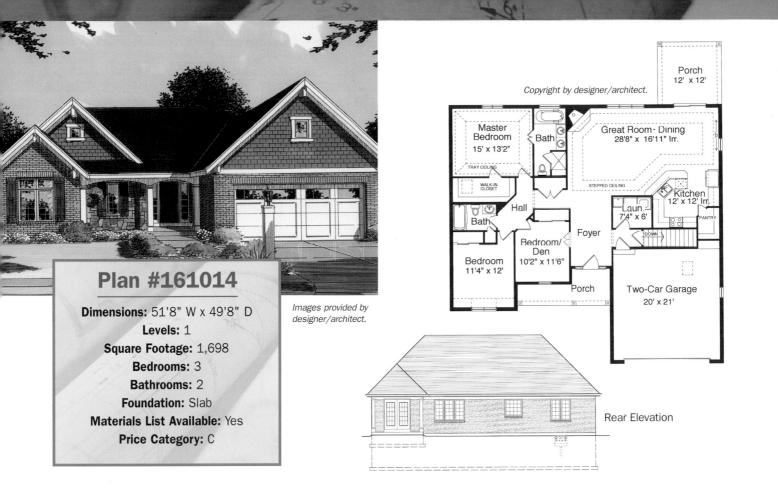

Plan #161014

Dimensions: 51'8" W x 49'8" D

Levels: 1

Square Footage: 1,698

Bedrooms: 3

Bathrooms: 2

Foundation: Slab

Materials List Available: Yes

Price Category: C

Images provided by designer/architect.

Rear Elevation

Plan #151054

Dimensions: 71'2" W x 54'10" D

Levels: 1

Square Footage: 1,746

Bedrooms: 3

Bathrooms: 2

Foundation: Crawl space or slab (basement option for fee)

CompleteCost List Available: Yes

Price Category: C

Images provided by designer/architect.

CAD FILE AVAILABLE

SMARTtip

Mixing and Matching Windows

Windows, both fixed and operable, are made in various styles and shapes. While mixing styles should be carefully avoided, a variety of interesting window sizes and shapes may nevertheless be combined to achieve symmetry, harmony, and rhythm on the exterior of a home.

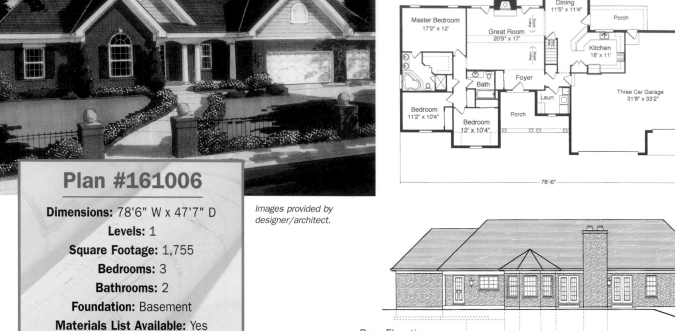

Copyright by designer/architect.

Images provided by designer/architect.

Plan #161006

Dimensions: 78'6" W x 47'7" D

Levels: 1

Square Footage: 1,755

Bedrooms: 3

Bathrooms: 2

Foundation: Basement

Materials List Available: Yes

Price Category: C

Rear Elevation

Copyright by designer/architect.

Images provided by designer/architect.

56'-0" Width

Plan #191003

Dimensions: 56' W x 42' D

Levels: 1

Square Footage: 1,785

Bedrooms: 3

Bathrooms: 3

Foundation: Crawl space, slab, or basement

Materials List Available: No

Price Category: C

Plan #221004

Dimensions: 67'8" W x 43' D

Levels: 1

Square Footage: 1,763

Bedrooms: 3

Bathrooms: 2

Foundation: Basement

Materials List Available: No

Price Category: C

Images provided by designer/architect.

You'll love the spacious feeling provided by the open design of this traditional ranch.

Features:

- Ceiling Height: 8 ft.

- Dining Room: This formal room is perfect for entertaining groups both large and small, and the open design makes it easy to serve.

- Living Room: The vaulted ceiling here and in the dining room adds to the elegance of these rooms. Use window treatments that emphasize these ceilings for a truly sumptuous look.

- Kitchen: Designed for practicality and efficiency, this kitchen will thrill all the cooks in the family. An attached dining nook makes a natural gathering place for friends and family.

- Master Suite: The private bath in this suite features a double vanity and whirlpool tub. You'll find a walk-in closet in the bedroom.

- Garage: You'll love the extra storage space in this two-car garage.

Rear Elevation

Copyright by designer/architect.

Planning Your Landscape

Landscapes change over the years. As plants grow, the overall look evolves from sparse to lush. Trees cast cool shade where the sun used to shine. Shrubs and hedges grow tall and dense enough to provide privacy. Perennials and ground covers spread to form colorful patches of foliage and flowers. Meanwhile, paths, arbors, fences, and other structures gain the patina of age.

Constant change over the years—sometimes rapid and dramatic, sometimes slow and subtle—is one of the joys of landscaping. It is also one of the challenges. Anticipating how fast plants will grow and how big they will eventually get is difficult, even for professional designers.

To illustrate the kinds of changes to expect in a planting, these pages show a landscape design at three different "ages." Even though a new planting may look sparse at first, it will soon fill in. And because of careful spacing, the planting will look as good in 10 to 15 years as it does after 3 to 5. It will, of course, look different, but that's part of the fun.

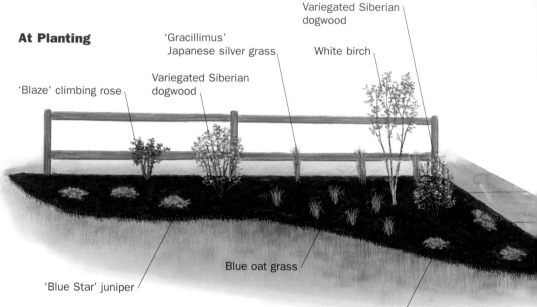

At Planting

'Blaze' climbing rose

'Gracillimus' Japanese silver grass

Variegated Siberian dogwood

Variegated Siberian dogwood

White birch

Blue oat grass

'Blue Star' juniper

'Blue Star' juniper

Three to Five Years

At Planting—Here's how the corner might appear in early summer immediately after planting. The white birch tree is only 5 to 6 ft. tall, with trunks no thicker than broomsticks. The variegated Siberian dogwoods each have a few main stems about 3 to 4 ft. tall. The 'Blaze' rose has just short stubs where the nursery cut back the old stems, but it will grow fast and may bloom the first year. The 'Blue Star' junipers are low mounds about 6 to 10 in. wide. The blue oat grass forms small, thin clumps of sparse foliage. The 'Gracillimus' Japanese silver grass may still be dormant, or it may have a short tuft of new foliage. Both grasses will grow vigorously the first year.

Three to Five Years—The birch tree has grown 1 to 2 ft. taller every year but is still quite slender. Near the base, it's starting to show the white bark typical of maturity. The variegated Siberian dogwoods are well established now. If you cut them to the ground every year or two in spring, they grow back 4 to 6 ft. tall by midsummer, with strong, straight stems. The 'Blaze' rose covers the fence, and you need to prune out a few of its older stems every spring. The slow-growing 'Blue Star' junipers make a series of low mounds; you still see them as individuals, not a continuous patch. The grasses have reached maturity and form lush, robust clumps. It would be a good idea to divide and replant them now, to keep them vigorous.

Ten to Fifteen Years—The birch tree is becoming a fine specimen, 20 to 30 ft. tall, with gleaming white bark on its trunks. Prune away the lower limbs up to 6 to 8 ft. above ground to expose its trunks and to keep it from crowding and shading the other plants. The variegated dogwoods and 'Blaze' rose continue to thrive and respond well to regular pruning. The 'Blue Star' junipers have finally merged into a continuous mass of glossy foliage. The blue oat grass and Japanese silver grass will still look good if they have been divided and replanted over the years. If you get tired of the grasses, you could replace them with cinnamon fern and astilbe, as shown here, or other perennials or shrubs.

Ten to Fifteen Years

Cinnamon fern

Astilbe

A Warm Welcome
Make a Pleasant Passage to Your Front Door

Why wait until a visitor reaches the front door to extend a cordial greeting? Have your landscape offer a friendly welcome and a helpful "Please come this way." Well-chosen plants and a revamped walkway not only make a visitor's short journey a pleasant one, but they can also enhance your home's most public face.

This simple arrangement of plants and paving produces an elegant entrance that deftly mixes formal and informal elements.

A wide walk of neatly fitted flagstones and a rectangular bed of roses have the feel of a small formal courtyard, complete with a pair of "standard" roses in planters, each displaying a mound of flowers atop a single stem. Clumps of ornamental grass rise from the paving like leafy fountains.

Gently curving beds of low-growing evergreens and shrub roses edge the flagstones, softening the formality and providing a comfortable transition to the lawn.

Morning glories and clematis climb simple trellises to brighten the walls of the house.

Flowers in pink, white, purple, and violet are abundant from early summer until frost. They are set off by the rich green foliage of the junipers and roses and the gray leaves of the catmint edging.

Add a bench, as shown here, so you can linger and enjoy the scene; in later years, the lovely star magnolia behind it will provide comfortable dappled shade.

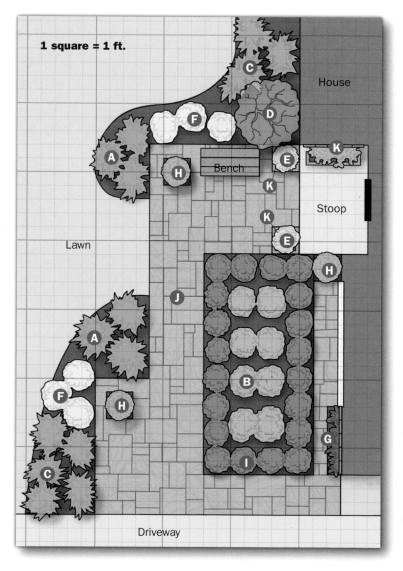

1 square = 1 ft.

Plants and Projects

Once established, these shrubs and perennials require little care beyond deadheading and an annual pruning. Ask the nursery where you buy the standard roses for advice on how to protect the plants in winter.

A **'Blue Star' juniper** *Juniperus squamata* (use 6 plants)
The sparkly blue foliage of this low-growing evergreen shrub neatly edges the opening onto the lawn.

B **'Bonica' rose** *Rosa* (use 8)
This deciduous shrub blooms from June until frost, producing clusters of double, soft pink flowers.

C **Dwarf creeping juniper**
Juniperis procumbens 'Nana' (use 8)
This low, spreading evergreen with prickly green foliage makes a tough, handsome ground cover.

D **Star magnolia** *Magnolia stellata* (use 1)
This small, multitrunked deciduous tree graces the entry with lightly scented white flowers in early spring.

E **'The Fairy' rose** *Rosa* (use 2)
Clusters of small, double, pale pink roses appear in abundance from early summer to frost. Buy plants

trained as standards at a nursery. Underplant with impatiens.

F **'White Meidiland' rose**
Rosa (use 6)
A low, spreading shrub, it is covered with clusters of lovely single white flowers all summer.

G **Jackman clematis** *Clematis* x *Jackmanii* (use 2)
Trained to a simple lattice, this deciduous vine produces large, showy, dark purple flowers for weeks in summer.

H **'Gracillimus' Japanese silver grass** *Miscanthus* (use 3)
The arching leaves of this perennial grass are topped by fluffy seed heads from late summer through winter.

I **'Six Hills Giant' catmint**
Nepeta x *faassenii* (use 20)
A perennial with violet-blue flowers and aromatic gray-green foliage edges the roses.

J **Flagstone paving**
Rectangular flagstones in random sizes.

K **Planters**
Simple wooden boxes contain blue-flowered annual morning glories (on the stoop, trained to a wooden lattice) and standard roses (in front of the stoop).

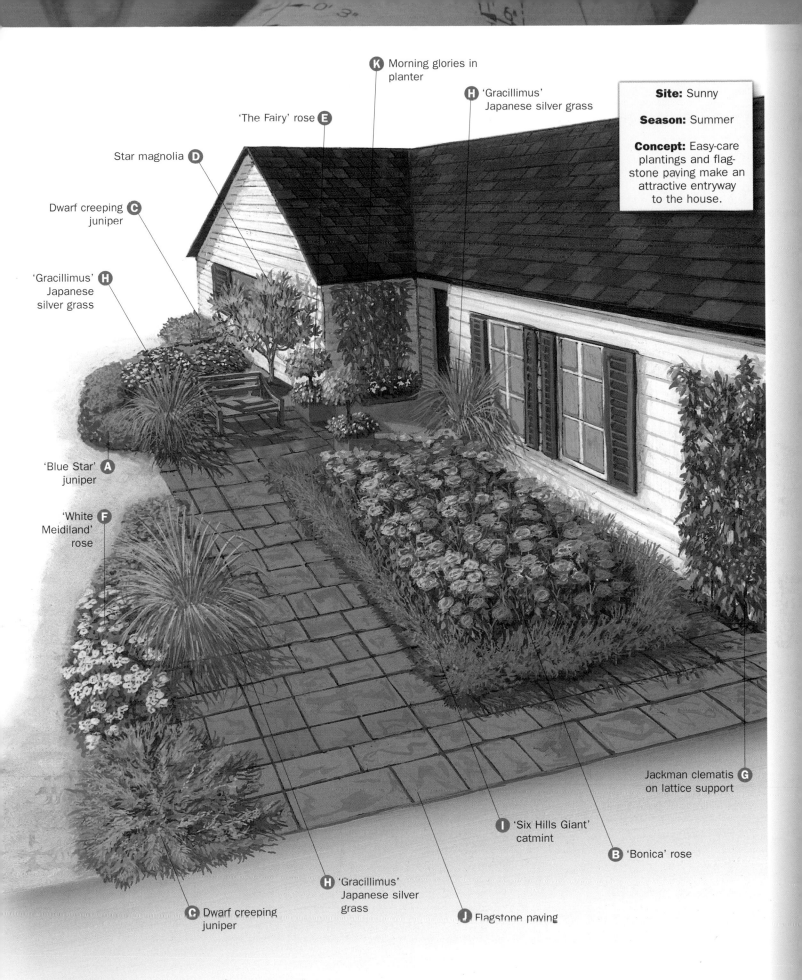

K Morning glories in planter

E 'The Fairy' rose

D Star magnolia

C Dwarf creeping juniper

H 'Gracillimus' Japanese silver grass

A 'Blue Star' juniper

F 'White Meidiland' rose

H 'Gracillimus' Japanese silver grass

H 'Gracillimus' Japanese silver grass

Site: Sunny

Season: Summer

Concept: Easy-care plantings and flag-stone paving make an attractive entryway to the house.

G Jackman clematis on lattice support

I 'Six Hills Giant' catmint

B 'Bonica' rose

C Dwarf creeping juniper

J Flagstone paving

Note: All plants are appropriate for USDA Hardiness Zones 4, 5, and 6.

A Step Up

Plant a Foundation Garden

'Techny' American **C**
arborvitae

R are is the home without foundation plantings. These simple skirtings of greenery hide unattractive concrete block underpinnings and help overcome the impression that the house is hovering a few feet above the ground. Useful as these plantings are, they are too often just monochromatic expanses of clipped yews, dull as dishwater. But, as this design shows, a durable, low-maintenance foundation planting can be more varied, more colorful, and more fun.

Broad-leaved and coniferous evergreen shrubs anchor this planting and provide four-season cover for the foundation. But they also offer contrasting shapes and textures and a range of colors from icy blue through a variety of greens to maroon.

What makes this design special is the smaller plants fronting the foundation shrubs. Including perenni-

als, grasses, and low shrubs in the mix expands the foundation planting into a small front-yard garden. From spring until frost, flowers in white, pink, magenta, and mauve stand out against the blue-and-green backdrop. When the last flower fades in autumn, the evergreen foliage takes center stage, serving through the winter as a welcome reminder that the world will green up again.

Germander **H**

'Sarah Bernhardt' **F**
peony

'Blue Star' juniper **D**

Plants and Projects

Eye-catching as the flowers in this planting are, the foliage is the key to its success in every season. The evergreens are attractive year-round. And each of the perennials has been chosen as much for its foliage as for its flowers. A thorough cleanup and maintenance pruning spring and fall will keep the planting looking its best.

A **'Wichita Blue' juniper** *Juniperus scopulorum* (use 1 plant)
This slow-growing, upright evergreen shrub has a neat pyramidal form and lovely silver-blue foliage and blue berries to add year-round color at the corner of the house.

B **'PJM' rhododendron**

Rhododendron (use 5)
An informal row of these hardy evergreen shrubs beautifully conceals the foundation. Vivid magenta flowers in early spring, small dark green leaves that turn maroon in winter, all on a compact plant.

C **'Techny' American arborvitae**
Thuja occidentalis (use 1)
This cone-shaped, slow-growing evergreen fills the corner near the front steps with fragrant, rich green, fine-textured foliage.

D **'Blue Star' juniper** *Juniperus squamata* (use 3)
The sparkly blue foliage and irregular mounded form of this low-growing evergreen shrub look great next to the peony and germander.

E **'Sea Urchin' blue fescue grass**
Festuca ovina var. *glauca* (use 3)
The very fine blue leaves of this perennial grass contrast handsomely with the dark green rhododendrons behind. Flower spikes rise above the neat, soft-looking mounds in early summer.

F **'Sarah Bernhardt' peony**
Paeonia (use 3)
A sentimental favorite, this perennial offers fragrant pink double flowers in early summer. Forms a multistemmed clump with attractive foliage that will look nice next to the steps through the summer.

G **White astilbe** *Astilbe* (use 3)
The lacy dark green foliage and fluffy white flower plumes of

this tough perennial stand out against the blue foliage of its neighbors. Flowers in June or July.

H **Germander** *Teucrium chamaedrys* (use 1)
This rugged little shrub forms a tidy mound of small, dark, shiny evergreen leaves next to the walk. Mauve flowers bloom in late summer.

I **'Sheffield' chrysanthemum**
Dendranthema x *grandiflorum* (use 1)
A longtime regional favorite, this hardy perennial forms a broad mound of fragrant gray-green foliage. Small, clear pink, daisylike blossoms cover the plant from September until frost.

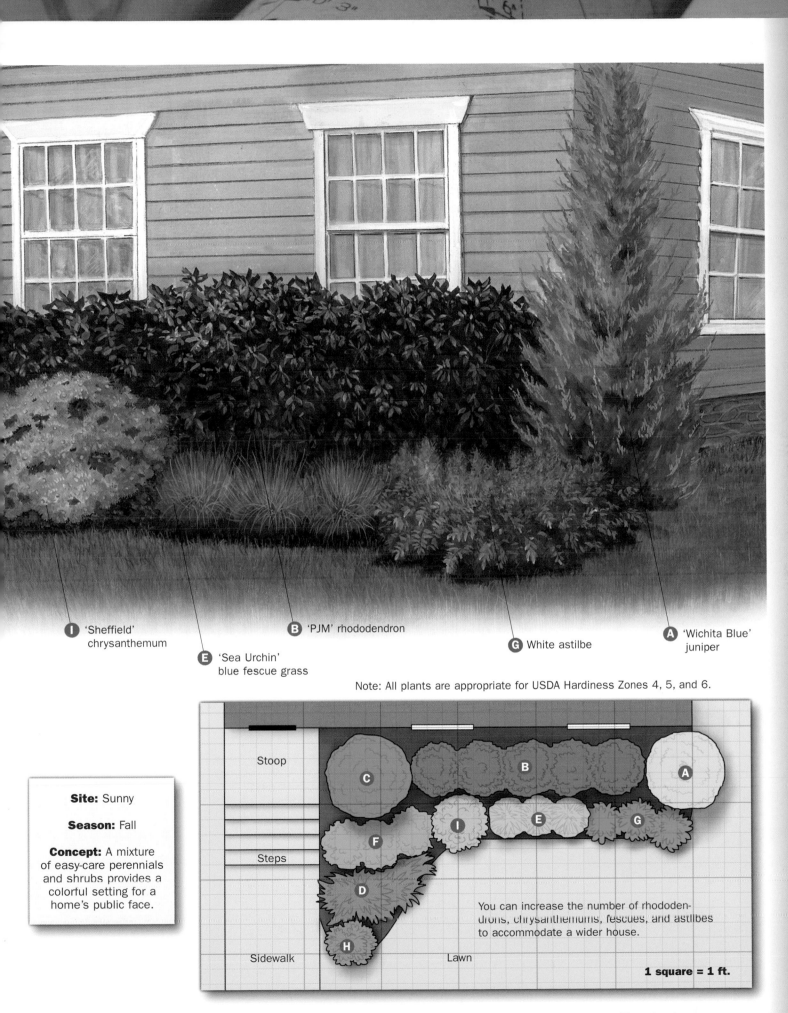

I 'Sheffield' chrysanthemum

E 'Sea Urchin' blue fescue grass

B 'PJM' rhododendron

G White astilbe

A 'Wichita Blue' juniper

Note: All plants are appropriate for USDA Hardiness Zones 4, 5, and 6.

Site: Sunny

Season: Fall

Concept: A mixture of easy-care perennials and shrubs provides a colorful setting for a home's public face.

Stoop

Steps

Sidewalk

Lawn

You can increase the number of rhododendrons, chrysanthemums, fescues, and astilbes to accommodate a wider house.

1 square = 1 ft.

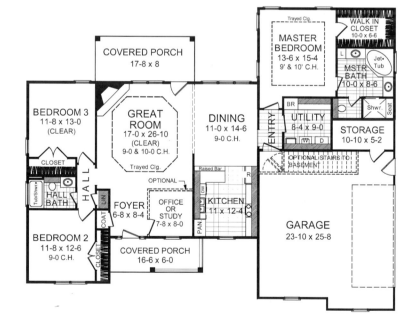

Plan #351042

Dimensions: 65'2" W x 53'4" D

Levels: 1

Square Footage: 1,801

Bedrooms: 3

Bathrooms: 2

Foundation: Crawl space or slab

Materials List Available: Yes

Price Category: D

Images provided by designer/architect.

This home features the popular split-floor plan layout and includes a spacious, open living area where your family can relax at the end of a long day.

Features:

- Great Room: This room just off the foyer features a tray ceiling and a corner fireplace.

- Kitchen: This well-equipped kitchen has a raised bar and is open into the dining room.

- Master Suite: This private area, located on the opposite side of the home from the secondary bedrooms, has a large walk-in closet and master bath.

- Bedrooms: These two additional bedrooms share a bathroom located in the hall.

Copyright by designer/architect.

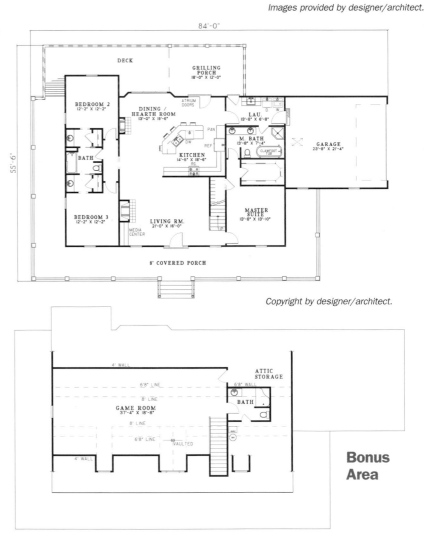

Plan #151089

Dimensions: 84' W x 55'6" D
Levels: 1
Square Footage: 1,921
Bedrooms: 3
Bathrooms: 3
Foundation: Crawl space, slab, or basement
CompleteCost List Available: Yes
Price Category: D

Images provided by designer/architect.

If your family loves to combine indoor and outdoor living, this home's fabulous porches and deck space make it perfect.

Features:

- **Porches:** A huge wraparound front porch, sizable rear porch, and deck that joins them give you space for entertaining or simply lounging.

- **Living Room:** A fireplace and built-in media center could be the focal points in this large room.

- **Hearth Room:** Open to both the living room and kitchen, this hearth room also features a fireplace.

- **Kitchen:** This step-saving kitchen includes ample storage and work space, as well as an angled bar it shares with the hearth room. Atrium doors lead to the rear porch.

- **Bonus Upper Level:** A large game room and a full bath make this area a favorite with the children.

Copyright by designer/architect.

Bonus Area

Plan #151005

Dimensions: 58' W x 54'10" D

Levels: 1

Square Footage: 1,940

Bedrooms: 4

Bathrooms: 2

Foundation: Crawl space, slab, or basement

CompleteCost List Available: Yes

Price Category: D

Images provided by designer/architect.

Copyright by designer/architect.

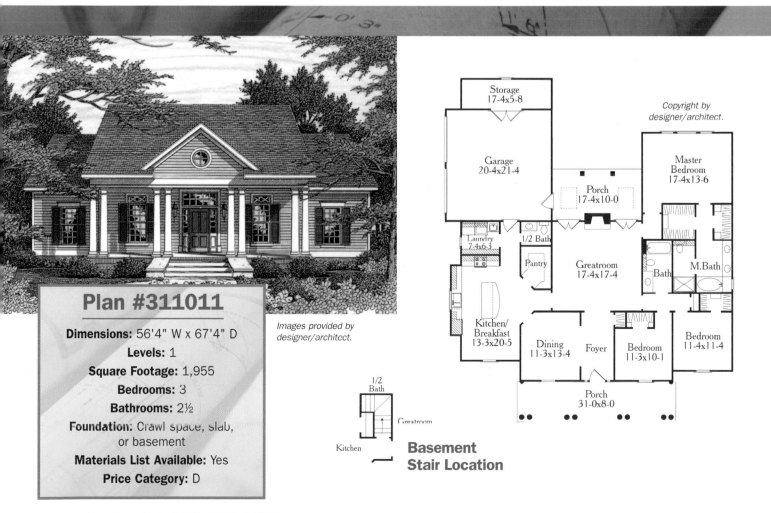

Plan #311011

Dimensions: 56'4" W x 67'4" D

Levels: 1

Square Footage: 1,955

Bedrooms: 3

Bathrooms: 2½

Foundation: Crawl space, slab, or basement

Materials List Available: Yes

Price Category: D

Images provided by designer/architect.

Copyright by designer/architect.

Basement Stair Location

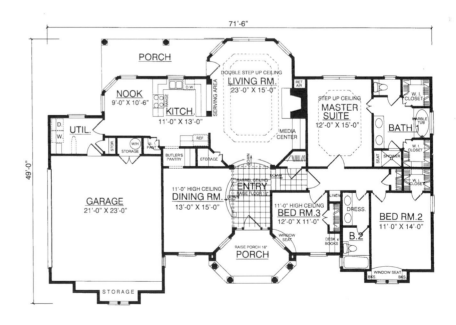

Plan #371042

Dimensions: 71'6" W x 49' D
Levels: 1
Square Footage: 1,999
Bedrooms: 3
Bathrooms: 2
Foundation: Slab
Materials List Available: No
Price Category: D

Ornate windows accent the exterior of this elegant French-style home—a dream come true.

Features:

- Entry: The raised porch will lead you into this beautiful tiled entry, with a barrel ceiling and columns separating it from a formal dining room.

- Living Room: This massive room has a double stepped-up ceiling and access to the rear porch. There is a built-in media center and charming fireplace.

- Kitchen: This gourmet kitchen with breakfast nook has a serving bar, which opens into the living room.

- Master Suite: This suite also has a stepped-up ceiling and a luxurious master bath with his and her vanities and walk-in closets.

- Bedrooms: Two additional large bedrooms share a convenient hall bathroom.

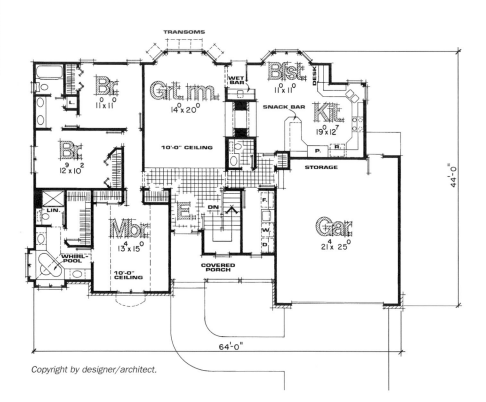

Plan #121051

Dimensions: 64' W x 44' D
Levels: 1
Square Footage: 1,808
Bedrooms: 3
Bathrooms: 2½
Foundation: Basement
Materials List Available: Yes
Price Category: D

You'll love the way that natural light pours into this home from the gorgeous windows you'll find in room after room.

Features:

- **Great Room:** You'll notice the bayed, transom-topped window in the great room as soon as you step into this lovely home. A wet-bar makes this great room a natural place for entertaining, and the see-through fireplace makes it cozy on chilly days and winter evenings.

- **Kitchen:** This well-designed kitchen will be a delight for everyone who cooks here, not only because of the ample counter and cabinet space but also because of its location in the home.

- **Master Suite:** Angled ceilings in both the bedroom and the bathroom of this suite make it feel luxurious, and the picturesque window in the bedroom gives it character. The bath includes a corner whirlpool tub where you'll love to relax at the end of the day.

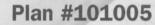

Plan #101005

Dimensions: 63' W x 57'2" D

Levels: 1

Square Footage: 1,992

Bedrooms: 3

Bathrooms: 2½

Foundation: Crawl space, slab, or basement

Materials List Available: Yes

Price Category: D

Images provided by designer/architect.

This midsized ranch is accented with Palladian windows and inviting front porch.

Features:

- Ceiling Height: 9 ft. unless otherwise noted.

- Special Ceilings: Tray or vaulted ceilings adorn the living room, family room, dining room, and master suite.

- Kitchen: This bright and airy kitchen is designed to be a pleasure in which to work. It shares a big bay window with the contiguous breakfast room.

- Breakfast Room: The light streaming in from the bay window makes this the perfect place to linger with coffee and the Sunday paper.

- Master Suite: This exceptional suite has a sitting area and direct access to the deck, as well as a full-featured bath, and spacious walk-in closet.

- Secondary Bedrooms: The other bedrooms each measure about 13 ft. x 11 ft. They have walk-in closets and share a "Jack-and-Jill" bath.

Rear View

Copyright by designer/architect.

Plan #141011

Dimensions: 54' W x 60'6" D

Levels: 1

Square Footage: 1,869

Bedrooms: 3

Bathrooms: 2

Foundation: Crawl space, slab, or basement

Materials List Available: Yes

Price Category: D

This home, as shown in the photograph, may differ from the actual blueprints. For more detailed information, please check the floor plans carefully.

Images provided by designer/architect.

The blending of brick and stone on this plan gives the home an old-world appeal.

Features:

• Ceiling Height: 8 ft. unless otherwise noted.

• Tall Ceilings: The main living areas feature dramatic 12-ft. ceilings.

• Open Plan: This home's open floor plan maximizes the use of space and makes it flexible. This main living area has plenty of room for large gatherings.

• Kitchen: The kitchen is integrated into the main living area. It features a breakfast room that is ideal for informal family meals.

• Master Suite: You'll enjoy unwinding at the end of the day in this luxurious space. It's located away from the rest of the house for maximum privacy.

• Secondary Bedrooms: You have the option of adding extra style to the secondary bedrooms by including volume ceilings.

Copyright by designer/architect.

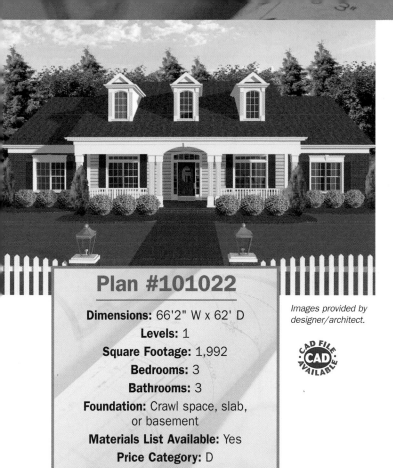

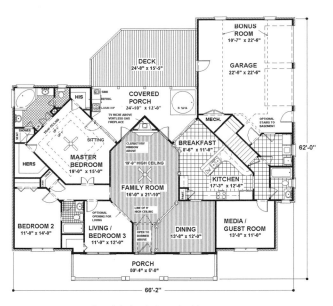

Plan #101022

Dimensions: 66'2" W x 62' D

Levels: 1

Square Footage: 1,992

Bedrooms: 3

Bathrooms: 3

Foundation: Crawl space, slab, or basement

Materials List Available: Yes

Price Category: D

Images provided by designer/architect.

CAD FILE AVAILABLE — CAD

Copyright by designer/architect.

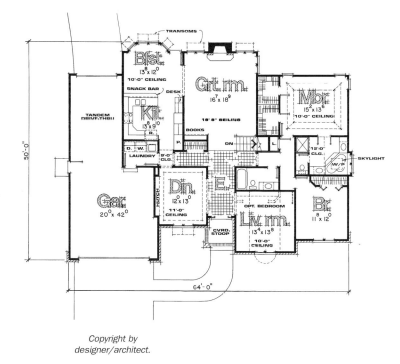

Plan #121050

Dimensions: 64' W x 50' D

Levels: 1

Square Footage: 1,996

Bedrooms: 2

Bathrooms: 2

Foundation: Basement

Materials List Available: Yes

Price Category: D

Images provided by designer/architect.

Copyright by designer/architect.

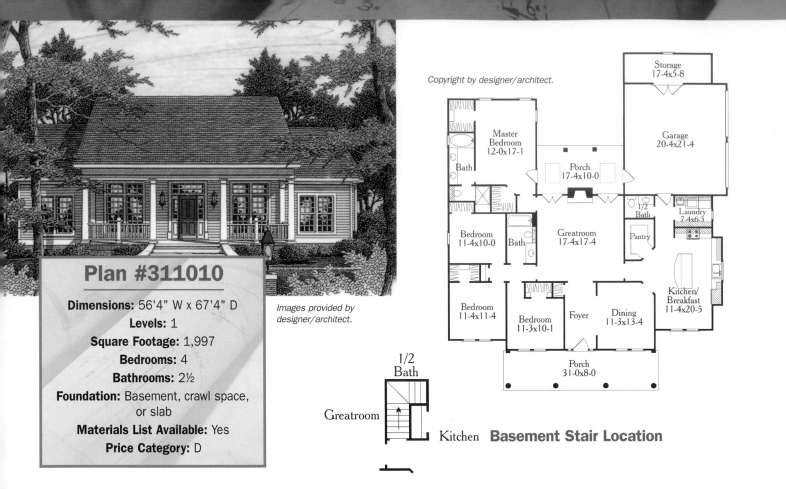

Images provided by designer/architect.

Plan #311010

Dimensions: 56'4" W x 67'4" D

Levels: 1

Square Footage: 1,997

Bedrooms: 4

Bathrooms: 2½

Foundation: Basement, crawl space, or slab

Materials List Available: Yes

Price Category: D

Basement Stair Location

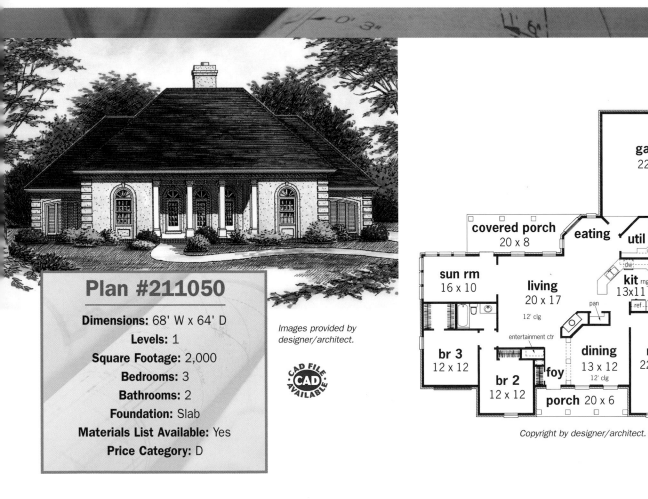

Plan #211050

Dimensions: 68' W x 64' D

Levels: 1

Square Footage: 2,000

Bedrooms: 3

Bathrooms: 2

Foundation: Slab

Materials List Available: Yes

Price Category: D

Images provided by designer/architect.

CAD FILE AVAILABLE

Plan #161008

Dimensions: 64'2" W x 46'6" D
Levels: 1
Square Footage: 1,860
Bedrooms: 3
Bathrooms: 2
Foundation: Slab
Materials List Available: No
Price Category: D

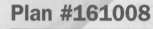

Images provided by designer/architect.

If you enjoy casual living and formal entertaining, this delightful floor plan will attract your eye.

Features:

- **Great Room:** A sloped ceiling and corner fireplace combine to provide this great room with an open and cozy atmosphere, perfect for relaxing evenings.

- **Kitchen:** This kitchen offers ample counter and cabinet space. A convenient snack bar provides a view to the breakfast area and great room

- **Master Suite:** Enjoy the elegance and style of this master suite, with its deluxe bath, large walk-in closet, and secluded alcove.

- **Laundry Room:** You will appreciate the ample counter space in this large laundry room with utility closet.

- **Porch:** From the breakfast area, enjoy a relaxed meal on this rear covered porch in warm weather.

Copyright by designer/architect.

SMARTtip

Espaliered Fruit Trees

Try a technique used by the royal gardeners at Versailles—espalier. They trained the fruit trees to grow flat against the walls, creating patterns. It's not difficult, especially if you go to a reputable nursery and purchase an apple or pear tree that has already been espaliered. Plant it against a flat surface that's in a sunny spot.

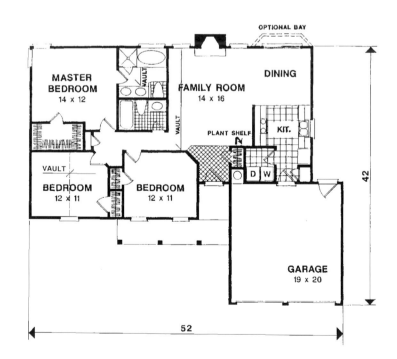

Plan #101023

Dimensions: 52' W x 42' D
Levels: 1
Square Footage: 1,197
Bedrooms: 3
Bathrooms: 2
Foundation: Crawl space, slab
Materials List Available: No
Price Category: C

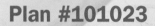

Images provided by designer/architect.

The open floor plan in this well-designed home makes everyone feel welcome in the public spaces but still allows privacy in the bedrooms.

Features:

- Family Room: A large fireplace flanked by windows and the vaulted ceiling are the focal points in this spacious room.

- Dining Area: Build the optional bay for an added design feature, or install sliding glass doors (and a back deck) to gain the maximum amount of natural light.

- Kitchen: A door to the garage and one to the adjacent laundry room both add convenience to this step-saving design.

- Master Suite: You'll love the walk-in closet and large corner windows here, as well as the bath with vaulted ceiling, tub, separate shower, and dual vanity.

- Additional Bedrooms: Both bedrooms have large closets and easy access to a nearby bath.

Copyright by designer/architect.

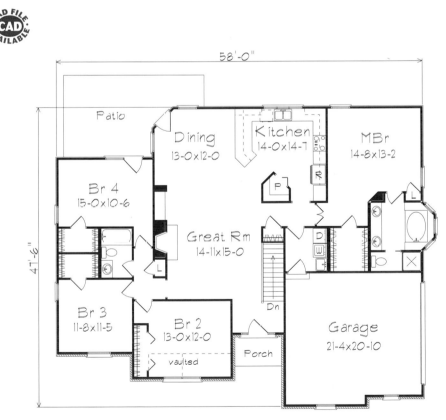

Plan #321020

Dimensions: 58' W x 47'6" D

Levels: 1

Square Footage: 1,882

Bedrooms: 4

Bathrooms: 2

Foundation: Basement

Materials List Available: Yes

Price Category: D

The interesting roofline will make this brick four-bedroom home stand out in the neighborhood.

Features:

- **Great Room:** Just off the entry, this large room has a cozy fireplace.

- **Dining Room:** This open room has access to the rear patio.

- **Kitchen:** This large kitchen, with its built-in pantry, has an abundance of cabinets and counter space.

- **Master Suite:** This inviting suite has a large walk-in closet and a master bath with a bay window.

- **Bedrooms:** Three additional bedrooms have large closets and share a common bathroom.

Images provided by designer/architect.

Copyright by designer/architect.

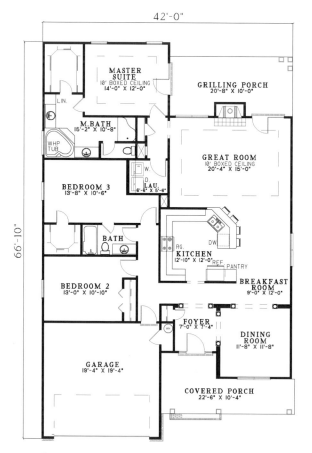

Plan #151008

Dimensions: 42' W x 66'10" D
Levels: 1
Square Footage: 1,892
Bedrooms: 3
Bathrooms: 2
Foundation: Crawl space, slab, basement, or daylight basement
CompleteCost List Available: Yes
Price Category: D

This cozy home features a foyer with 8-in. columns and a wide-open welcoming great room and kitchen.

Features:

- Great Room/Kitchen: Enjoy the fireplace in the great room while seated at the kitchen island or in the breakfast room. Access to the rear patio and covered porch makes this room a natural spot for family as well as for entertaining.

- Dining Room: For a formal evening, entertain in this dining room, with its grand entrance through elegant 8-in. columns.

- Master Suite: Luxuriate in the privacy of this master suite, with its 10-ft. ceiling and private access to the covered porch. The master bath pampers you with a whirlpool tub, separate vanities, a shower, and a walk-in closet.

- Bedrooms: A bedroom with walk-in closet and private access to full bath is a cozy retreat, while the other bedroom makes room for one more!

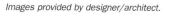

Copyright by designer/architect.

Plan #221015

Dimensions: 69'8" W x 46' D

Levels: 1

Square Footage: 1,926

Bedrooms: 3

Bathrooms: 2½

Foundation: Basement; optional walk-out basement available for extra fee

Materials List Available: No

Price Category: D

Images provided by designer/architect.

Rear Elevation

You'll love the open plan in this lovely ranch and admire its many features, which are usually reserved for much larger homes.

Features:

- Ceiling Height: 8 ft.

- Great Room: A vaulted ceiling and tall windows surrounding the centrally located fireplace give distinction to this handsome room.

- Dining Room: Positioned just off the entry, this formal room makes a lovely spot for quiet dinner parties.

- Dining Nook: This nook sits between the kitchen and the great room. Central doors in the bayed area open to the backyard.

- Kitchen: An island will invite visitors while you cook in this well-planned kitchen, with its corner pantry and ample counter space.

- Master Suite: A tray ceiling, bay window, walk-in closet, and bath with whirlpool tub, dual-sink vanity, and standing shower pamper you here.

Copyright by designer/architect.

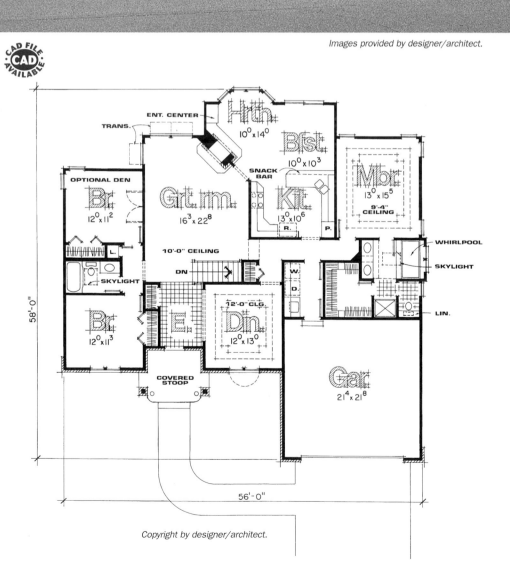

Plan #121001

Dimensions: 56' W x 58' D
Levels: 1
Square Footage: 1,911
Bedrooms: 3
Bathrooms: 2
Foundation: Basement
Materials List Available: Yes
Price Category: D

Detailed, soaring ceilings and top-notch amenities set this distinctive home apart.

Features:

- Ceiling Height: 8 ft. except as noted.

- Great Room: A soaring ceiling and six tall transom-topped windows make this a light and airy spot for entertaining. At the back of the home, a see-through fireplace in this great room is joined by a built-in entertainment center.

- Formal Dining Room: The entry enjoys a pleasing view of this dining room's detailed 12-ft. ceiling and picture window.

- Hearth Room: This bayed room shares the see-through fireplace with the great room.

- Master Suite: Enjoy the stars and the sun in the private bath's whirlpool and separate shower. The bath features the same decorative ceiling as the dining room.

Images provided by designer/architect.

Copyright by designer/architect.

Plan #151117

Dimensions: 66' W x 55' D

Levels: 1

Square Footage: 1,957

Bedrooms: 3

Bathrooms: 3

Foundation: Crawl space, slab, or basement

CompleteCost List Available: Yes

Price Category: D

You'll love this home if you have a family-centered lifestyle and enjoy an active social life.

Features:

- Foyer: A 10-ft. ceiling sets the tone for this home.

- Great Room: A 10-ft. boxed ceiling and fireplace are the highlights of this room, which also has a door leading to the rear covered porch.

- Dining Room: Columns mark the entry from the foyer to this lovely formal dining room.

- Study: Add the French doors from the foyer to transform bedroom 3, with its vaulted ceiling, into a quiet study.

- Kitchen: This large kitchen includes a pantry and shares an eating bar with the adjoining, bayed breakfast room.

- Master Suite: You'll love the access to the rear porch, as well as the bath with every amenity, in this suite.

Images provided by designer/architect.

Copyright by designer/architect.

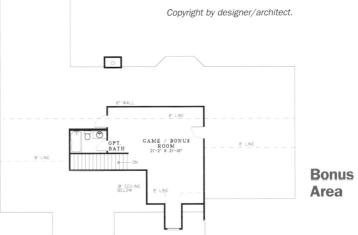

Bonus Area

Plan #211039

Dimensions: 62' W x 64' D

Levels: 1

Square Footage: 1,868

Bedrooms: 3

Bathrooms: 2

Foundation: Slab

Materials List Available: Yes

Price Category: D

Images provided by designer/architect.

Copyright by designer/architect.

Floor plan labels: sto 11 x 6, sto 11 x 6, garage 22 x 22, patio, br 2 14 x 12, living 20 x 16, util 10 x 9, bath, his, 1/2 wall, hers, mbr 18 x 14, foy, dining 12 x 12, kit 12 x 11, lazy susan, porch 17 x 4, br 3 13 x 12, eating 12 x 10

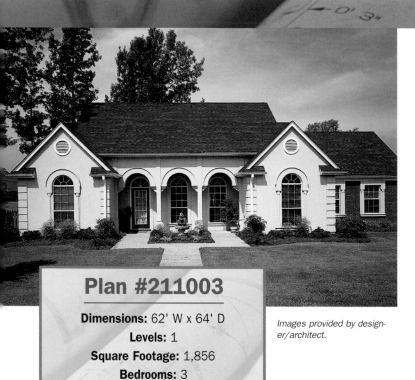

Plan #211003

Dimensions: 62' W x 64' D

Levels: 1

Square Footage: 1,856

Bedrooms: 3

Bathrooms: 2

Foundation: Crawl space or slab

Materials List Available: Yes

Price Category: D

Images provided by designer/architect.

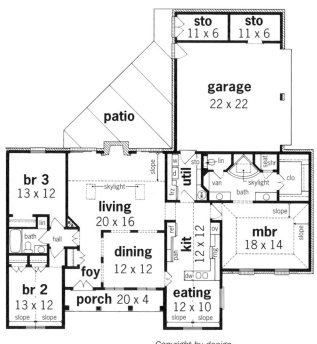

Copyright by designer/architect.

Floor plan labels: sto 11 x 6, sto 11 x 6, garage 22 x 22, patio, br 3 13 x 12, living 20 x 16, util, skylight, van, bath, seat, clo, mbr 18 x 14, hall, foy, dining 12 x 12, kit 12 x 12, br 2 13 x 12, porch 20 x 4, eating 12 x 10

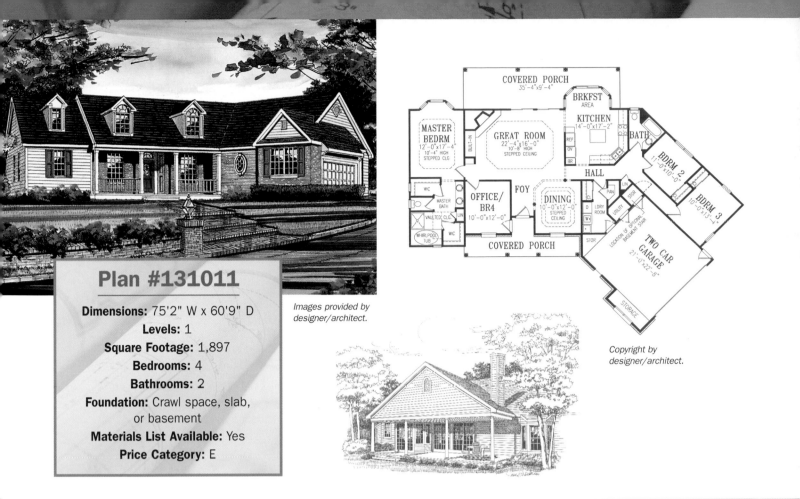

Plan #131011

Dimensions: 75'2" W x 60'9" D

Levels: 1

Square Footage: 1,897

Bedrooms: 4

Bathrooms: 2

Foundation: Crawl space, slab, or basement

Materials List Available: Yes

Price Category: E

Images provided by designer/architect.

Copyright by designer/architect.

Plan #221014

Dimensions: 72' W x 44'8" D

Levels: 1

Square Footage: 1,906

Bedrooms: 3

Bathrooms: 2½

Foundation: Basement

Materials List Available: No

Price Category: D

Images provided by designer/architect.

CAD FILE AVAILABLE

Copyright by designer/architect.

Rear Elevation

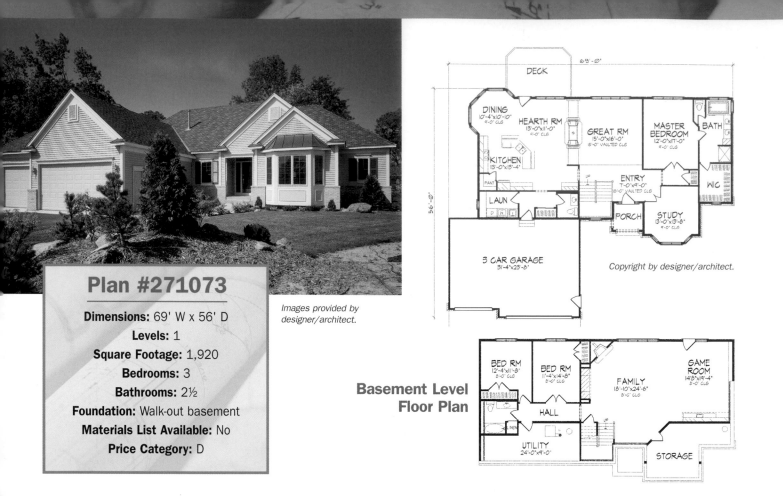

Images provided by designer/architect.

Copyright by designer/architect.

Basement Level Floor Plan

Plan #271073

Dimensions: 69' W x 56' D

Levels: 1

Square Footage: 1,920

Bedrooms: 3

Bathrooms: 2½

Foundation: Walk-out basement

Materials List Available: No

Price Category: D

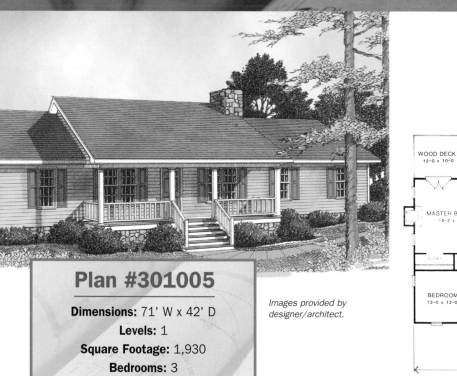

Images provided by designer/architect.

Copyright by designer/architect.

Plan #301005

Dimensions: 71' W x 42' D

Levels: 1

Square Footage: 1,930

Bedrooms: 3

Bathrooms: 2

Foundation: Crawl space, slab

Materials List Available: Yes

Price Category: D

Plan #131016

Dimensions: 75' W x 45' D
Levels: 1
Square Footage: 1,902
Bedrooms: 3
Bathrooms: 2
Foundation: Crawl space, slab, or basement
Materials List Available: Yes
Price Category: E

Images provided by designer/architect.

If traditional country looks appeal to you, you'll be delighted by the wraparound covered porch that forms the entryway to this comfortable home.

Features:

- **Great Room:** Sit by the fireplace in this room with feature walls so large that they'll suit a home theater or large media center.

- **Kitchen:** Overlooking the great room, this well-designed kitchen has great cabinets and ample counter space to make all your cooking and cleaning a pleasure.

- **Master Suite:** A large bay window makes the bedroom in this private suite sophisticated, and two walk-in closets make it practical. You'll love to relax in the master bath, whether in the whirlpool tub or the separate shower. A dual-sink vanity completes the amenities in this room.

- **Garage:** Find extra storage space in this two-bayed, attached garage.

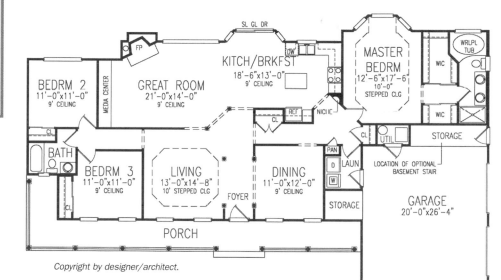

Copyright by designer/architect.

Great Room.

Plan #131044

Dimensions: 57'6" W x 42'4" D
Levels: 1
Square Footage: 1,994
Bedrooms: 3
Bathrooms: 2
Foundation: Crawl space, slab, or basement
Materials List Available: Yes
Price Category: E

Under a covered porch, Victorian-detailed bay windows grace each side of the brick-faced facade at the center of this ranch-style home, giving it a formal air.

Features:

- Ceiling Height: 10-ft. ceilings grace the central living area and the master bedroom of this home.
- Foyer: Round top windows make this area and the flanking rooms bright and cheery.
- Great Room: A fireplace and built-ins that are visible from anywhere in this large room make it a natural gathering place for friends and family.
- Optional Office: Use the room just off the central hall as a home office, fourth bedroom, or study.
- Master Suite: You'll love the bay window, tray ceiling, two walk-in closets, and private bath.
- Bonus Space: Finish this large area in the attic for extra living space, or use it for storage.

Rear Elevation

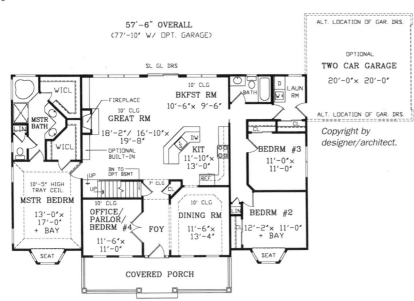

Copyright by designer/architect.

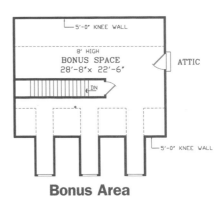

Bonus Area

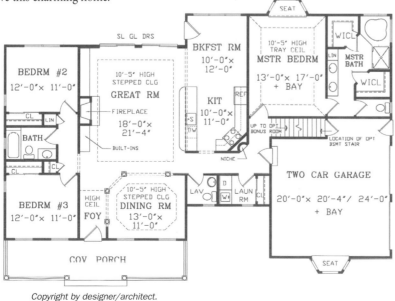

Plan #131035

Dimensions: 65'4" W x 45'10" D
Levels: 1
Square Footage: 1,892
Bedrooms: 3
Bathrooms: 2½
Foundation: Crawl space, slab, or basement
Materials List Available: Yes
Price Category: D

Images provided by designer/architect.

Families who love a mixture of traditional — a big front porch, simple roofline, and bay windows—and contemporary—an open floor plan—will love this charming home.

Features:

• Great Room: Central to this home, the open living and entertaining areas allow the family to gather effortlessly and create the perfect spot for entertaining.

• Dining Room: Volume ceilings both here and in the great room further enhance the spaciousness the open floor plan creates.

• Master Suite: Positioned on the opposite end of the other two bedrooms in the split-bedroom plan, this master suite gives an unusual amount of privacy and quiet in a home of this size.

• Bonus Room: Located over the attached garage, this bonus room gives you a place to finish for a study or a separate game room.

Rear Elevation

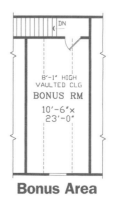

Bonus Area

Copyright by designer/architect.

Plan #131015

Dimensions: 57'4" W x 56'10" D

Levels: 1

Square Footage: 1,860

Bedrooms: 3

Bathrooms: 2

Foundation: Crawl space, slab, or basement

Materials List Available: Yes

Price Category: E

This home, as shown in the photograph, may differ from the actual blue-prints. For more detailed information, please check the floor plans carefully.

Images provided by designer/architect.

The mixture of country charm and formal elegance is sure to thrill any family looking for a distinctive and comfortable home.

Features:

• Great Room: Separated from the dining room by a columned arch, this spacious room has a stepped ceiling, a built-in media center, and a fireplace. French doors within a rear bay lead to the large backyard patio at the rear of the house.

• Dining Room: Graced by a bay window, this formal room has an impressive 11-ft. 6-in.-high stepped ceiling.

• Breakfast Room: With a 12-ft. sloped ceiling, this room shares an eating bar with the kitchen.

• Master Bedroom: The 10-ft. tray ceiling and bay window contribute elegance, and the walk-in closet and bath with a bayed nook, whirlpool tub, and separate shower make it practical.

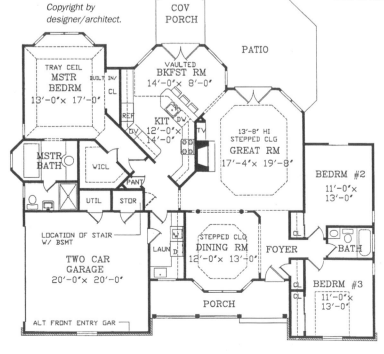

Copyright by designer/architect.

Rear Elevation

Great Room

Plan #161085

Dimensions: 67'2" W x 46'2" D
Levels: 1
Square Footage: 1,979
Bedrooms: 3
Bathrooms: 2
Foundation: Walk-out Basement
Materials List Available: No
Price Category: D

Images provided by designer/architect.

This nicely designed floor plan features step-saving convenience, high ceilings, furniture alcoves, and a delightful outdoor living space.

Features:

- Dining Room: This formal room and the great room form a large gathering space, and a grand opening to the breakfast area expands the living area.

- Kitchen: The snack bar defines this kitchen and offers additional seating. The breakfast area is surrounded by windows and provides a bright and cheery place to start the day.

- Master Suite: This suite enjoys a luxurious bath, and two additional bedrooms complete the main floor.

- Basement: This house comes with a full walk-out basement, which can be finished for additional square footage.

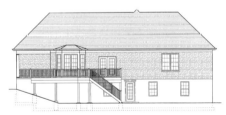

Rear Elevation

Left Side Elevation

Right Side Elevation

Copyright by designer/architect.

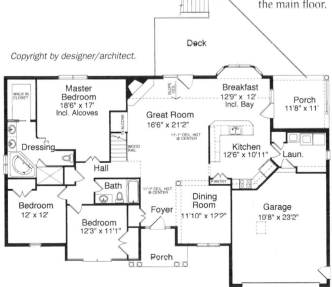

The Right Light

Lighting is one of the most important design elements in any home. Coordinating all of your artificial lighting sources—lamps, recessed or track lighting, sconces, ceiling-mounted fixtures, even pendants—can make the difference between a place that is warm and welcoming or one that is dark and depressing. In addition, light can be used in more focused ways—whether that be illuminating your desk in a home office or minimizing reflection as you watch a DVD on your big-screen television.

Light even has the power to visually reconfigure space, making rooms seem larger or smaller than they are. Lastly, the smart use of lighting can shine attention on architectural high points while obscuring less desirable details.

Lighting Plans

The rooms in your new home will combine the three types of lighting: ambient, task, and accent light. How you plan to use the room will determine the amount and type of lighting you will need. Although there are some general rules and an actual formula to determine how many watts of light to use for every square foot of space in your house, you must be the ultimate judge of your lighting needs.

General Lighting

Ambient Light. Because this is the soft diffused overall light that fills a room, ambient lighting is also called general lighting. Obviously, it is critical to the mood of a room. Aside from natural light, there are numerous artificial sources of ambient light. You can use all or some of them for your home.

Ceiling Fixtures. Standard ceiling-mounted fixtures, such as pendants and chandeliers, and recessed canisters are good sources of general lighting.

Sconces and Torcheres. Wall fixtures usually direct light upward, where it washes the wall and is reflected back into the room. Other possible sources of good general lighting are lamps with opaque shades. But the important thing to remember is that ambient light is inconspicuous. Although you know the source of the light, the glow is diffused. Of course, never use an exposed bulb, which is much too harsh.

How bright you should make the rooms in your new home depends on the way and the time of day the room will be used. To create the precise level of light, wire ambient light sources to dimmer switches. This puts you in control and allows you to easily

Recessed accent lighting highlights the painting and the shelves of collectibles.

adjust the light level. For example, in a family room you may want subdued lighting for watching a movie, and stronger, more cheerful lighting when you're hosting a kid's birthday party.

Task Lighting

Task lighting focuses on a specific area. It illuminates the work surface—whether it be the kitchen counter or the top of your desk in a home office. Metal architects' lamps, under-cabinet lights, reading lamps, and desk lamps are all excellent examples

Wall sconces, above left, placed on both sides of a bathroom mirror are good sources of light for applying makeup and general grooming.

Track-mounted spotlights, above right, serve a number of lighting needs. Here some provide general lighting while others accentuate the wall of art.

Use light to set off a collection, right, of personal objects. Here the items alone draw attention, but the lighting makes this area a focal point of the room.

of task lighting. Optimally, task lights should be angled between you and the work. A reading lamp functions best, after all, when it is positioned behind you and over your shoulder. Aiming light directly on a surface creates glare, which causes eye strain.

In bathrooms, include task lights for grooming. Sconces on either side of the mirror are preferable to a strip of light above the mirror because the latter will cast shadows. If the room is small, the sconces may serve as general lighting as well.

Accent Lighting

Designers like to use accent lighting because it is decorative and often dramatic. Accent lighting draws attention to a favorite work of art, a recessed niche on a stairway landing, or a tall plant at the end of a long room, for example. Designers agree that when you want to highlight something special, be sure the light source is concealed in order not to detract from the object you are spotlighting.

Room-by-Room Guide to Lighting

With lighting, one size doesn't fit all. Each room presents its own lighting challenges and solutions. Think outside of the box. Recessed lighting, for example, can be tucked away under bookshelves, not just in the ceiling; track lighting can be installed in a circular pattern to mirror a room with sweeping curves rather than in straight strips. Here are some other strategies for lighting each of your new rooms.

Family/Play Room. Pendants or chandeliers are obvious choices here if headroom is not an issue. Add recessed lighting in the corners or near doors and windows. Or if the room is designed for active play, install recessed lighting throughout. Use lamps or track lighting for areas that will be used for reading or hobbies. And don't forget about accent lighting to highlight wall-hung photographs or paintings.

Media/TV Room. No light should be brighter than the TV screen. Instead of one bright light source, try several low-level lights—recessed lighting, lamps, and lighting under shelves. Three-way bulbs or dimmers are often the best solution. Remember: light should be behind you, not between you and the screen.

Home Office. A good lighting arrangement combines indirect overhead illumination with table lamps. Indirect light means that the light is softy diffused throughout the home office, not shining down on you. Use a desktop lamp, preferably an adjustable fixture, to focus light on the task at hand and to deflect glare from the computer screen. Install unobtrusive light fixtures in a hutch above the work surface or create a light bridge, a horizontal strip of wood with a light built into it, fastened to the underside of two upper cabinets.

In media room, try to keep the lighting levels below that of the TV.

Bedrooms. Any number of lighting combinations could work in this room, but generally an overhead fixture that you flip on when you first enter the room is practical and, depending on your choice of fixture, stylish. For a more intimate mood, wiring bedside lamps to a light switch will also work. A must-have is a swing-arm reading lamp with a narrow beam of light that enables you to finish your novel while your spouse gets some shuteye. These types of reading lamps are responsible for saving more than one marriage.

Bathrooms. As with a home office, you need ambient (general) light (to help you find your way to the toilet or shower without tripping) and task lighting (for personal grooming). The ideal task lighting should come from both sides of the mirror at eye level.

Kitchens. Team up general illumination—recessed or ceiling-mounted fixtures installed about 12 to 15 inches from the front of the upper cabinets is a good choice and a fixture or two over the sink—with under-the-cabinet task lighting for food preparation. Install decorative wood trim to hide the light strips.

Home Workshop. A workable solution that has stood the test of time is fluorescent fixtures at regular intervals along the ceiling and work lights for specific tasks. Installing a strip of outlets along the length of a worktable and plugging in lights, either portable ones or those attached to the underside of the cabinet, provides illumination on demand.

Staircase. Sufficient light is critical around staircases, where one false step can lead to injury. As a rule, figure you will need at least one 60-watt fixture per 10 feet of running stairs. Try recessed lighting in the ceiling, or for a more dramatic look, install lighting in several recessed niches along the staircase wall that won't invade the stair area.

Light home offices, right, using indirect general lighting combined with desk-mounted task lighting.

Kitchens, below, require overhead ambient lighting and concentrated task lighting over work surfaces.

For workshops, bottom, install overhead lights that won't cast shadows on the work.

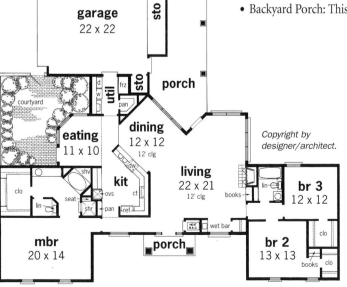

Plan #211049

Dimensions: 73' W x 66' D
Levels: 1
Square Footage: 2,023
Bedrooms: 3
Bathrooms: 2
Foundation: Slab
Materials List Available: Yes
Price Category: D

Images provided by designer/architect.

This European-style home features an open floor plan that maximizes use and flexibility of space.

Features:

- Ceiling Height: 8 ft. unless otherwise noted.

- Living/Dining Area: This combined living-and-dining area features high ceilings, which make the large area seem even more spacious. Corner windows will fill the room with light. The wet bar and cozy fireplace make this the perfect place for entertaining.

- Backyard Porch: This huge covered backyard

porch is accessible from the living/dining area, so the entire party can step outdoors on a warm summer night.

- Kitchen: More than just efficient, this modern kitchen is actually an exciting place to cook. It features a dramatic high ceiling and plenty of work space.

- Utility Area: Located off the kitchen, this area has extra freezer space, a walk-in pantry, and access to the garage.

- Eating Nook: Informal family meals will be a true delight in this nook that adjoins the kitchen and faces a lovely private courtyard.

Copyright by designer/architect.

SMARTtip
Outdoor Lighting Safety

Lighting is necessary for walkways, paths, stairways, and transition areas (from the deck to the yard, hot tub, or pool) to prevent accidents. Choose from low-voltage rail, path, and post lighting for these areas. The corners of planters or built-in seating should also be delineated with lighting. Consider installing floodlights near doorways or large open spaces for security reasons.

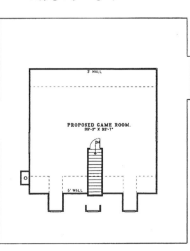

Plan #151105

Dimensions: 60'6" W x 91'4" D

Levels: 1

Square Footage: 2,013

Bedrooms: 4

Bathrooms: 2

Foundation: Crawl space or slab; basement for fee

CompleteCost List Available: Yes

Price Category: D

Images provided by designer/architect.

If you've always wanted a wraparound porch with columns, this could be your dream home.

Features:

- **Great Room:** Just off the foyer, this spacious room features a handsome fireplace where friends and family are sure to gather.

- **Dining Room:** Columns set off this dining room, and the large window area allows natural lighting during the day.

- **Kitchen:** Open to the dining room, this well-planned kitchen features a large central island with a sink and a dishwasher on one side and an eating bar on the other.

- **Breakfast Room:** You'll love the unusual shape of this room and its windows overlooking the rear porch. Access to the porch is from a hallway here.

- **Master Suite:** Enjoy two walk-in closets, plus a bath with a corner whirlpool tub, glass shower, linen closet, vanity, and compartmentalized toilet.

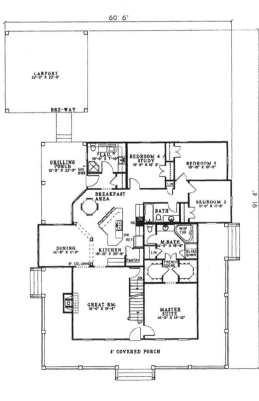

Bonus Area

Copyright by designer/architect.

Plan #161026

Dimensions: 67'6" W x 63'6" D
Levels: 1
Square Footage: 2,041
Bedrooms: 3
Bathrooms: 2
Foundation: Basement
Materials List Available: No
Price Category: D

Images provided by designer/architect.

You'll love the special features of this home, which has been designed for efficiency and comfort.

Features:

• Foyer: This raised foyer offers a view through the great room and beyond it to the covered deck.

• Great Room: Elegant windows allow versatility — decorate casually or more formally.

• Kitchen: You'll find ample counter space and cabinets in this spacious room, which adjoins the dining room and opens onto the rear yard.

• Library: Curl up on the window seat that wraps around the tower in this quiet spot.

• Laundry Room: A tub makes this large room practical for crafts as well as laundry.

• Master Suite: A vaulted ceiling gives grace to the sitting area, and the garden bath with a walk-in closet and whirlpool tub adds luxury.

Rear Elevation

Main Level Floor Plan

Basement Level Floor Plan

Copyright by designer/architect.

Left Side Elevation

Right Side Elevation

Front View

Living Room

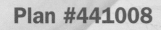

Plan #441008

Dimensions: 60' W x 50' D
Levels: 1
Square Footage: 2,001
Bedrooms: 3
Bathrooms: 2
Foundation: Crawl space;
slab or basement available for fee
Materials List Available: No
Price Category: D

A fine design for a country setting, this one-story plan offers a quaint covered porch at the entry, cedar shingles in the gables, and stonework at the foundation line.

Features:

- **Entry:** The pretty package on the outside is prelude to the fine floor plan on the inside. It begins at this entry foyer, which opens on the right to a den with a 9-ft.-high ceiling and space for a desk or closet.

- **Great Room:** This entertaining area is vaulted and contains a fireplace and optional media center. The rear windows allow a view onto the rear deck.

- **Kitchen:** Open to the dining room and great room to form one large space, this kitchen boasts a raised bar and a built-in desk.

- **Master Suite:** The vaulted ceiling in this master suite adds an elegant touch. The master bath features a dual vanities and a spa tub.

Rear Elevation

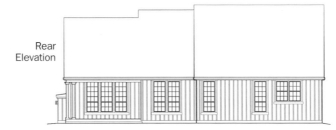

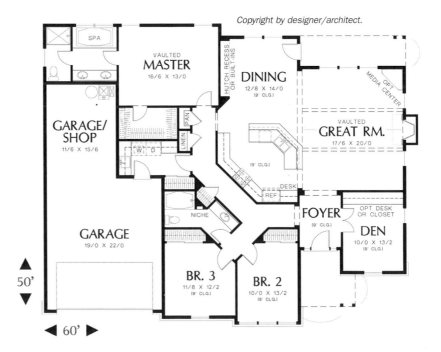

Plan #351008

Dimensions: 64'6"W x 61'4" D

Levels: 1

Square Footage: 2,002

Bedrooms: 3

Bathrooms: 2

Foundation: Crawl space or basement

Materials List Available: Yes

Price Category: E

Images provided by designer/architect.

This home has the charming appeal of a quaint cottage that you might find in an old village in the English countryside. It's a unique design that maximizes every inch of its usable space.

Features:

- **Great Room:** This room has a vaulted ceiling and built-in units on each side of the fireplace.

- **Kitchen:** This kitchen boasts a raised bar open to the breakfast area; the room is also open to the dining room.

- **Master Suite:** The bedroom retreat features a raised ceiling and a walk-in closet. The bathroom has a double vanity, large walk-in closet, and soaking tub.

- **Bedrooms:** Two bedrooms share a common bathroom and have large closets.

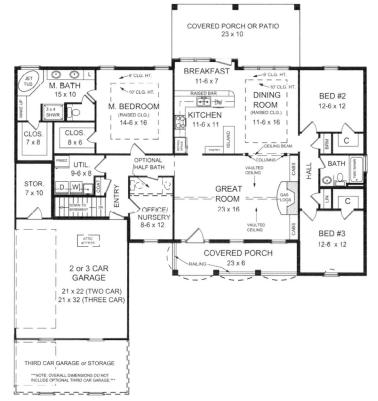

Copyright by designer/architect.

Plan #371056

Dimensions: 77'8" W x 60'1" D

Levels: 1

Square Footage: 2,043

Bedrooms: 3

Bathrooms: 2

Foundation: Slab

Materials List Available: No

Price Category: D

This classic country charmer has it all, large front porch, dormer windows, and beautiful bay windows.

Features:

- **Dining Room:** Once inside you will find a tiled entry that leads you into this elegant room set off by wood columns.

- **Living Room:** This large gathering area has a 9-ft.-high ceiling and a cozy fireplace, which opens into a cozy nook.

- **Kitchen:** This spacious island kitchen has plenty of counter space and a pantry with brick around the oven, making it a unique feature.

- **Master Suite:** This suite features a private bathroom with his and her walk-in closets and double vanities.

- **Bedrooms:** Two secondary bedrooms have large closets and share a hall bathroom.

Images provided by designer/architect.

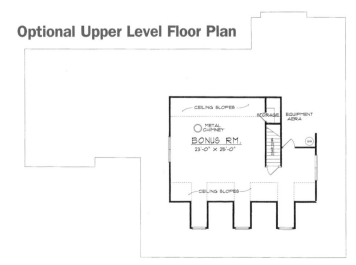

Optional Upper Level Floor Plan

Plan #151050

Dimensions: 69'2" W x 74'10" D
Levels: 1
Square Footage: 2,096
Bedrooms: 3
Bathrooms: 2½
Foundation: Crawl space, slab, or basement
CompleteCost List Available: Yes
Price Category: D

Images provided by designer/architect.

You'll love this spacious home for both its elegance and its convenient design.

Features:

- Ceiling Height: 8 ft.

- Great Room: A 9-ft. boxed ceiling complements this large room, which sits just beyond the front gallery. A fireplace and door to the rear porch make it a natural gathering spot.

- Kitchen: This well-designed kitchen includes a central work island and shares an angled eating bar with the adjacent breakfast room.

- Breakfast Room: This room's bay window is gorgeous, and the door to the garage is practical.

- Master Suite: You'll love the 9-ft. boxed ceiling in the bedroom and the vaulted ceiling in the bath, which also includes two walk-in closets, a corner whirlpool tub, split vanities, a shower, and a separate toilet room.

- Workshop: A huge workshop with half-bath is ideal for anyone who loves to build or repair.

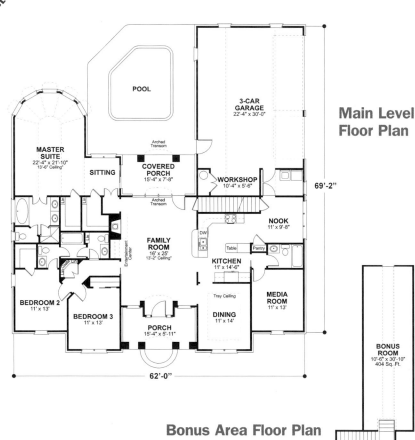

Plan #101033

Dimensions: 62' W x 69'2" D

Levels: 1

Square Footage: 2,260

Bedrooms: 3

Bathrooms: 3

Foundation: Basement

Material List Available: No

Price Category: E

Images provided by designer/architect.

The standing-seam roof over the entry porch makes this home stand out.

Features:

- Family Room: This gathering area features an over-13-ft.-tall ceiling, a built-in entertainment center, and a fireplace.

- Kitchen: This large kitchen has a built-in pantry and is open to the breakfast nook.

- Master Suite: This suite provides a dramatic extended bow-window wall with a clear view to the pool. It also offers his and her walk-in closets, a sitting area, and direct access to the covered rear porch.

- Bedrooms: The two additional bedrooms share a Jack-and-Jill bathroom Bedroom 2 has a walk-in closet.

Main Level Floor Plan

Bonus Area Floor Plan

Copyright by designer/architect.

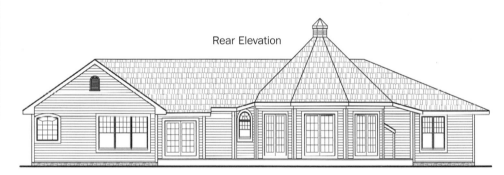

Plan #131019

Dimensions: 83'6" W x 53'4" D
Levels: 1
Square Footage: 2,243
Bedrooms: 3
Bathrooms: 2½
Foundation: Crawl space, slab, or basement
Materials List Available: Yes
Price Category: F

Images provided by designer/architect.

Rear Elevation

Drama marks this contemporary, angled ranch-style home which can be placed to suit any site, even the most difficult.

Features:

- **Great Room:** Imagine having an octagonal great room! The shape alone makes it spectacular, but the view to the backyard from its four exterior sides adds to the impression it creates, and you'll love its 16-ft. tray ceiling, fireplace, and wall designed to fit a large entertainment center.

- **Kitchen:** This room is adjacent to and visually connected to the great room but has excellent features of its own that make it an easy place to cook or clean.

- **Master Suite:** Separated from the other bedrooms, this suite is planned for privacy. You'll love the bath here and look forward to the quiet you can find at the end of the day.

- **Additional Bedrooms:** In a wing of their own, the other two bedrooms share a bath.

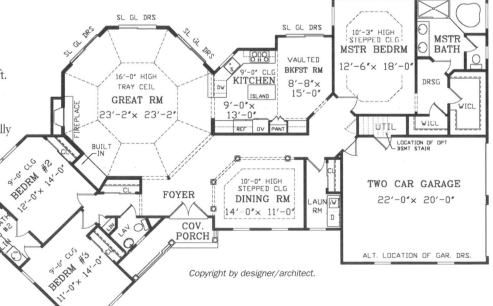

Copyright by designer/architect.

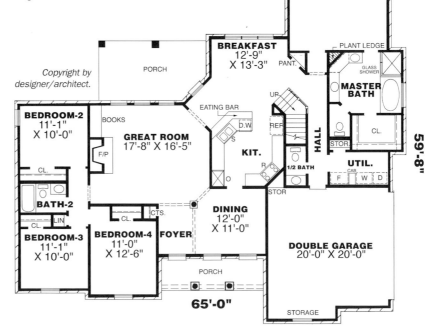

Plan #241002

Dimensions: 65' W x 59'8" D
Levels: 1
Square Footage: 2,154
Bedrooms: 4
Bathrooms: 2½
Foundation: Slab
Materials List Available: No
Price Category: D

Attractive corner quoins add style and grace to the elegance portrayed by the French-style roof and arched windows of this lovely split-bedroom home.

SMARTtip

Planting

Does the size of your yard or budget preclude a separate structure? You could carve a corner out of the garage if there's a window nearby. But you need access to water. That's why a utility or laundry room can double as a potting place. Set a large shelf under the window for seedlings, and reserve a cabinet for storing supplies.

Images provided by designer/architect.

Features:

- **Great Room:** From the foyer, guests enter this spacious and comfortable great room, which features a fireplace, built-in bookshelves, and a grand view of a wonderful covered porch.

- **Kitchen:** Designed for total convenience and easy work patterns, this kitchen features ample counter space and cabinets, an eating bar that adjoins a large breakfast area, and easy access to the great room and formal dining room.

- **Master Suite:** You can enjoy the relaxing comfort of this luxurious master suite—separated for privacy—which features an oversized whirlpool tub, his and her vanities, and a separate shower.

- **Additional Bedrooms:** Three secondary bedrooms share a full bath.

Copyright by designer/architect.

Plan #481156

Dimensions: 78' W x 62'6" D

Levels: 1

Square Footage: 2,109

Bedrooms: 1

Bathrooms: 1

Foundation: Walkout

Materials List Available: No

Price Category: D

Images provided by designer/architect.

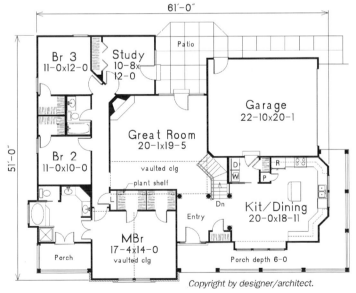

Copyright by designer/architect.

Plan #321030

Dimensions: 61' W x 51' D

Levels: 1

Square Footage: 2,029

Bedrooms: 4

Bathrooms: 2

Foundation: Crawl space, slab, basement, or walk-out

Materials List Available: Yes

Price Category: D

Images provided by designer/architect.

SMARTtip

Measuring Angles

A sure-fire way to accurately measure the wall-frame acute angle is to cut a piece of scrap lumber to emulate the angle, and then measure it.

Plan #651128

Dimensions: 39' W x 92' D

Levels: 1

Square Footage: 2,169

Bedrooms: 3

Bathrooms: 2

Foundation: Slab

Materials List Available: No

Price Category: D

Images provided by designer/architect.

Copyright by designer/architect.

The eye-catching columns at the front of this home make it unique and attractive.

Features:

• Great Room: Step into the home into this beautiful great room, with its fireplace and arched entryways into the dining room.

• Kitchen: This open and airy kitchen has an angled island in order to help with cooking or to provide a place to have a quick snack. The adjoining breakfast nook and keeping room are wonderful places to gather with friends and family.

• Master Suite: Located at the rear of the home for added privacy, this master suite features his and her walk-in closets, a tub, and a dual sink vanity.

Plan #151004

Dimensions: 64'8" W x 62'1" D

Levels: 1

Square Footage: 2,107

Bedrooms: 4

Bathrooms: 2½

Foundation: Basement, slab, crawl space

CompleteCost List Available: Yes

Price Category: D

Images provided by designer/architect.

You'll love the spacious feeling in this comfortable home designed for a family.

Features:

• Foyer: A 10-ft. ceiling greets you in this home.

• Great Room: A 10-ft. ceiling complements this large room, with its fireplace, built-in cabinets, and easy access to the rear covered porch.

• Dining Room: The 9-ft. boxed ceiling in this large room helps to create a beautiful formal feeling.

• Kitchen: The island in this kitchen is open to the breakfast room for true convenience.

• Breakfast Room: Morning light will stream through the bay window here.

• Master Suite: A 9-ft. pan ceiling adds a distinctive note to this room with access to the rear porch. In the bath, you'll find a whirlpool tub, separate shower, double vanities, and two walk-in closets.

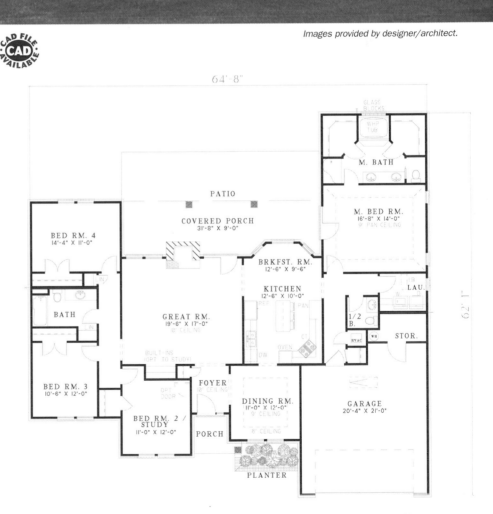

Copyright by designer/architect.

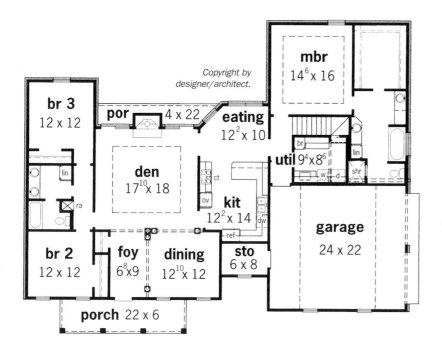

Plan #201084

Dimensions: 66'10" W x 54'5" D

Levels: 1

Square Footage: 2,056

Bedrooms: 3

Bathrooms: 2

Foundation: Crawl space, slab

Materials List Available: Yes

Price Category: D

Images provided by designer/architect.

This classic family home features beautiful country styling with lots of curb appeal.

Features:

• Ceiling Height: 8 ft.

• Open Plan: When guests arrive, they'll enter a foyer that is open to the dining room and den. This open area makes the home seem especially spacious and offers the flexibility for all kinds of entertaining and family activities.

• Kitchen: You'll love preparing meals in this large, well-designed kitchen. There's plenty of counter space, and the breakfast bar is perfect impromptu family meals.

• Master Suite: This spacious and elegant master suite is separated from the other bedroom for maximum privacy.

• Bonus Room: This unfinished bonus room awaits the time to add another bedroom or a home office.

• Garage: This attached garage offers parking for two cars, plus plenty of storage space.

Copyright by designer/architect.

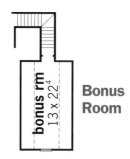

Bonus Room

Plan #171015

Dimensions: 79' W x 52' D

Levels: 1

Square Footage: 2,089

Bedrooms: 3

Bathrooms: 2½

Foundation: Crawl space or slab

Materials List Available: Yes

Price Category: D

Images provided by designer/architect.

This lovely three-bedroom country home, with a bonus room above the garage, is a perfect family home.

Features:

- **Dining Room:** This formal room and the great room form a large gathering space with a 12-ft.-high ceiling.

- **Kitchen:** The raised bar defines this kitchen and offers additional seating.

- **Master Suite:** This suite, located on the opposite side of the home from the secondary bedrooms, enjoys a luxurious bath with his and her walk-in closets.

- **Bedrooms:** Two secondary bedrooms have large closets and share a hall bathroom.

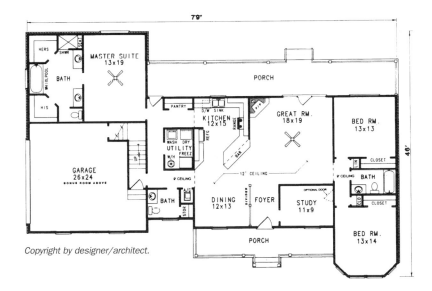

Copyright by designer/architect.

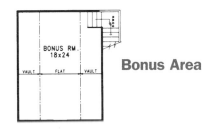

Bonus Area

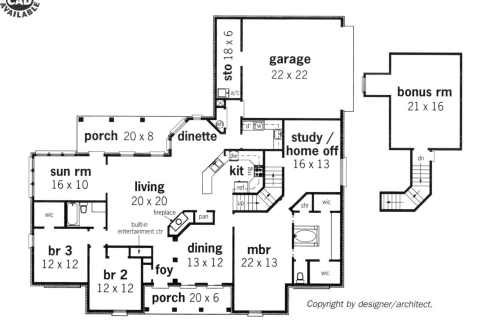

Images provided by designer/architect.

Plan #211059

Dimensions: 68' W x 84' D
Levels: 1
Square Footage: 2,299
Bedrooms: 3
Bathrooms: 2
Foundation: Slab, basement
Materials List Available: No
Price Category: E

This well designed home features plenty of space and all the amenities you seek.

Features:

- Ceiling Height: 9 ft.

- Living Room: This living room is the center of the home's activity. It boasts an attractive, unique angled fireplace and a built-in entertainment room.

- Sunroom: This glass room fills the living room with light. In fact, if you open its interior door on a sunny winter day, it can bring solar heat into the home. The sunroom also has direct access to the porch.

- Master Suite: This suite is located opposite the other bedrooms for maximum privacy. This is truly a master retreat. The private bath features two convenient entries, his and her walk-in closets, dual-sink vanity, luxurious tub, and separate shower.

- Bonus Room: Located over the garage, this room offers 352 ft. of additional space.

Copyright by designer/architect.

SMARTtip

Outdoor Decorating

Arrange outdoor spaces as you would an interior room. Choose a dominant element around which everything else flows. It can be a pool, a fire pit, or the garden. One major furniture piece, such as a dining table, can anchor an area.

Plan #151048

Dimensions: 60'6" W x 69'2" D

Levels: 1

Square Footage: 2,238

Bedrooms: 4

Bathrooms: 2

Foundation: Crawl space, slab (basement option for fee)

CompleteCost List Available: Yes

Price Category: C

This grand brick home, with four bedrooms, has room for everyone.

Features:

- **Great Room:** This room has a fireplace with two glass doors on either side for access to the rear grilling porch.

- **Dining Room:** Located just off the foyer, this room, which has a view of the front yard, is open to the great room.

- **Kitchen:** This kitchen, with a raised bar, is open to the breakfast room.

- **Master Suite:** This restful area, located on the opposite side of the home from the secondary bedrooms, features a private bathroom with a walk-in closet and double vanities.

- **Bedrooms:** Three secondary bedrooms have large closets and share a hall bathroom.

Copyright by designer/architect.

Images provided by designer/architect.

Copyright by designer/architect.

Plan #151045

Dimensions: 68'6" W x 65' D

Levels: 1

Square Footage: 2,250

Bedrooms: 4

Bathrooms: 2

Foundation: Crawl space, slab (basement option for fee)

CompleteCost List Available: Yes

Price Category: E

CAD FILE AVAILABLE

Images provided by designer/architect.

Copyright by designer/architect.

Plan #171004

Dimensions: 72' W x 52' D

Levels: 1

Square Footage: 2,256

Bedrooms: 3

Bathrooms: 2

Foundation: Crawl space, slab

Materials List Available: Yes

Price Category: E

SMARTtip

Windows – Privacy

You can easily stencil a work of art onto a windowpane, perhaps only as a border around the edge. Choose or create a design that gives you as little or as much privacy and light control as you need. Use a ready-made stencil or a piece of openwork fabric such as lace, or mask a design onto the glass using tape and a razor knife. Then apply glass paint or frosted glass spray, referring to the instructions and guidelines that come with the product.

Images provided by designer/architect.

Optional Bonus Space Floor Plan

Plan #151109

Dimensions: 59'9" W x 64'7" D

Levels: 1

Square Footage: 2,132

Bedrooms: 3

Bathrooms: 2

Foundation: Crawl space, slab (basement option for fee)

CompleteCost List Available: Yes

Price Category: D

Images provided by designer/architect.

Front Elevation

Plan #111006

Dimensions: 56' W x 67' D

Levels: 1

Square Footage: 2,241

Bedrooms: 4

Bathrooms: 2½

Foundation: Slab

Materials List Available: No

Price Category: F

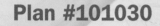

Plan #101030

Dimensions: 63' W x 63' D

Levels: 1

Square Footage: 2,071

Bedrooms: 3

Bathrooms: 2½

Foundation: Crawl space or basement

Materials List Available: No

Price Category: D

This lovely three-bedroom brick home with an optional bonus room above the three-car garage is just what you've been looking for.

Features:

• **Family Room:** This large room, with its high ceiling and cozy fireplace, is great for entertaining.

• **Kitchen:** This kitchen boasts a built-in pantry and a peninsula opening into the breakfast nook.

• **Master Suite:** This suite, with its 14-ft.-high ceiling and private sitting area, is a perfect place to relax after a long day. The bath has a double vanity, large walk-in closet, and soaking tub.

• **Bedrooms:** Two additional bedrooms feature walk-in closets and share a private bathroom.

CAD FILE AVAILABLE

SCREENED PORCH
15'-4" x 13'-10"

DECK
11' x 7'-6"

MASTER SUITE
21'-4" x 14'-2"
14' Ceiling

SITTING

BEDROOM 3
13' x 11'

BRKFST
11' x 10'-10"

8' High Opening

FAMILY
16' x 24'-1"
13'10" Ceiling

KITCHEN
13' x 9'-6"

Up to Bonus Room

DW

10' Ceiling

Dn

BEDROOM 2
13' x 11'

9' Ceiling

DINING
11' x 12'
Tray Ceiling

LIVING
11' x 12'
13'10" Ceiling

PORCH
15'-4" x 5'-4"

3-CAR SIDE-LOAD GARAGE
21'-4" x 33'-6"

63'-0"

63'-0"

OPT. BONUS ROOM
11'-4" x 33'-6"
434 Sq. Ft.

Bonus Area

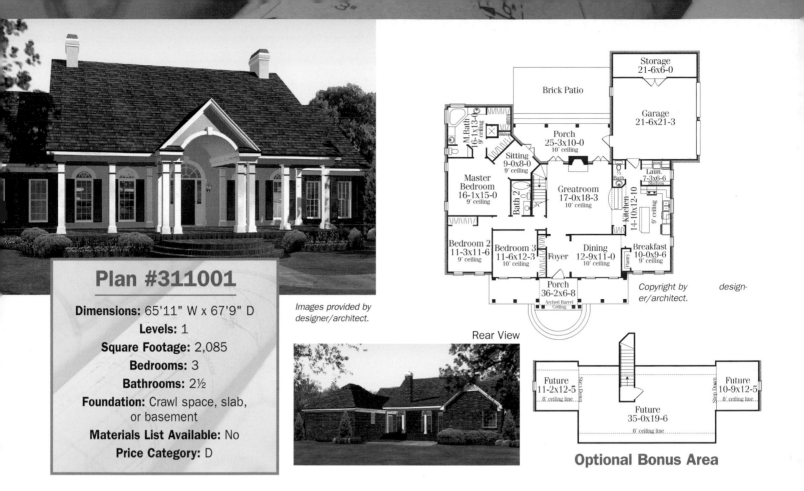

Plan #311001

Dimensions: 65'11" W x 67'9" D

Levels: 1

Square Footage: 2,085

Bedrooms: 3

Bathrooms: 2½

Foundation: Crawl space, slab, or basement

Materials List Available: No

Price Category: D

Images provided by designer/architect.

Copyright by designer/architect.

Rear View

Optional Bonus Area

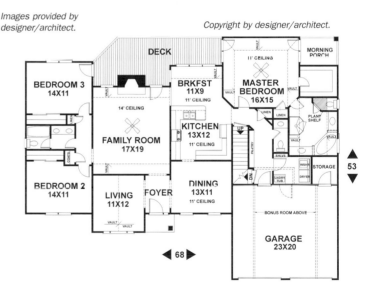

Plan #101008

Dimensions: 68' W x 53' D

Levels: 1

Square Footage: 2,088

Bedrooms: 3

Bathrooms: 2½

Foundation: Crawl space, slab or basement

Materials List Available: Yes

Price Category: E

Images provided by designer/architect.

Copyright by designer/architect.

CAD FILE AVAILABLE

SMARTtip

Accentuating Your Bathroom with Details

No matter how big or small the room, details will pull the style together. Some of the best details that you can include are the smallest—drawer pulls from an antique store or shells in a glass jar or just left on the countertop. Add period flavor with crown molding, or dress up contemporary fixtures with polished stone fittings.

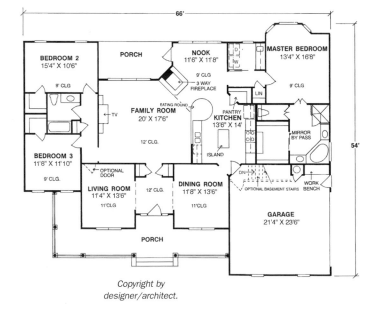

Plan #121178

Dimensions: 66' W x 54' D
Levels: 1
Square Footage: 2,126
Bedrooms: 3
Bathrooms: 2
Foundation: Slab; basement for fee
Material List Available: Yes
Price Category: D

Images provided by designer/architect.

• Master Suite: You will never want to leave this master suite, with its windowed bedroom, 9-ft. ceiling, mirror bypass, toilet, tub, and his and her sinks.

This home is as beautiful inside as it is outside, with little details that will truly make it feel unique.

Features:

• Porches: The front porch is perfect for welcoming guests to your home, or greeting the children after school. After dinner, relax on the rear porch while watching the stars.

• Family Room: A beautiful 12-ft. ceiling, windows to the porch, and three-way fire place make this room wonderful for relaxing with friends and family.

• Kitchen: This kitchen's efficient layout is sure to delight the family chef. A large workspace, pantry, and center island make meal prep a pleasure. The eating area and snack bar are perfect for quick meals or catching up with the family. The three-way fireplace can be enjoyed from here in the kitchen, the nook, or the family room.

Copyright by designer/architect.

Plan #351007

Dimensions: 73'8"W x 53'2" D

Levels: 1

Square Footage: 2,251

Bedrooms: 3

Bathrooms: 2½

Foundation: Crawl space, slab, or basement

Materials List Available: Yes

Price Category: E

This three-bedroom brick home with arched window offers traditional styling that features an open floor plan.

Features:

- **Great Room:** This room has a 12-ft.-high ceiling and a corner fireplace.

- **Kitchen:** This kitchen boasts a built-in pantry and a raised bar open to the breakfast area.

- **Dining Room:** This area features a vaulted ceiling and a view of the front yard.

- **Master Bedroom:** This private room has an office and access to the rear porch.

- **Master Bath:** This bathroom has a double vanity, large walk-in closet, and soaking tub.

Images provided by designer/architect.

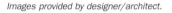

Bonus Room

Copyright by designer/architect.

Plan #121034

Dimensions: 92'8" W x 59'4" D

Levels: 1

Square Footage: 2,223

Bedrooms: 1

Bathrooms: 2½

Foundation: Basement; crawl space for a fee

Materials List Available: Yes

Price Category: E

Images provided by designer/architect.

CAD FILE AVAILABLE

Copyright by designer/architect.

Optional Basement Level Floor Plan

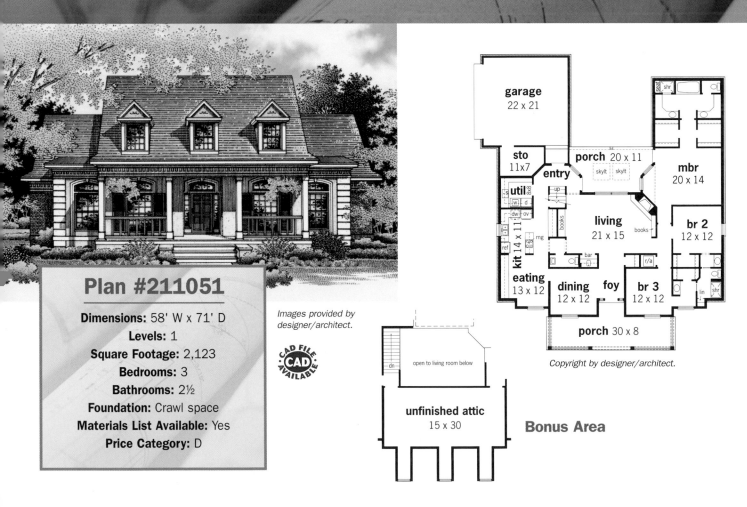

Plan #211051

Dimensions: 58' W x 71' D

Levels: 1

Square Footage: 2,123

Bedrooms: 3

Bathrooms: 2½

Foundation: Crawl space

Materials List Available: Yes

Price Category: D

Images provided by designer/architect.

CAD FILE AVAILABLE

Copyright by designer/architect.

Bonus Area

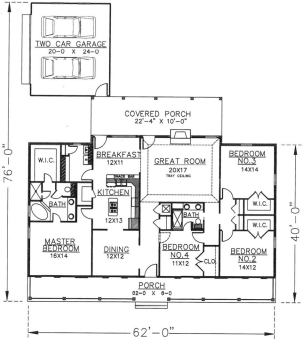

Plan #191009

Dimensions: 62' W x 76' D

Levels: 1

Square Footage: 2,172

Bedrooms: 4

Bathrooms: 2

Foundation: Crawl space, slab

Materials List Available: No

Price Category: D

Images provided by designer/architect.

Copyright by designer/architect.

Plan #171003

Dimensions: 69' W x 64' D

Levels: 1

Square Footage: 2,098

Bedrooms: 3

Bathrooms: 3

Foundation: Crawl space, slab

Materials List Available: Yes

Price Category: D

Images provided by designer/architect.

Copyright by designer/architect.

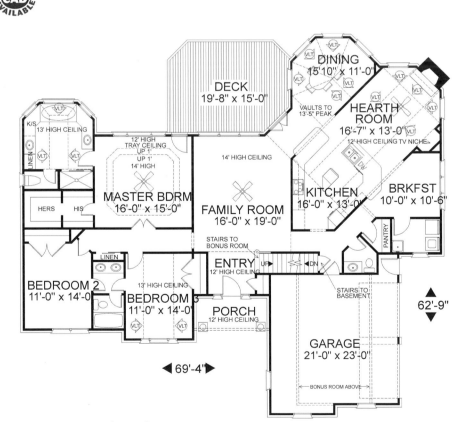

Plan #101012

Dimensions: 69'4" W x 62'9" D

Levels: 1

Square Footage: 2,288

Bedrooms: 3

Bathrooms: 2½

Foundation: Crawl space, slab, basement or walkout

Materials List Available: No

Price Category: E

Images provided by designer/architect.

This classic brick ranch boasts traditional styling and an exciting up-to-date floor plan.

Features:

• Ceiling Height: 9 ft. unless otherwise noted.

• Front Porch: Guests will be welcome by this inviting front porch, which features a 12-ft. ceiling.

• Family Room: This warm and inviting room measures 16 ft. x 19 ft. It features a 14-ft. ceiling and a rear wall of windows. French doors lead to an enormous deck.

• Kitchen: This unique angled kitchen is open to the hearth room and eating areas, all of which enjoy vaulted ceilings and are surrounded by windows. The hearth room has a TV niche.

• Master Suite: This 16-ft. x 15-ft. master suite is truly sumptuous, with its 12-ft. ceiling, sitting area, two walk-in closets, and full-featured bath.

• Bonus Room: Here is plenty of storage or room for future expansion. Just beyond the entry are stairs leading to a bonus room measuring approximately 12 ft. x 21 ft.

Copyright by designer/architect.

Plan #371058

Dimensions: 67'6" W x 53' D

Levels: 1

Square Footage: 2,195

Bedrooms: 4

Bathrooms: 2

Foundation: Slab

Materials List Available: No

Price Category: D

This traditionally classic brick four-bedroom home is loaded with charm.

Features:

- **Living Room:** The tiled entry takes you into this spacious room with a view of the backyard.

- **Family Room:** The living room's see-through fireplace opens into this large room with a double-stepped-up ceiling.

- **Kitchen:** A charming breakfast nook leads to this gourmet kitchen.

- **Dining Room:** Just off the kitchen, this formal room boasts a 10-foot-high ceiling.

- **Master Suite:** This massive sleeping suite has a sloped ceiling. The private bath has his and her vanities and two walk-in closets.

- **Bedrooms:** The three additional large bedrooms, all with sloped ceilings, share a common bathroom.

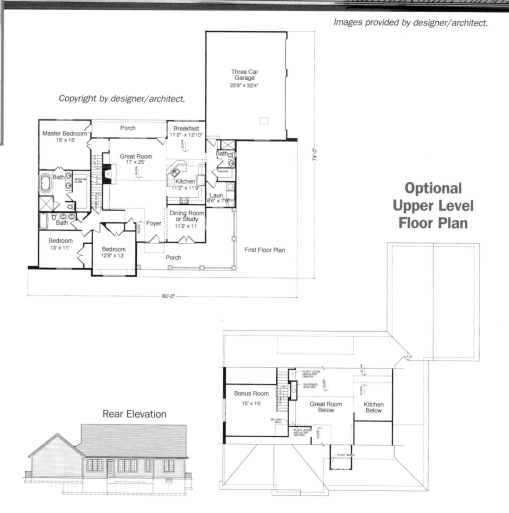

Plan #161072

Dimensions: 80' W x 74' D
Levels: 1
Square Footage: 2,183
Bedrooms: 3
Bathrooms: 3
Foundation: Basement
Materials List Available: Yes
Price Category: D

Features that make this house a spectacular home include a wraparound porch, a stone-and-siding exterior, and a garage that is set to the rear.

Features:

- **Great Room:** This large gathering area boasts a sloped ceiling, gas fireplace, and a series of windows that offer a view to the rear porch.

- **Breakfast Room:** This spacious breakfast room becomes a great place to start the day, with its surrounding windows and sloped ceiling.

- **Kitchen:** A snack bar and an abundance of counter space create this delightful kitchen. The room set in front of the kitchen can function as a formal dining room or a private study.

- **Master Suite:** This area is designed to pamper the homeowner with its comfortable private bath.

- **Bedrooms:** Two secondary bedrooms have large closets and share a hall bathroom.

Optional Upper Level Floor Plan

Rear Elevation

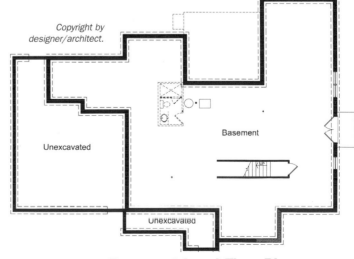

Plan #161160

Dimensions: 73'10" W x 58' D

Levels: 1

Square Footage: 2,230

Bedrooms: 3

Bathrooms: 2½

Foundation: Walkout

Material List Available: Yes

Price Category: E

Images provided by designer/architect.

This charming home will draw the warm affection of its occupants, guests, and neighbors alike.

CAD FILE AVAILABLE

Features:

• **Great Room:** Find peace at the center of your home with this comfortable space, which is perfect for entertaining friends or just quietly lounging by the fireplace.

• **Kitchen:** This efficiently designed space is situated between the sunlit breakfast area and the formal dining room for simple mealtime transitions. On warm days, move your meal out onto the screened-in deck.

• **Master Suite:** This master suite features a walk-in closet and a compartmentalized full bath with his and her vanities, large tub, and separate standing shower.

• **Secondary Bedrooms:** Two additional bedrooms feature wide closets and proximity to a full bathroom. Don't need three bedrooms? Use the third as a library.

Rear Elevation

Main Level Floor Plan

Copyright by designer/architect.

Basement Level Floor Plan

Plan #131006

Dimensions: 61' W x 53'6" D
Levels: 1
Square Footage: 2,193
Bedrooms: 3
Bathrooms: 2
Foundation: Crawl space, slab, or basement
Materials List Available: Yes
Price Category: E

SMARTtip

Give It Another Chance

Bear in mind that even if an item has lost its luster, it can take on a new life in the great outdoors. And it often happens that something that looks tired when it's indoors can add a new and invigorating, or even eccentric, charm to a porch, patio, or garden room. A lone peeling wooden shutter, a section of fencing, an old metal headboard, a rusty bike — any of these items or others like them can find new life in the garden. While peeling paint adds to the charm of some of these things, a couple of new coats may rejuvenate or preserve others.

Images provided by designer/architect.

This compact home is perfect for a small lot, but even so, has all the features of a much larger home, thanks to its space-saving interior design that lets one area flow into the next.

Features:

• Great Room: This wonderful room is sure to be the heart of your home. Visually, it flows from the foyer and dining room to the rear of the house, giving you enough space to create a private nook or two in it or treat it as a single, large room.

• Dining Room: Emphasize the formality of this room by decorating with subdued colors and sumptuous fabrics.

• Kitchen: Designed for efficiency, this kitchen features ample counter space and cabinets in a layout guaranteed to please you.

• Master Suite: You'll love the amenities in this private master suite, with its lovely bedroom and a bath filled with contemporary fixtures.

Rear View

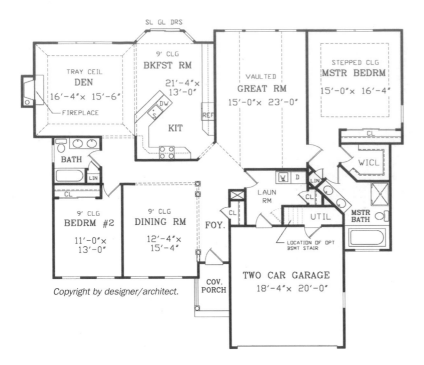

TRAY CEIL
DEN
16'-4" x 15'-6"
FIREPLACE

SL GL DRS

9' CLG
BKFST RM
21'-4" x
13'-0"

KIT

REF

DW
S

BATH

LIN

CL

9' CLG
BEDRM #2
11'-0" x
13'-0"

9' CLG
DINING RM
12'-4" x
15'-4"

FOY.

COV.
PORCH

VAULTED
GREAT RM
15'-0" x 23'-0"

STEPPED CLG
MSTR BEDRM
15'-0" x 16'-4"

CL

WICL

W D

LIN

CL

LAUN
RM

CL

LOCATION OF OPT
BSMT STAIR

UTIL

MSTR
BATH

TWO CAR GARAGE
18'-4" x 20'-0"

Copyright by designer/architect.

Alternate Floor Plan

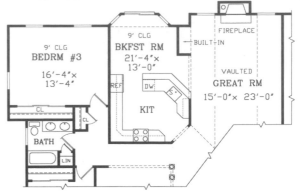

FIREPLACE

BUILT-IN

9' CLG
BEDRM #3
16'-4" x
13'-4"

9' CLG
BKFST RM
21'-4" x
13'-0"

REF

CL

CL

BATH

LIN

DW
S

KIT

VAULTED
GREAT RM
15'-0" x 23'-0"

Foyer / Dining Room

Kitchen

Great Room

Plan #351052

Dimensions: 79'4" W x 53'6" D

Levels: 1

Square Footage: 2,100

Bedrooms: 3

Bathrooms: 3

Foundation: Basement, crawl space, or slab

Materials List Available: Yes

Price Category: F

Images provided by designer/architect.

This elegant brick home features a spacious living area inside a classic exterior.

Features:

• Great Room: The great room and the sun room are vaulted with gas logs and windows on the rear with transoms above for plenty of light.

• Kitchen: This beautiful kitchen holds all the amenities you ever wanted, with a raised breakfast bar and a separate dining area.

• Master Suite: Your master suite will be envied, with its his and her bath, enormous closets, jet tub, and walk-in shower.

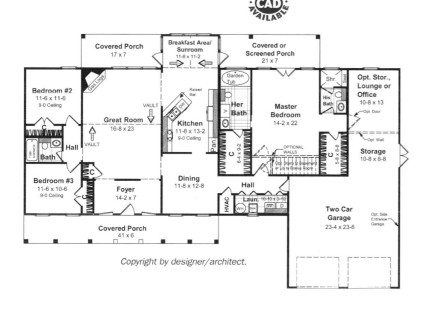

Copyright by designer/architect.

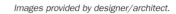

Bonus Area

Rear View

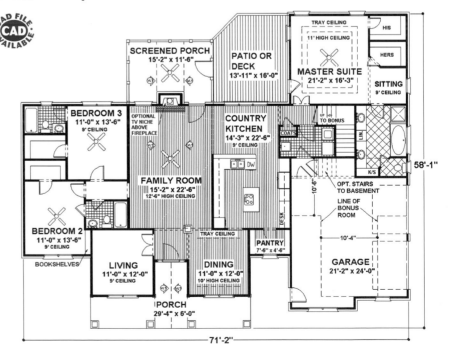

Plan #101011

Dimensions: 71'2" W x 58'1" D

Levels: 1

Square Footage: 2,184

Bedrooms: 3

Bathrooms: 3

Foundation: Crawl space, slab, basement or walkout

Materials List Available: No

Price Category: E

A classic design and spacious interior add up to a flexible design suitable to any modern lifestyle.

Features:

- Ceiling Height: 9 ft. unless otherwise noted.

- Dining Room: A decorative square column and a tray ceiling adorn this elegant dining room.

- Screened Porch: Enjoy summer breezes in style by stepping out of the French doors into this vaulted screened porch.

- Kitchen: Does everyone want to hang out in the kitchen while you are cooking? No problem. True to the home's country style, this huge 14-ft.-3-in. x 22-ft.-6-in. has plenty of room for helpers. This area is open to the vaulted family room.

- Patio or Deck: This pleasant outdoor area is accessible from both the screened porch and the master bedroom.

- Master Suite: This luxurious suite includes a double tray ceiling, a sitting area, two walk-in closets, and an exquisite bath.

Copyright by designer/architect.

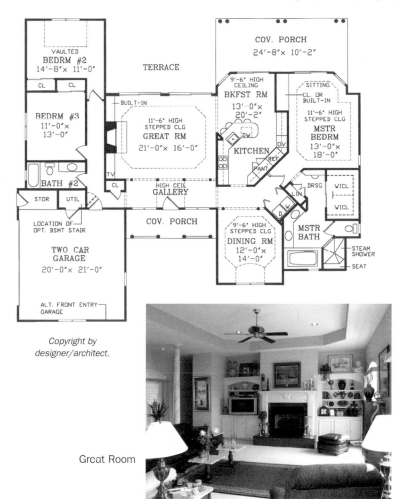

Plan #131009

Dimensions: 64'10" W x 57'8" D
Levels: 1
Square Footage: 2,018
Bedrooms: 3
Bathrooms: 2
Foundation: Crawl space, slab, or basement
Materials List Available: Yes
Price Category: D

Images provided by designer/architect.

The pavilion-styled great room at the heart of this H-shaped ranch gives it an unusual elegance that you're sure to enjoy.

Features:

- **Great Room:** The tray ceiling sets off this room, and a fireplace warms it on chilly nights and cool days. Two sets of sliding glass doors leading to the backyard terrace let in natural light and create an efficient traffic flow.

- **Kitchen:** Designed for a gourmet cook, this kitchen features a snack bar that everyone will enjoy and easy access to the breakfast room.

- **Breakfast Room:** Open to the columned rear porch, this breakfast room is an ideal spot for company or family brunches.

- **Master Suite:** A sitting area and access to the porch make the bedroom luxurious, while the private bath featuring a whirlpool tub creates a spa atmosphere.

Copyright by designer/architect.

Great Room

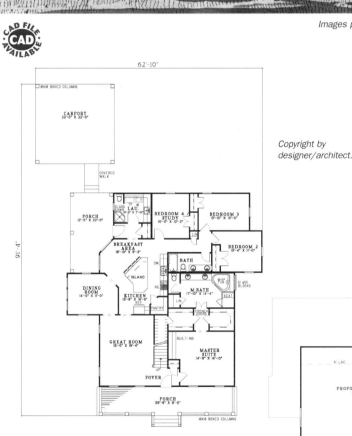

Plan #151113

Dimensions: 62'10" W x 91'4" D

Levels: 1

Square Footage: 2,186

Bedrooms: 4

Bathrooms: 3

Foundation: Crawl space, slab, or basement

CompleteCost List Available: Yes

Price Category: D

Images provided by designer/architect.

Copyright by designer/architect.

The porch on this four-bedroom ranch welcomes you home.

Features:

- **Great Room:** You'll find this large room just off the foyer.

- **Dining Room:** This room, with a view of the side yard, is located adjacent to the kitchen and the great room.

- **Kitchen:** This island kitchen, with a built-in pantry, is open to the breakfast area.

- **Master Suite:** This suite features his and her walk-in closets and a private bathroom with double vanities and whirlpool tub.

- **Bedrooms:** Three secondary bedrooms have large closets and share a hall bathroom.

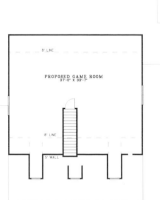

Optional Bonus Area Floor Plan

Plan #101010

Dimensions: 70' W x 47' D

Levels: 1

Square Footage: 2,187

Bedrooms: 4

Bathrooms: 2½

Foundation: Crawl space, slab, or basement

Materials List Available: Yes

Price Category: E

This stately ranch features a brick-and-stucco exterior, layered trim, and copper roofing returns.

Features:

- Ceiling Height: 11 ft. unless otherwise noted.

- Special Ceilings: Vaulted and raised ceilings adorn the living room, family room, dining room, foyer, kitchen, breakfast room, and master suite.

- Kitchen: This roomy kitchen is brightened by an abundance of windows.

- Breakfast Room: Located off the kitchen, this breakfast room is the perfect spot for informal family meals.

- Master Suite: This truly exceptional master suite features a bath, and a spacious walk in closet.

- Morning Porch: Step out of the master bedroom, and greet the day on this lovely porch.

- Additional Bedrooms: The three additional bedrooms each measure approximately 11 ft. x 12 ft. Two of them have walk-in closets.

Images provided by designer/architect.

CAD FILE AVAILABLE

Copyright by designer/architect.

SMARTtip

Using Slipcovers in Your Dining Area

Change the look of your dining room by slipcovering chairs. Short-skirted slipcovers give a more informal appearance; fabrics in graphic patterns, such as checks or floral prints, complement this style of slipcover best. Long-skirted covers are elegant additions to a formal dining room, particularly in solid color or tone-on-tone fabrics. Ties, buttons, or trim can add personality.

Plan #151034

Dimensions: 58'6" W x 64'6" D
Levels: 1
Square Footage: 2,133
Bedrooms: 3
Bathrooms: 2
Foundation: Crawl space, slab, or basement
CompleteCost List Available: Yes
Price Category: D

You'll love the high ceilings, open floor plan, and contemporary design features in this home.

Features:

- Great Room: A pass-through tiled fireplace between this lovely large room and the adjacent hearth room allows you to notice the mirror effect created by the 10-ft. boxed ceilings in both rooms.

- Dining Room: An 11-ft. ceiling and 8-in. boxed column give formality to this lovely room, where you're certain to entertain.

- Kitchen: If you're a cook, this room may become your favorite spot in the house, thanks to its great design, which includes plenty of work and storage space, and a very practical layout.

- Master Suite: A 10-ft. boxed ceiling gives elegance to this room. A pocket door opens to the private bath, with its huge walk-in closet, glass-blocked whirlpool tub, separate glass shower, and private toilet room.

This home, as shown in the photograph, may differ from the actual blueprints. For more detailed information, please check the floor plans carefully.

Images provided by designer/architect.

Copyright by designer/architect.

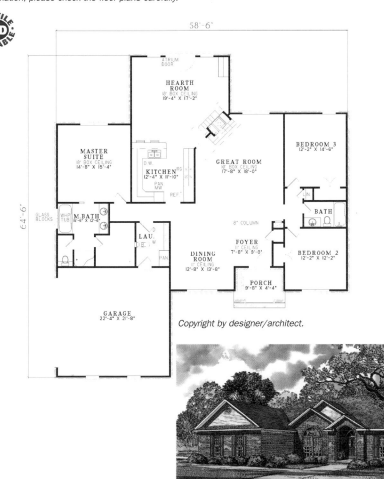

Rendering reflects floor plan

Plan #151083

Dimensions: 63'4" W x 58'6" D

Levels: 1

Square Footage: 2,034

Bedrooms: 4

Bathrooms: 2

Foundation: Crawl space, slab (basement option for fee)

CompleteCost List Available: Yes

Price Category: D

This grand brick home, with four bedrooms, will look great in any neighborhood.

CAD FILE AVAILABLE

Features:

- Great Room: This gathering room has a two-sided fireplace, which it shares with the hearth room.

- Dining Room: Just off the foyer is this room, with a view of the front yard.

- Kitchen: This kitchen, with a raised bar, is open to the hearth room.

- Master Suite: This suite, located on the opposite side of the home from the secondary bedrooms, features a private bathroom with a walk-in closet and double vanities.

- Bedrooms: Three secondary bedrooms have large closets and share a hall bathroom.

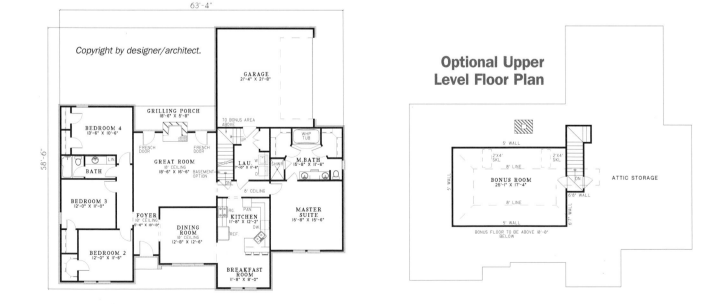

Copyright by designer/architect.

Optional Upper Level Floor Plan

Copyright by
designer/architect.

Rear Elevation

Plan #221018

Dimensions: 67' W x 53' D

Levels: 1

Square Footage: 2,007

Bedrooms: 3

Bathrooms: 2

Foundation: Basement

Materials List Available: No

Price Category: D

Images provided by designer/architect.

CAD FILE AVAILABLE

Plan #111015

Dimensions: 64' W x 58' D

Levels: 1

Square Footage: 2,208

Bedrooms: 4

Bathrooms: 2

Foundation: Slab

Materials List Available: No

Price Category: F

Images provided by designer/architect.

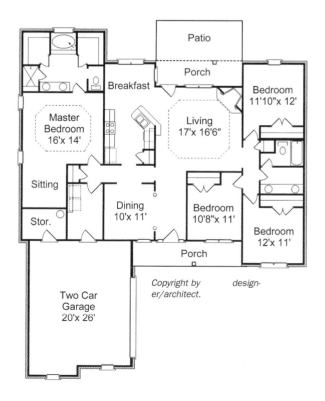

Copyright by   designer/architect.

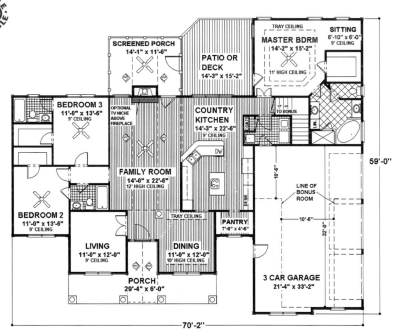

Plan #101009

Dimensions: 70'2" W x 59' D

Levels: 1

Square Footage: 2,097

Bedrooms: 3

Bathrooms: 3

Foundation: Crawl space, slab or basement

Materials List Available: Yes

Price Category: E

Round columns enhance this country porch design, which will nestle into any neighborhood.

Features:

- Ceiling Height: 9 ft. unless otherwise noted.

- Family Room: This large family room seems even more spacious, thanks to the vaulted ceiling. It's the perfect spot for all kinds of family activities.

- Dining Room: This elegant dining room is adorned with a decorative round column and a tray ceiling.

- Kitchen: You'll love the convenience of this enormous 14-ft.-3-in. x 22-ft.-6-in. country kitchen, which is open to the family room.

- Screened Porch: A French door leads to this breezy porch, with its vaulted ceiling.

- Master Suite: This sumptuous suite includes a double tray ceiling, a sitting area, a large walk-in closet, and a luxurious bath.

- Patio or Deck: This area is accessible from both the screened porch and master suite.

Copyright by designer/architect.

SMARTtip

Single-Level Decks

A single-level deck can use a strong vertical element, such as a pergola or a gazebo, to make it interesting. A simple and less-expensive option is a potted conical shrub or a clematis growing on a trellis.

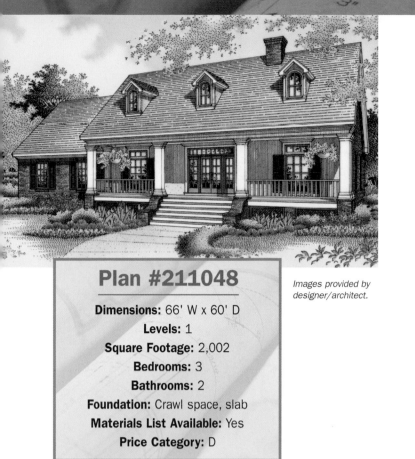

Images provided by designer/architect.

Plan #211048

Dimensions: 66' W x 60' D

Levels: 1

Square Footage: 2,002

Bedrooms: 3

Bathrooms: 2

Foundation: Crawl space, slab

Materials List Available: Yes

Price Category: D

Copyright by designer/architect.

Floor plan labels: office 14 x 9, storage, garage 22 x 22, util 9x6, kit 13x11, mbr 15 x 14, deck, eating 10 x 8, porch 15 x 12, dining 14 x 12, living 17 x 16, entry, br 3 12 x 11, br 2 13 x 11, porch 44 x 6, skylight

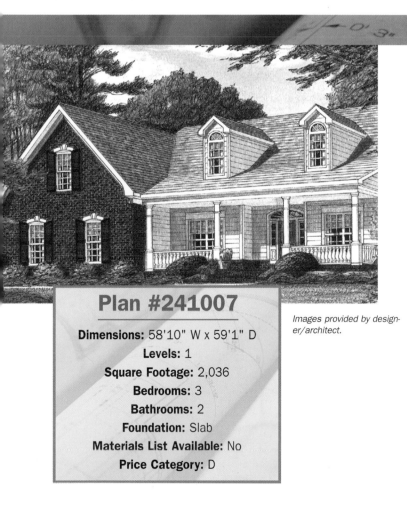

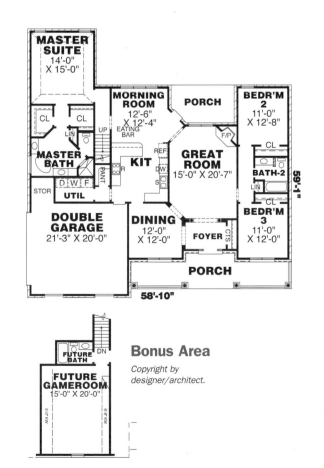

Images provided by designer/architect.

Plan #241007

Dimensions: 58'10" W x 59'1" D

Levels: 1

Square Footage: 2,036

Bedrooms: 3

Bathrooms: 2

Foundation: Slab

Materials List Available: No

Price Category: D

Floor plan labels: MASTER SUITE 14'-0" X 15'-0", MASTER BATH, UTIL, DOUBLE GARAGE 21'-3" X 20'-0", MORNING ROOM 12'-6" X 12'-4", EATING BAR, KIT, DINING 12'-0" X 12'-0", PORCH, GREAT ROOM 15'-0" X 20'-7", FOYER, BEDR'M 2 11'-0" X 12'-8", BATH-2, BEDR'M 3 11'-0" X 12'-0", PORCH, 58'-10", 59'-1"

Bonus Area

FUTURE BATH, FUTURE GAMEROOM 15'-0" X 20'-0"

Copyright by designer/architect.

Plan #271076

Dimensions: 69' W x 57' D

Levels: 1

Square Footage: 2,188

Bedrooms: 1

Bathrooms: 1½

Foundation: Walk-out basement

Materials List Available: No

Price Category: D

This stunning home, with its optional finished basement plan to add two more bedrooms, would be perfect for your growing family.

Features:

• Great Room: This room with tray ceiling has a fireplace with built-in cabinets on either side.

• Kitchen: This island kitchen, with dinette area, is open to the great room.

• Master Bedroom: This room features a tray ceiling and a view of the backyard.

• Master Bath: This private bath has a walk-in closet and double vanities.

Optional Basement Level Floor Plan

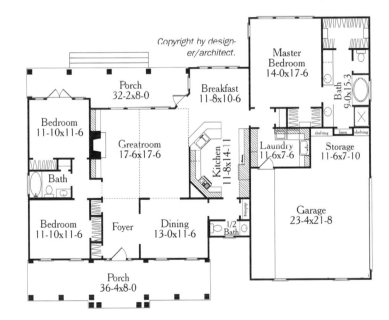

Plan #311004

Dimensions: 68'2" W x 57'4" D

Levels: 1

Square Footage: 2,046

Bedrooms: 3

Bathrooms: 2½

Foundation: Crawl space, slab, or basement

Materials List Available: Yes

Price Category: D

The open design of the public spaces in this home makes it ideal for an active family life or frequent entertaining.

Features:

• **Great Room:** Open to the foyer, this spacious room has a fireplace flanked by built-ins and a bank of windows at the rear.

• **Dining Room:** This large front room is convenient to the kitchen but isolated enough to be just right for a formal dinner party or a casual family meal.

• **Kitchen:** The angled work space creates efficient traffic patterns, and the snack bar makes it easy for small visitors to share the news of their day.

• **Breakfast Room:** The expansive window area lights this room, and the door to the rear porch makes outside entertaining easy.

• **Master Suite:** You'll feel coddled by the large window area, two walk-in closets, and bath with two vanities, tub, and shower.

Images provided by designer/architect.

Copyright by designer/architect.

Rear View

Plan #351047

Dimensions: 64' W x 54'4" D

Levels: 1

Square Footage: 2,001

Bedrooms: 3

Bathrooms: 2

Foundation: Crawl space, slab, or basement

Materials List Available: Yes

Price Category: E

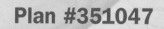

This home incorporates a unique design that maximizes every inch of its usable space to give you more for less.

Features:

- **Great Room:** This large room features a vaulted ceiling and a gas fireplace that has built-in cabinets on each side.

- **Kitchen:** This kitchen has a raised bar and is open to the sunroom and dining room.

- **Dining Room:** This gracious room has a view of the backyard and a raised ceiling.

- **Master Suite:** This area boasts a raised ceiling and a walk-in closet. There is also a private master bath with walk-in closet.

- **Bedrooms:** These two additional bedrooms share a bathroom located in the hall.

Clutter-Cutting Tips for Your Home

One of the great things about moving into a new home is all that new, uncluttered closet space you gain. But if you are like most homeowners, storage of all types will quickly become scarce, especially in a smaller cottage home. Here are some tips for expanding and organizing storage space.

Shelving Types

Shelving is an easy and economical way to add extra storage space in almost any part of your home—along walls, inside closets, and even in the basement or garage. Building shelves doesn't usually require a lot of skill or specialized tools, so this is one project just about any do-it-yourselfer can handle. And unless you decide to use hardwood—which looks great but costs a bundle—it won't cost a lot to install them either.

Solid wood shelving is the way to go when you want to show off the wood or your work.

Plywood and particleboard offer a couple of advantages when it comes to shelving, though. They cost less than solid wood, and can be bought faced with decorative surfaces. They also come in sheets, which makes them ideal for a really wide

Home offices require a mix of storage options: open shelving, drawers, and file cabinets.

shelf. Inexpensive, manufactured storage units ready for assembly often are made from melamine-coated particleboard.

Wood trim will help match your new shelves to the rest of the room or add some interesting detail. Trim is also a handy way to hide seams, gaps, exposed edges of plywood, and other blemishes. You can get trim in either hardwood or softwood. If you plan on finishing a project with stain or sealer, make sure the trim

matches the wood you used for the rest of the project.

Bracket Options

There are two basic types of ready-to-hang shelving supports: stationary shelf brackets and shelving standards. Stationary brackets come in many sizes and styles, and range from utilitarian to decorative. Shelving standards are slotted metal strips that support various types of shelf brackets.

Mounting Brackets

For maximum strength, anchor shelf supports to wall studs. If your shelf will carry a light load, you can anchor its supports between studs with mollies or toggle bolts. Attaching supports directly to the studs is always better, though, because sooner or later something heavy will wind up on the shelf. Use masonry anchors to attach shelf supports to brick or concrete. You can also attach shelf supports to a ledger attached to wall studs with 3-inch drywall screws.

Ready-made shelving, above, offers a quick alternative to building your own shelves.

Mud rooms and areas near the entrance the family uses most should have storage for coats, hats, and boots.

Shelf Standards. Metal shelf standards can be mounted directly to walls or, for a more decorative look, you can insert the standards in grooves routed into the wood itself or into hardwood strips.

Cut the standards to fit with a hacksaw, and attach them to wall studs with 3-inch drywall screws. Use a carpenter's level to make sure that both standards are plumb and that the corresponding mounting slots are level. Mount standards 6 inches from the ends of shelving to prevent sagging. For long wall shelves, install standards every 48 inches.

Many kitchen and closet storage systems use wire grids that attach to walls with molded plastic brackets. If you anticipate light loads, you can mount these brackets to drywall using the screws and expansion anchors usually included with such systems. But for heavier loads, use drywall screws to fasten the brackets directly to the wall studs.

Customized Storage

Built-in storage units are an excellent way to make the most of existing storage space in your home. Ready-made or custom-made built-in shelving units, entertainment centers, kitchen cabinets, medicine cabinets, window seats, and under-bed drawers are not only inexpensive and easy to assemble, they allow you to add a unique, personalized touch to your living spaces.

Built-in Shelving

A built-in shelving unit can create valuable storage capacity from an overlooked wall space, such as the area between windows or between a door and its adjacent corner. To construct the shelving, you'll need 1x10 or 1x12 lumber for side panels, top and base panels, and shelves; four 2x2 strips for spreaders; trim molding to conceal gaps along the top and bottom of the unit; 12d common nails and 6d finishing nails. If the unit will be bearing heavy loads, use hardwood boards, and make sure that the shelves span no more than 36 inches. To make installation easier, cut the side pieces an inch shorter than the ceiling height. (This way, you'll be able to tilt the unit into position without scraping the ceiling.) Paint or stain the wood pieces before assembling the unit. Hang the shelves from pegs or end clips inserted into holes drilled in the side pieces.

Adding Closet Space

What homeowner, even a new homeowner, hasn't complained about having too little closet space? Fortunately, there are almost always ways to find a bit more closet space or to make the closet space you have more efficient. Often, it isn't the space that is lacking but how the space is organized that is the problem. The trick is to find ways to help you organize the space.

Ventilated closet systems help keep your belongings neat and within easy reach.

Organizing Systems. The easiest and most obvious solution is one of the many commercial closet organizing systems now on the market. There are a number of configurations available, and you can customize most systems to meet your needs. Constructing your own version of a commercial closet organizer is another option. With a combination of shelves and plywood partitions, you can divide a closet into storage zones, with a single clothes pole on one side for full-length garments; double clothes poles on the other side for half-length garments like jackets, skirts, or slacks; a column of narrow shelves between the two for folded items or shoes; and one or more closet-wide shelves on top.

Before designing a closet system, above, inventory all of the items you want to store in the closet.

Metal shelf standards can provide a quick solution for creating shelving in areas where it is needed.

Copyright by designer/architect.

Plan #321037

Dimensions: 78'8" W x 50'6" D

Levels: 1

Square Footage: 2,397

Bedrooms: 3

Bathrooms: 2

Foundation: Walkout

Materials List Available: Yes

Price Category: E

Images provided by designer/architect.

CAD FILE AVAILABLE

Optional Basement Level Floor Plan

Plan #241008

Dimensions: 65' W x 56'8" D

Levels: 1

Square Footage: 2,526

Bedrooms: 4

Bathrooms: 3

Foundation: Crawl space, slab or basement

Materials List Available: No

Price Category: E

Images provided by designer/architect.

Copyright by designer/architect.

Optional Bonus Area Floor Plan

Plan #401023

Dimensions: 76' W x 63'4" D
Levels: 1
Square Footage: 2,806
Bedrooms: 3
Bathrooms: 2½
Foundation: Basement, walkout
Materials List Available: Yes
Price Category: F

The lower level of this magnificent home includes unfinished space that could have a future as a den and a family room with a fireplace. This level could also house extra bedrooms or an in-law suite.

Features:

- Foyer: On the main level, this foyer spills into a tray ceiling living room with a fireplace and an arched, floor-to-ceiling window wall.

- Family Room: Up from the foyer, a hall introduces this vaulted room with built-in media center and French doors that open to an expansive railed deck.

- Kitchen: Featured in this gourmet kitchen are a food-preparation island with a salad sink, double-door pantry, corner-window sink, and breakfast bay.

- Master Bedroom: The vaulted master bedroom opens to the deck, and the deluxe bath offers a raised whirlpool spa and a double-bowl vanity under a skylight.

Images provided by designer/architect.

- Bedroom: Two family bedrooms share a compartmented bathroom.

Foyer

Master Bathroom

Rear Elevation

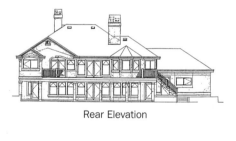
Right Side Elevation

Left Side Elevation

Rear View

Front View

Master Bedroom

Kitchen

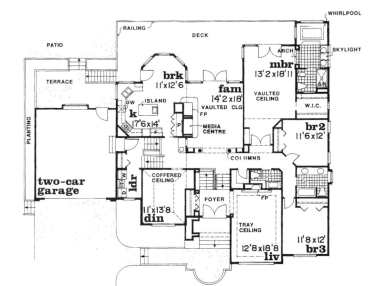

Copyright by designer/architect.

Optional Floor Plan

Plan #101013

Dimensions: 71'4" W x 65'3" D

Levels: 1

Square Footage: 2,564

Bedrooms: 3

Bathrooms: 2½

Foundation: Basement

Materials List Available: Yes

Price Category: F

This exciting design combines a striking classic exterior with a highly functional floor plan.

Features:

• Ceiling Height: 9 ft. unless otherwise noted.

• Family Room: This warm and inviting room measures 18 ft. x 22 ft. It features a 14-ft. ceiling and a rear wall of windows. French doors lead to an enormous deck.

• Kitchen: This unique angled kitchen is open to the hearth room and eating areas, all of which enjoy vaulted ceilings and are surrounded by windows. The hearth room has a TV niche.

• Master Suite: This 19-ft. x 18-ft. master suite is truly sumptuous, with its 12-ft. ceiling, sitting area, two walk-in closets, and full-featured bath.

• Secondary Bedrooms: Each of the secondary bedrooms measures 11 ft. x 14 ft. and has direct access to a shared bath.

Copyright by designer/architect.

• Bonus Room: Just beyond the entry are stairs leading to this bonus room, which measures approximately 12 ft. x 21 ft.—plenty of room for storage or future expansion.

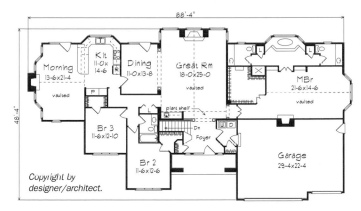

Plan #321018

Dimensions: 88'4" W x 48'4" D
Levels: 1
Square Footage: 2,523
Bedrooms: 3
Bathrooms: 2
Foundation: Basement
Materials List Available: Yes
Price Category: E

Images provided by designer/architect.

CAD FILE AVAILABLE

Copyright by designer/architect.

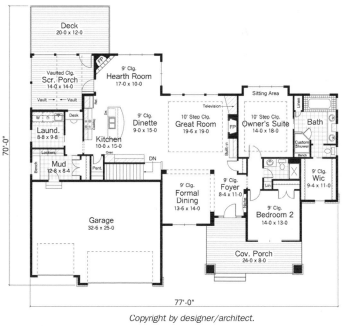

Plan #481158

Dimensions: 77' W x 58' D
Levels: 1
Square Footage: 2,311
Bedrooms: 2
Bathrooms: 2
Foundation: Walkout
Materials List Available: No
Price Category: E

Images provided by designer/architect.

Copyright by designer/architect.

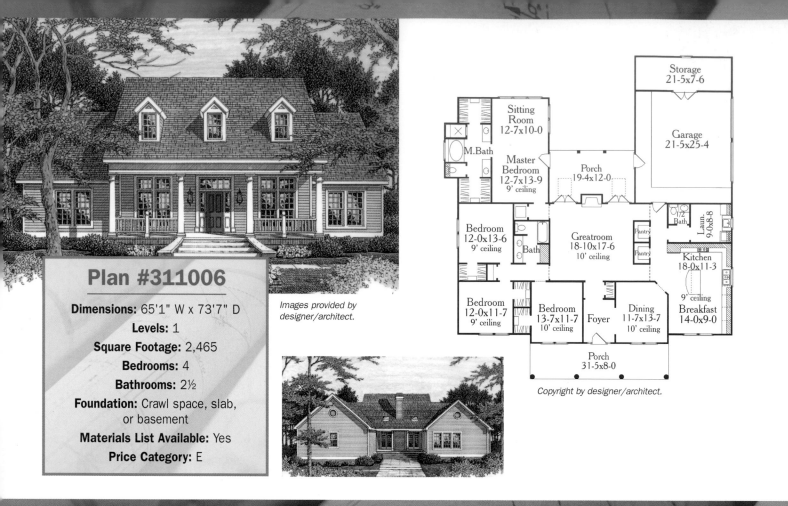

Plan #311006

Dimensions: 65'1" W x 73'7" D

Levels: 1

Square Footage: 2,465

Bedrooms: 4

Bathrooms: 2½

Foundation: Crawl space, slab, or basement

Materials List Available: Yes

Price Category: E

Images provided by designer/architect.

Storage 21-5x7-6
Garage 21-5x25-4
Sitting Room 12-7x10-0
M.Bath
Master Bedroom 12-7x13-9 9' ceiling
Porch 19-4x12-0
½ Bath
Laun. 9-0x8-8
Bedroom 12-0x13-6 9' ceiling
Bath
Greatroom 18-10x17-6 10' ceiling
Pantry
Pantry
Kitchen 18-0x11-3 9' ceiling
Bedroom 12-0x11-7 9' ceiling
Bedroom 13-7x11-7 10' ceiling
Foyer
Dining 11-7x13-7 10' ceiling
Breakfast 14-0x9-0
Porch 31-5x8-0

Copyright by designer/architect.

Plan #161066

Dimensions: 62'8" W x 57'11" D

Levels: 1

Square Footage: 2,078

Bedrooms: 3

Bathrooms: 2

Foundation: Basement, walkout basement

Materials List Available: Yes

Price Category: D

Images provided by designer/architect.

Rear Elevation

Deck
Dining 19'5" x 11'
Great Room 23'8" x 18'4"
Master Bedroom 17'1" x 13'4"
Kitchen 15'8" x 11'
WALK-IN CLOSET
Dressing
Hall
Foyer
Laun.
Bath
Bedroom 13'8" x 11'
Garage 20' x 22'
Porch
Bedroom 13' x 11'
57'-11"
62'-8"

Copyright by designer/architect.

Plan #321019

Dimensions: 70'8" W x 70' D

Levels: 1

Square Footage: 2,452

Bedrooms: 4

Bathrooms: 2½

Foundation: Basement

Materials List Available: Yes

Price Category: E

Images provided by designer/architect.

Copyright by designer/architect.

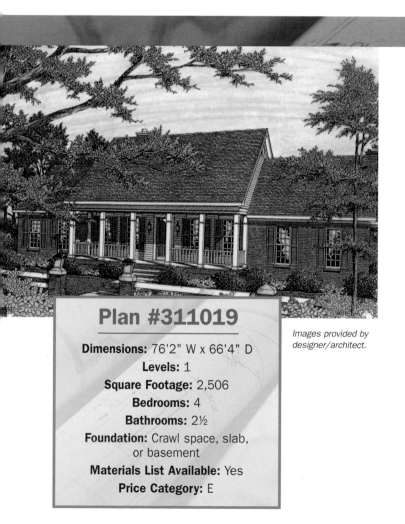

Plan #311019

Dimensions: 76'2" W x 66'4" D

Levels: 1

Square Footage: 2,506

Bedrooms: 4

Bathrooms: 2½

Foundation: Crawl space, slab, or basement

Materials List Available: Yes

Price Category: E

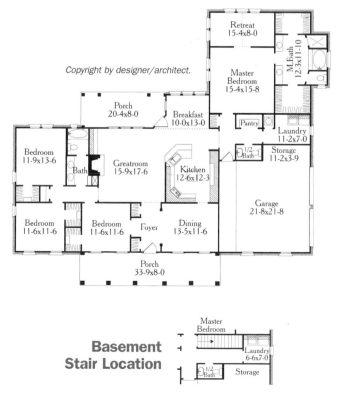

Images provided by designer/architect.

Copyright by designer/architect.

Basement Stair Location

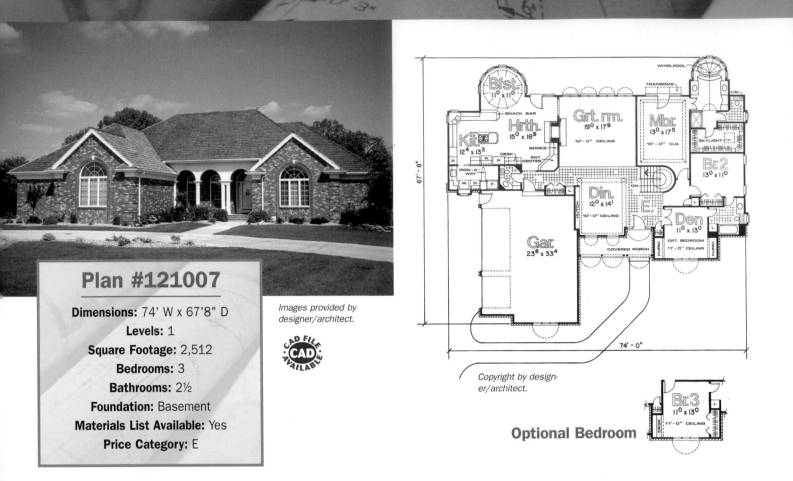

Plan #121007

Dimensions: 74' W x 67'8" D

Levels: 1

Square Footage: 2,512

Bedrooms: 3

Bathrooms: 2½

Foundation: Basement

Materials List Available: Yes

Price Category: E

Images provided by designer/architect.

CAD FILE AVAILABLE

Copyright by designer/architect.

Optional Bedroom

Plan #321032

Dimensions: 109' W x 57'6" D

Levels: 1

Square Footage: 4,826

Bedrooms: 4

Bathrooms: 2½

Foundation: Walk-out basement

Materials List Available: Yes

Price Category: I

Images provided by designer/architect.

CAD FILE AVAILABLE

Copyright by designer/architect.

Optional Basement Level Floor Plan

Main Level Floor Plan

Dressing

Sitting
11'2" x 7'9"
Irregular

Breakfast
13'6" x 13'11"
Irregular

Hearth Room
22'11" x 17'1"
Irregular

Bath

Master Bedroom
17'8" x 17'4"
Irregular

WALK-IN CLOSET

Great Room
19'5" x 17'8"

Kitchen
16'10" x 17'11"
Irregular

Bath

Hall

WALK-IN CLOSET

DOWN

Hall

Garage
21'4" x 40'11"

Bedroom
13'4" x 14'0"

WALK-IN CLOSET

Bath

Bedroom
13'4" x 12'3"
Irregular

Foyer

Dining Room
14'4" x 15'7"
Irregular

Laun.

Porch

69'-4"

84'-6"

Copyright by designer/architect.

Images provided by designer/architect.

Plan #161028

Dimensions: 84'6" W x 69'4" D

Levels: 1

Square Footage: 3,570

Optional Finished Basement Sq. Ft.: 2,367

Bedrooms: 3

Bathrooms: 3½

Foundation: Basement

Materials List Available: Yes

Price Category: H

Office
12'10" x 11'8"
Irregular

Bedroom
12'6" x 14'11"
Irregular

Raised Bar

Billiards Room
19'8" x 15'11"
Irregular

WALK-IN CLOSET

Media Area
20'0" x 13'6"
Irregular

Bath

Hall

Game Room
14'11" x 9'6"

Unexcavated

Basement Level Floor Plan

Basement

Exercise Area
13'8" x 12'5"

Unexc.

Plan #161180

Dimensions: 68'2" W x 64'9" D

Levels: 1

Square Footage: 2,437

Bedrooms: 3

Bathrooms: 2

Foundation: Basement

Materials List Available: Yes

Price Category: E

Images provided by designer/architect

Garage
23'-7" x 33'-3"

Porch

Copyright by designer/architect.

Great Room
16'-8" x 22'-11"

Breakfast
12'-8" x 12'-2"

15'-1" HIGH CLG

Bath

Walk In Closet

Kitchen
12'-8" x 14'-6"

Bedroom
13' x 11'-4"

Wood Rail

DOWN

Pantry

Lin.

Closet

Bath

Cubbies

Hall

Master Bedroom
14'-1" x 16'-3"

Closet

Foyer
9'-1" HIGH CLG

Laundry
9'-4" x 7'-9"

Dining Room
12'-1" x 14'-5"

Closet

Bedroom
13' x 12'-1"

Porch

Unexcavated

Unexcavated

Basement

Unex.

Foundation Plan

Optional Basement Level Floor Plan

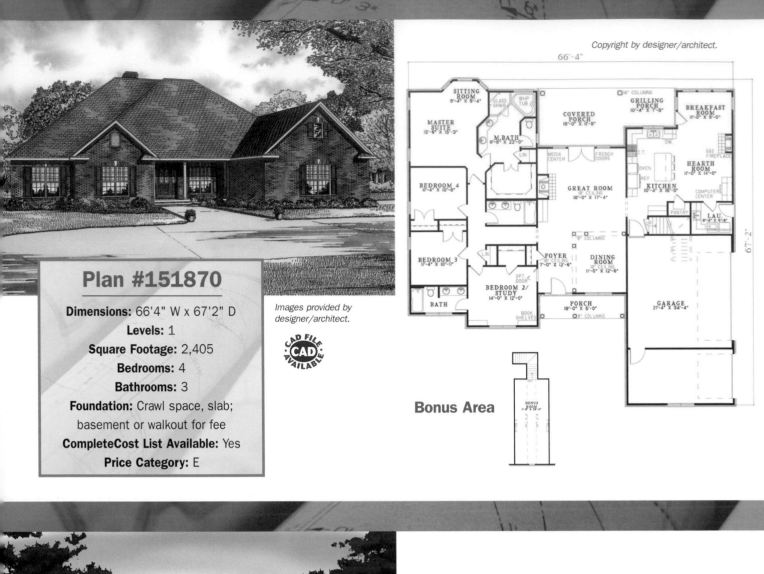

Copyright by designer/architect.

Bonus Area

Plan #151870

Dimensions: 66'4" W x 67'2" D

Levels: 1

Square Footage: 2,405

Bedrooms: 4

Bathrooms: 3

Foundation: Crawl space, slab; basement or walkout for fee

CompleteCost List Available: Yes

Price Category: E

Images provided by designer/architect.

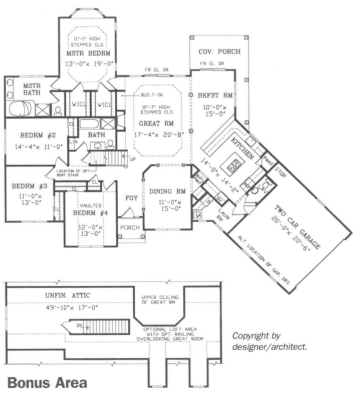

Copyright by designer/architect.

Bonus Area

Plan #131045

Dimensions: 81'4" W x 68'3" D

Levels: 1

Square Footage: 2,347

Bedrooms: 4

Bathrooms: 2½

Foundation: Crawl space, slab, or basement

Materials List Available: Yes

Price Category: E

Images provided by designer/architect.

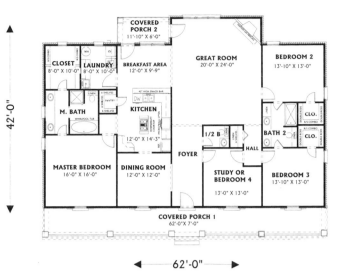

Copyright by designer/architect.

Images provided by designer/architect.

Plan #191027

Dimensions: 62' W x 42' D

Levels: 1

Square Footage: 2,354

Bedrooms: 4

Bathrooms: 2½

Foundation: Crawl space

Materials List Available: No

Price Category: E

COVERED PORCH 2 11'-10" X 6'-0"

CLOSET 8'-0" X 10'-0"

LAUNDRY 8'-0" X 10'-0"

BREAKFAST AREA 12'-0" X 9'-9"

GREAT ROOM 20'-0" X 24'-0"

BEDROOM 2 13'-10" X 13'-0"

M. BATH

KITCHEN 12'-0" X 14'-3"

1/2 B

BATH 2

CLO.

CLO.

MASTER BEDROOM 16'-0" X 16'-0"

DINING ROOM 12'-0" X 12'-0"

FOYER

HALL

STUDY OR BEDROOM 4 13'-0" X 13'-0"

BEDROOM 3 13'-10" X 13'-0"

COVERED PORCH 1 62'-0" X 7'-0"

42'-0"

62'-0"

Plan #211009

Dimensions: 72' W x 60' D

Levels: 1

Square Footage: 2,396

Bedrooms: 4

Bathrooms: 2

Foundation: Slab

Materials List Available: Yes

Price Category: E

Images provided by designer/architect.

CAD FILE AVAILABLE

Copyright by designer/architect.

patio

mbr 16 x 15

wic

sky light

br 2 16 x 11

porch 18 x 8

bkfst 10 x10

sto 12 x 9

br 3 12 x 12

util

living 20 x 20

kit 14 x 10

garage 22 x 22

br 4 14 x 12

foy 16x5

porch 16 x 4

dining 17 x 14

SMARTtip

Ornaments in a Garden

Placement is everything with ornaments in a garden. Some elements are best sitting by themselves. Others are better when they are part of a cohesive whole, perhaps placed in the greenery at a corner or flanking a structure.

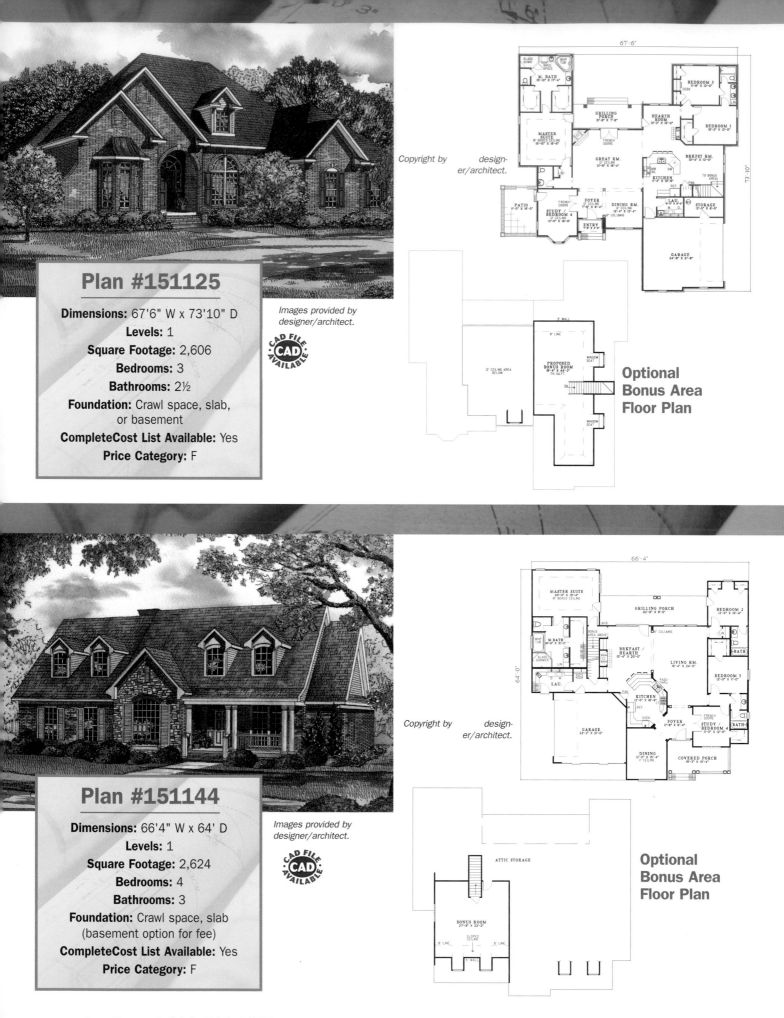

Plan #151125

Dimensions: 67'6" W x 73'10" D

Levels: 1

Square Footage: 2,606

Bedrooms: 3

Bathrooms: 2½

Foundation: Crawl space, slab, or basement

CompleteCost List Available: Yes

Price Category: F

Copyright by designer/architect.

Images provided by designer/architect.

Optional Bonus Area Floor Plan

Plan #151144

Dimensions: 66'4" W x 64' D

Levels: 1

Square Footage: 2,624

Bedrooms: 4

Bathrooms: 3

Foundation: Crawl space, slab (basement option for fee)

CompleteCost List Available: Yes

Price Category: F

Copyright by designer/architect.

Images provided by designer/architect.

Optional Bonus Area Floor Plan

Plan #151057

Dimensions: 73'6" W x 80'6" D

Levels: 1

Square Footage: 2,951

Bedrooms: 4

Bathrooms: 3

Foundation: Crawl space, slab, or basement

CompleteCost List Available: Yes

Price Category: F

Images provided by designer/architect.

CAD FILE AVAILABLE

Plan #151060

Dimensions: 80'11" W x 95'8" D

Levels: 1

Square Footage: 3,554

Bedrooms: 3

Bathrooms: 3

Foundation: Crawl space, slab basement, or walkout

CompleteCost List Available: Yes

Price Category: F

Images provided by designer/architect.

CAD FILE AVAILABLE

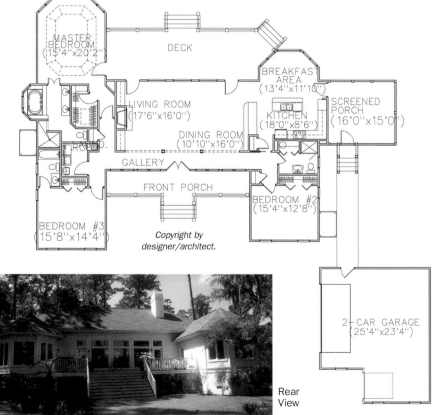

Plan #521017

Dimensions: 94'11" W x 94'10" D
Levels: 1
Square Footage: 2,359
Bedrooms: 3
Bathrooms: 3
Foundation: Slab
Material List Available: No
Price Category: E

Images provided by designer/architect.

This country-style ranch home is ideal for a growing family. The covered front porch houses a window-lined exterior, illustrating to guests how open and welcoming the home is.

CAD FILE AVAILABLE

Features:

- **Living Room:** This large space features a fireplace and built-in storage, and it opens onto the large deck, which is perfect for barbecues and soaking up the sun.

- **Kitchen:** An efficient and convenient design, this L-shaped kitchen includes an island with sinks and a raised bar. It opens into the breakfast room and open dining area and onto the screened porch. The space is ideal for warm indoor meals or fun, insect-free meals outside.

- **Master Suite:** Lined with windows, this already-spacious area opens up in sunlit comfort. Amenities include a walk-in closet and full master bath, which includes dual sinks, a large standing shower, and an over-sized tub set beneath bay windows.

- **Secondary Bedrooms:** Both bedrooms include a large closet, access to a full bathroom, and enough space to accommodate any design you can create.

- **Garage:** This two-car garage includes extra space for storage or hobbies and is far enough from the house for all the hammer strokes and buzzing saws of a busy workshop without disturbing the household.

MASTER BEDROOM (15'4"x20'2")

DECK

BREAKFAST AREA (13'4"x11'10")

LIVING ROOM (17'6"x16'0")

KITCHEN (18'0"x8'6")

SCREENED PORCH (16'0"x15'0")

DINING ROOM (10'10"x16'0")

GALLERY

FRONT PORCH

BEDROOM #2 (15'4"x12'8")

BEDROOM #3 (15'8"x14'4")

Copyright by designer/architect.

Rear View

2-CAR GARAGE (25'4"x23'4")

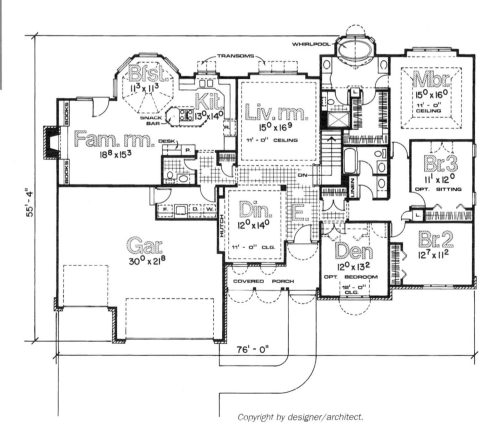

Plan #121003

Dimensions: 76' W x 55'4" D
Levels: 1
Square Footage: 2,498
Bedrooms: 4
Bathrooms: 2½
Foundation: Basement
Materials List Available: Yes
Price Category: E

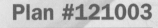
Images provided by designer/architect.

Repeated arches bring style and distinction to the interior and exterior of this spacious home.

Features:

- Ceiling Height: 8 ft. except as noted.

- Den: A decorative volume ceiling helps make this spacious retreat the perfect place to relax after a long day.

- Formal Living Room: The decorative volume ceiling carries through to the living room that invites large formal gatherings.

- Formal Dining Room: There's plenty of room for all the guests to move into this gracious formal space that also features a decorative volume ceiling.

- Master Suite: Retire to this suite with its glamorous bayed whirlpool, his and her vanities, and a walk-in closet.

- Optional Sitting Room: With the addition of French doors, one of the bedrooms can be converted into a sitting room for the master suite.

Copyright by designer/architect.

Plan #321007

Dimensions: 76' W x 55'2" D

Levels: 1

Square Footage: 2,695

Bedrooms: 3

Bathrooms: 2½

Foundation: Basement

Materials List Available: Yes

Price Category: F

Images provided by designer/architect.

SMARTtip

Decorative Poles

Drapery poles are supported by the brackets fastened to the window frame or wall. The brackets that are provided with the poles generally coordinate and blend in with the pole finish. Brackets can be simple but also decorative. If you opt for a spectacular, attention-grabbing bracket, consider choosing less showy finials for the ends of the pole.

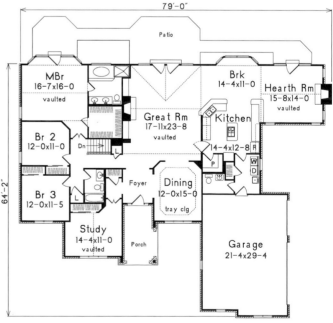

Plan #321028

Dimensions: 79' W x 64'2" D

Levels: 1

Square Footage: 2,723

Bedrooms: 3

Bathrooms: 2½

Foundation: Basement

Materials List Available: Yes

Price Category: F

Images provided by designer/architect.

Plan #201069

Dimensions: 70'10" W x 64'10" D

Levels: 1

Square Footage: 2,735

Bedrooms: 4

Bathrooms: 3½

Foundation: Crawl space, slab

Materials List Available: Yes

Price Category: F

Images provided by designer/architect.

Copyright by designer/architect.

Floor plan labels: br 4 12 x 12 · br 3 12 x 12 · br 2 12 x 12 · porch 31⁸ x 6 · eating 11¹⁰ x 12 · den 20² x 18 · kit 11 x 12 · living 12 x 14 · foy · dining 11¹⁰ x 15 · mbr 22⁴ x 16 · util · sto 10x8⁶ · garage 22⁴ x 22 · open sto · por

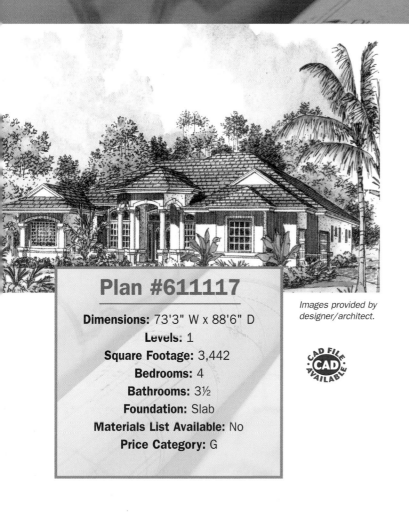

Plan #611117

Dimensions: 73'3" W x 88'6" D

Levels: 1

Square Footage: 3,442

Bedrooms: 4

Bathrooms: 3½

Foundation: Slab

Materials List Available: No

Price Category: G

Images provided by designer/architect.

CAD FILE AVAILABLE

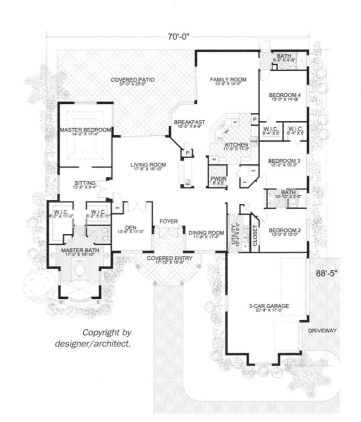

Copyright by designer/architect.

Floor plan labels: COVERED PATIO 37'-0" X 23'-0" · FAMILY ROOM 13'-9" X 14'-0" · BATH 6'-0" X 4'-6" · BEDROOM 4 13'-0" X 14'-0" · MASTER BEDROOM 14'-2" X 17'-4" · BREAKFAST 10'-0" X 8'-9" · KITCHEN 11'-5" X 11'-0" · W.I.C. 6'-4" X 5' · W.I.C. 6'-4" X 5' · BEDROOM 3 13'-0" X 13'-0" · LIVING ROOM 17'-8" X 16'-0" · SITTING 12'-8" X 9'-4" · PWDR 6' X 5' · BATH 10'-10" X 6'-0" · W.I.C. 6'-2" X 11'-0" · W.I.C. 6'-2" X 5'-11" · DEN 13'-6" X 11'-0" · FOYER · DINING ROOM 11'-8" X 17'-4" · UTILITY 10'-4" X 9'-6" · CLOSET · BEDROOM 2 13'-0" X 17'-0" · MASTER BATH 17'-0" X 19'-10" · COVERED ENTRY 17'-10" X 6'-0" · 3-CAR GARAGE 22'-9" X 17'-0" · DRIVEWAY · 70'-0" · 88'-5"

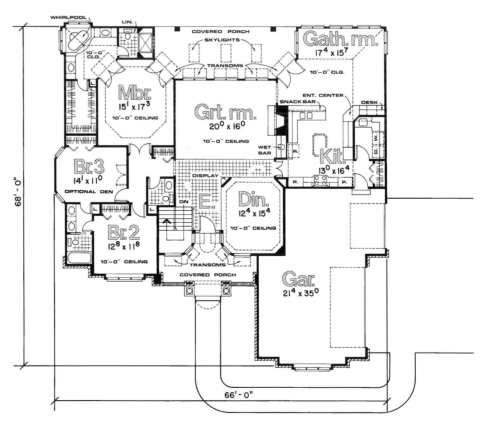

Plan #121053

Dimensions: 66' W x 68' D

Levels: 1

Square Footage: 2,456

Bedrooms: 3

Bathrooms: 2½

Foundation: Basement

Materials List Available: Yes

Price Category: E

Images provided by designer/architect.

If you're looking for a home that gives comfort at every turn, this could be the one.

Features:

- **Entry:** Airy and open, this entry imparts a welcoming feeling.

- **Great Room:** You'll love the style built into this centrally located room. A row of transom-topped windows adds natural light, and a fireplace gives it character.

- **Dining Room:** Just off the entry for convenience, this formal room has a boxed ceiling that accentuates its interesting angled shape.

- **Gathering Room:** This lovely room features an angled ceiling, snack bar, built-in entertainment center, built-in desk, and abundance of windows. A door leads to the large, covered rear porch with skylights.

- **Master Suite:** Relax in comfort after a long day, or sit on the adjoining, covered rear porch to enjoy the evening breezes.

Copyright by designer/architect.

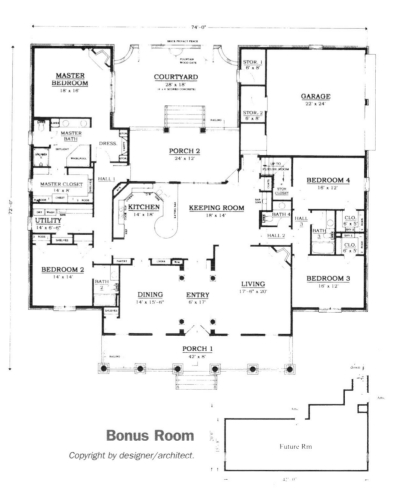

Plan #171013

Dimensions: 74' W x 72' D

Levels: 1

Square Footage: 3,084

Bedrooms: 4

Bathrooms: 3½

Foundation: Slab, crawl space

Materials List Available: Yes

Price Category: G

Impressive porch columns add to the country charm of this amenity-filled family home.

Features:

- Ceiling Height: 10 ft.

- Foyer: The sense of style continues from the front porch into this foyer, which opens to the formal dining room and the living room.

- Dining Room: Two handsome support columns accentuate the elegance of this dining room.

- Living Room: This living room features a cozy corner fireplace and plenty of room for the entire family to gather and relax.

- Kitchen: You'll be inspired to new culinary heights in this kitchen, which offers plenty of counter space, a snack bar, a built-in pantry, and a china closet.

- Master Suite: The bedroom of this master suite has a fireplace and overlooks a rear courtyard. The bath has two vanities a large walk-in closet, a deluxe tub, a walk-in shower, and a skylight.

Images provided by designer/architect.

Bonus Room

Copyright by designer/architect.

Plan #151001

Dimensions: 70' W x 88'2" D
Levels: 1
Square Footage: 3,124
Bedrooms: 4
Bathrooms: 3½
Foundation: Crawl space, slab
CompleteCost List Available: Yes
Price Category: G

This home, as shown in the photograph, may differ from the actual blueprints. For more detailed information, please check the floor plans carefully.

Images provided by designer/architect.

Copyright by designer/architect.

From the double front doors to sleek arches, columns, and a gallery with arched openings to the bedrooms, you'll love this elegant home.

Features:

• Grand Room: With a 13-ft. pan ceiling and column entry, this room opens to the rear covered porch as well as through French doors to the bay-windowed morning room that, in turn, leads to the gathering room.

• Gathering Room: A majestic fireplace, built-in entertainment center, and book shelves give comfort and ease.

• Kitchen: A double oven, built-in desk, and a work island add up to a design for efficiency.

• Master Suite: Enjoy the practicality of walk-in closets, the comfort of a private sitting area, and the convenience of an adjacent study or nursery. The bath features a step-up whirlpool tub and separate shower.

Color

No other decorating component has more power and greater effect at such little cost than color. It can fill a space and make furnishings look fresh and new. Color can also show off fine architectural details or downplay a room's structural flaws. A particular color can make a cold room cozy, while another hue can cool down a sunny cooker. And color comes cheap, giving a tremendous impact for your decorating dollar: elbow grease, supplies, prep work, and paint will all cost pretty much the same if you choose a gorgeous hue over plain white.

But finding the color—the right color—isn't easy. Where do you begin to look? Like the economy, color has leading indicators. You have a market basket full of choices, and there are lots of signposts to direct you where to go.

The Lay of the Land

For the past 200 years, white has been the most popular choice for American home exteriors. And it still is, followed by tan, brown, and beige. You can play it safe and follow the leader. But you should also think about the architecture of your house and where you live when you're considering exterior color. For example, traditional Colonials have a color-combination range of about two that look appropriate: white with black or green shutters and gray with white trim. Mediterranean-style houses typically pick up the colors of terra-cotta and the tile that are indigenous to the regions that developed the architecture—France, Italy, and Spain. A ranch-style house shouldn't be overdone—it is, after all, usually a modest structure. On the other hand, a cottage can be fanciful. Whimsical colors also look charming on Victorian houses in San Francisco, but they would be out of place in conservative Scarsdale, New York, where you must

check with the local building board even when you want to change the exterior color of your house.

How's the Weather?

Like exteriors, interiors often take their color cues from their environs and local traditions. In the rainy and often chilly Pacific Northwest, cozy blanket plaids in strong reds and black abound. In the hot-and-arid climate of the West, indigo or brown ticking-stripes and faded denim look appropriately casual and cool. Subtle grays and neutrals, reflecting steel, lime-stone, and concrete, look apropos for sophisticated city life. In extremely warm southern climates, the brilliant sun tends to overpower lighter colors. That explains the popularity of strong hues in tropical, sun-drenched locales.

Natural Light. That's the one you don't pay for. Its direction and intensity greatly affects color. A room with a window that faces trees will look markedly different in summer, when warm white sunlight is filtered through the leaves, than in winter, when the trees are bare and the color of natural light takes on a cool blue cast. Time of day affects color, too. Yellow walls that are pleasant and cheerful in the early morning can be stifling and blinding in the afternoon. That's because afternoon

The yellow-colored wall, above, complements the antique painted dresser.

Warm neutral-color walls, opposite, and touches of red make this bedroom cozy.

sun is stronger than morning sun.

When you're choosing a color for an interior, always view it at different times of day, but especially during the hours in which you will inhabit the room.

Artificial Light. Because artificial light affects color rendition as much as natural light, don't judge a color in the typically chilly fluorescence of a hardware store. The very same color chip will look completely different when you bring it home, which is why it's so important to test out a paint color in your own home. Most fluorescent light is bluish and distorts colors. It depresses red and exaggerates green, for example. A romantic faded rose on your dining room walls will just wash out in the kitchen if your use a fluorescent light there. Incandescent light, the type produced by the standard bulbs you probably use in your chandelier and in most of your home's light fixtures, is warm but slightly yellow. Halogen light, which comes from another newer type of incandescent bulb, is white and the closest to natural sunlight. Of all three types of bulbs, halogen is truest in rendering color.

 # red

RED is powerful, dramatic, motivating. Red is also hospitable, and it stimulates the appetite, which makes it a favorite choice for dining rooms. Some studies have indicated that a red room actually makes people feel warmer.

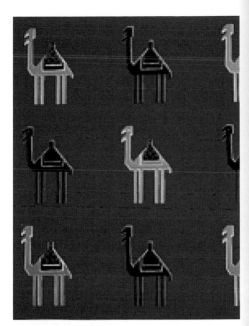

yellow

YELLOW illuminates the colors it surrounds. It warms rooms that receive northern light but can be too bright in a sunny room. It's best for daytime rooms, not bedrooms. It has a short range, which means as white is added to yellow, it disappears. Yellow highlights and calls attention to features—think of bright taxicabs.

green

GREEN is tranquil, nurturing, rejuvenating. It is a psychological primary, and because it is mixed from yellow and blue, it can appear both warm and cool. Time seems to pass more quickly in green rooms. Perhaps that's why waiting rooms off-stage are called "green rooms."

 **neutrals**

GRAY goes with all colors—it is a good neighbor. Various tones of gray range from dark charcoal to pale oyster.

BLACK (technically the absence of color) enhances and brightens other colors, making for livelier decorating schemes when used as an accent.

 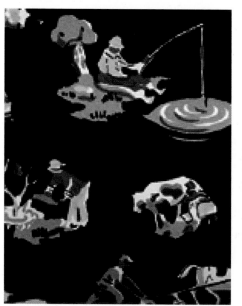 

pink

PINK is perceived as outgoing and active. It's also a color that flatters skin tones. Hot shades are invigorating, while soft, toned-down versions can be relaxed and charming.

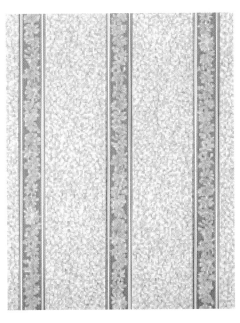

 **blue**

BLUE, with its associations of sea and sky, offers serenity, which is why it is a favorite in bedrooms. Studies have shown that people think better in blue rooms. Perhaps that explains the popularity of the navy blue suit. Cooler blues show this color's melancholy side, however.

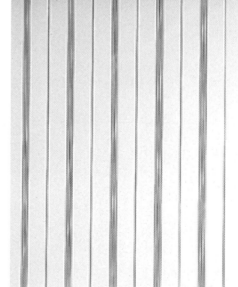

Plan #211055

Dimensions: 88' W x 64' D

Levels: 1

Square Footage: 2,394

Bedrooms: 3

Bathrooms: 2

Foundation: Crawl space

Materials List Available: Yes

Price Category: E

Images provided by designer/architect.

CAD FILE CAD AVAILABLE

Copyright by designer/architect.

garage 26 x 21

sto 16 x 5

porch

owner's retreat & master suite 19 x 15

master bath

br 2 12 x 12

living 20 x 18

kit

dining 13 x 12

parlor/ br 4 12 x 11

br 3 12 x 12

porch

Plan #111030

Dimensions: 74'10" W x 85'5" D

Levels: 1

Square Footage: 2,905

Bedrooms: 4

Bathrooms: 3

Foundation: Slab

Materials List Available: No

Price Category: G

Images provided by designer/architect.

Copyright by designer/architect.

Master Bedroom 17'5"x 18'1"

Master Bath

Walk-In Closet

Porch

Patio

Porch

Bedroom 13'3"x 13'1"

Breakfast 13'9"x 12'5"

Bedroom 11'1"x 12'1"

Bath

Kitchen

Living 20'3"x 20'7"

Bath

Utility 8'9"x 8'3"

13'9"x 18'1"

Bedroom 13'3"x 12'1"

Dining 12'9"x 15'1"

Foyer 7'3"x 7'7"

Two-Car Garage 21'3"x 27'9"

Porch

Unfinished Gameroom 14'1"x 27'9"

Bonus Gameroom

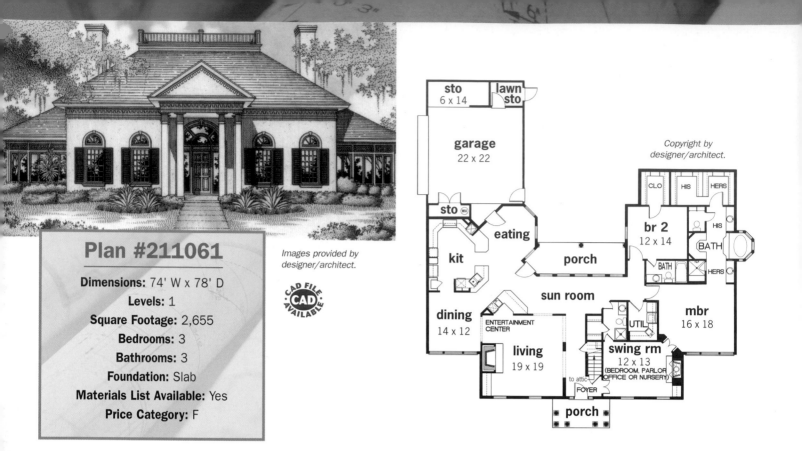

Plan #211061

Dimensions: 74' W x 78' D

Levels: 1

Square Footage: 2,655

Bedrooms: 3

Bathrooms: 3

Foundation: Slab

Materials List Available: Yes

Price Category: F

Images provided by designer/architect.

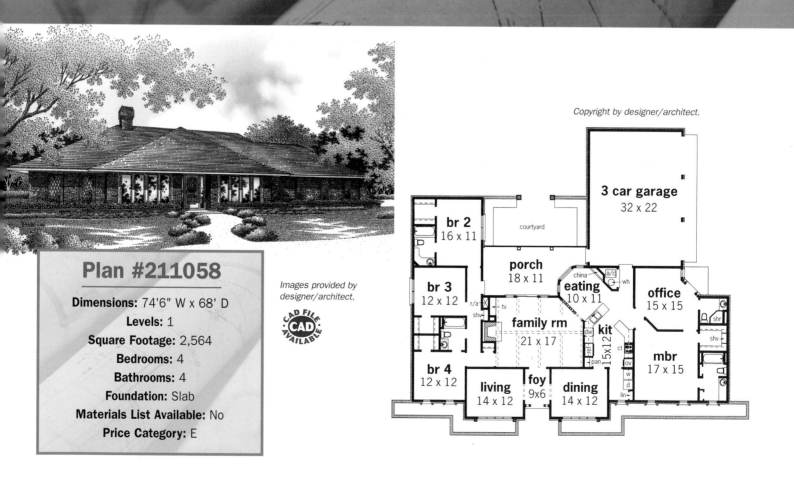

Plan #211058

Dimensions: 74'6" W x 68' D

Levels: 1

Square Footage: 2,564

Bedrooms: 4

Bathrooms: 4

Foundation: Slab

Materials List Available: No

Price Category: E

Images provided by designer/architect.

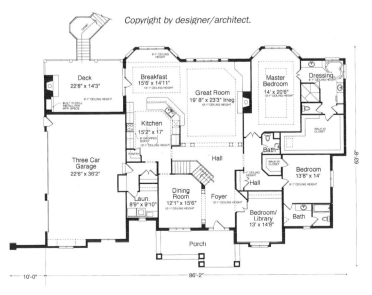

Plan #161056

Dimensions: 86'2" W x 63'8" D
Levels: 1
Square Footage: 3,171
Bedrooms: 3
Bathrooms: 2½
Foundation: Basement or walkout
Material List Available: Yes
Price Category: G

This home is dedicated to comfort and high lifestyle and sets the standard for excellence.

Images provided by designer/architect.

Features:

- **Open Plan:** A wraparound island with seating is adorned with pillars and arched openings, and it separates the kitchen from the great room and breakfast room. This design element allows the rooms to remain visually open and, paired with a 9-ft. ceiling height, creates a spacious area.

- **Great Room:** A gas fireplace warms this gathering area, and the wall of windows across the rear brings the outdoors in. The built-in entertainment center will be a hit with the entire family.

- **Master Suite:** Delighting you with its size and luxury, this retreat enjoys a stepped ceiling in the sleeping area. The master bath features a garden bathtub and an oversized walk-in closet.

- **Lower Level:** Open stairs introduce this lower level, which mimics the size of the first floor, and, with a 9-ft. ceiling height, offers the same elegant feel of the first floor. Additional bedrooms, a game room, an exercise area, and storage are available options.

Copyright by designer/architect.

Optional Basement Level Floor Plan

Plan #151002

Dimensions: 67' W x 66' D

Levels: 1

Square Footage: 2,444

Bedrooms: 3

Bathrooms: 2½

Foundation: Crawl space, slab, or basement

CompleteCost List Available: Yes

Price Category: E

Images provided by designer/architect.

This home, as shown in the photograph, may differ from the actual blueprints. For more detailed information, please check the floor plans carefully.

Copyright by designer/architect.

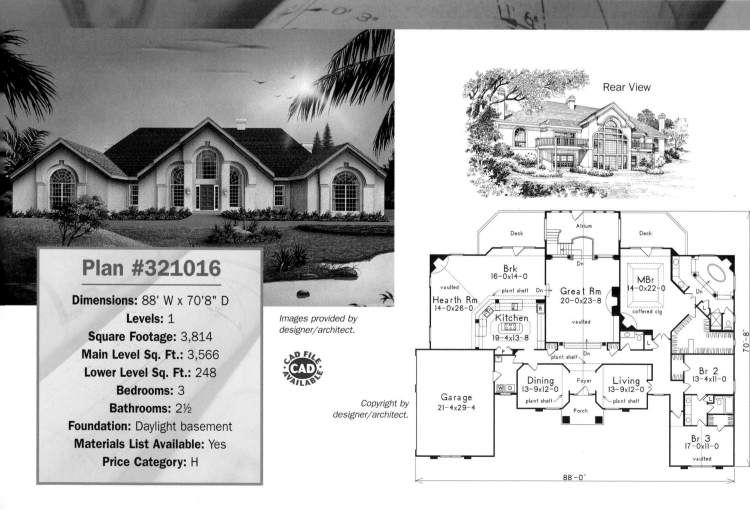

Plan #321016

Dimensions: 88' W x 70'8" D

Levels: 1

Square Footage: 3,814

Main Level Sq. Ft.: 3,566

Lower Level Sq. Ft.: 248

Bedrooms: 3

Bathrooms: 2½

Foundation: Daylight basement

Materials List Available: Yes

Price Category: H

Images provided by designer/architect.

Copyright by designer/architect.

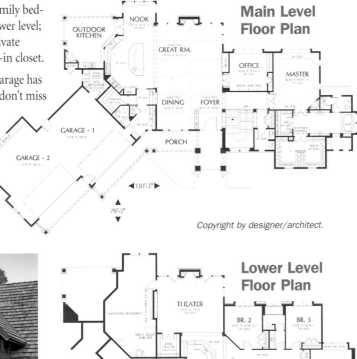

Plan #441015

Dimensions: 130'3" W x 79'3" D
Levels: 1
Square Footage: 4,732
Main Level Sq. Ft.: 2,902
Lower Level Sq. Ft.: 1,830
Bedrooms: 4
Bathrooms: 3 full, 2 half
Foundation: Walkout basement
Materials List Available: No
Price Category: I

An artful use of stone was employed on the exterior of this rustic hillside home to complement other architectural elements, such as the angled, oversize four-car garage and the substantial roofline.

CAD FILE AVAILABLE

Features:

- **Great Room:** This massive vaulted room features a large stone fireplace at one end and a formal dining area at the other. A built-in media center and double doors separate the great room from a home office with its own hearth and built-ins.

- **Kitchen:** This kitchen features a walk-in pantry and snack counter and opens to a skylighted outdoor kitchen. Its appointments include a cooktop and a corner fireplace.

- **Home Theatre:** This space has a built-in viewing screen, a fireplace, and double terrace access.

- **Master Suite:** This private space is found at the other side of the home. Look closely for

expansive his and her walk-in closets, a spa tub, a skylighted double vanity area, and a corner fireplace in the salon.

- **Bedrooms:** Three family bedrooms are on the lower level; bedroom 4 has a private bathroom and walk-in closet.

- **Garage:** This large garage has room for four cars; don't miss the dog shower and grooming station just off the garage.

Entry

Main Level Floor Plan

Lower Level Floor Plan

Plan #271074

Dimensions: 68' W x 86' D

Levels: 1

Square Footage: 2,400

Bedrooms: 4

Bathrooms: 3

Foundation: Crawl space or slab

Materials List Available: No

Price Category: E

Perfect for families with aging relatives or boomerang children, this home includes a completely separate suite at the rear.

Features:

• **Living Room:** A corner fireplace casts a friendly glow over this gathering space.

• **Kitchen:** This efficient space offers a serving bar that extends toward the eating nook

and the formal dining room.

• **Master Suite:** A cathedral ceiling presides over this deluxe suite, which boasts a whirlpool tub, dual-sink vanity, and walk-in closet.

• **In-law Suite:** This separate wing has its own vaulted living room, plus a kitchen, a dining room, and a bedroom suite.

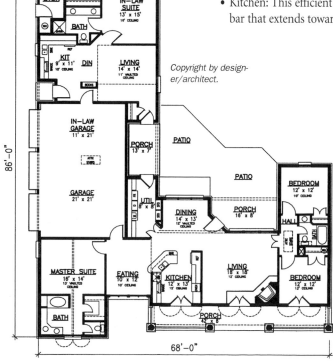

Copyright by designer/architect.

SMARTtip

Adding Professional Flair to Window Treatments

You can give your window treatment designs a professional look by using decorator tricks to customize readymades or dress your own home-sewn designs. These could include contrast linings, tassels, cording, ribbons, or couture trimmings such as buttons, coins, or bows applied to edges. Another trick is to sew a fine wire into the hem of curtains or valances to create a pliable edge that you can shape yourself. Small weights that you can sew into the hem of drapery panels or jabots will make them hang better. For more inspiration look at fashion magazines and visit showrooms.

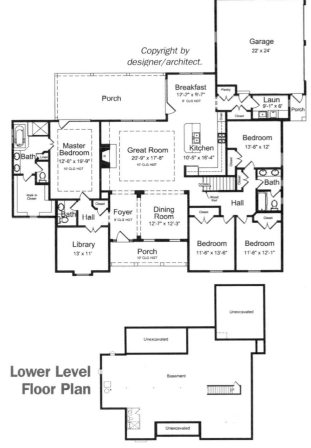

Images provided by designer/architect.

CAD FILE AVAILABLE

Plan #161225

Dimensions: 73'10" W x 69'4" D

Levels: 1

Square Footage: 2,591

Bedrooms: 4

Bathrooms: 2½

Foundation: Basement

Materials List Available: Yes

Price Category: E

Lower Level Floor Plan

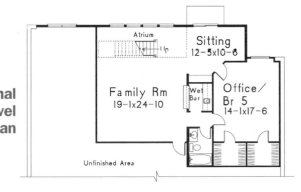

Images provided by designer/architect.

CAD FILE AVAILABLE

Plan #321034

Dimensions: 75'8" W x 52'6" D

Levels: 1

Square Footage: 3,508

Bedrooms: 4

Bathrooms: 3

Foundation: Basement, walk-out

Materials List Available: Yes

Price Category: H

Optional Basement Level Floor Plan

Plan #111007

Dimensions: 72' W x 91' D

Levels: 1

Square Footage: 3,668

Bedrooms: 4

Bathrooms: 3½

Foundation: Crawl space

Materials List Available: No

Price Category: I

Images provided by designer/architect.

Copyright by designer/architect.

Floor plan labels: Bedroom 15'7"x 13', WIC, Bath, Dressing, Porch, Breakfast 14'1"x 14'8", Master Bedroom 17'11"x 17'6", Bedroom 11'7"x 12'1", TV, Living 22'1"x 23'11", Kitchen 14'1"x 15', WIC, WIC, Master Bath, Bath, Dress, WIC, Hunting Room 11'7"x 7'3", Bedroom 13'1"x 16'3", Foyer 6'9"x14', Dining 14'1"x 14'1", 1/2 Bath, Utility 9'11"x 9'9", Workshop 11'11"x 11'7", Porch, Two-Car Garage 23'3"x 24'8", Extra Storage 12'3"x 7'9"

Plan #321005

Dimensions: 69' W x 53'8" D

Levels: 1

Square Footage: 2,483

Bedrooms: 3

Bathrooms: 2

Foundation: Basement

Materials List Available: Yes

Price Category: E

Images provided by designer/architect.

Copyright by designer/architect.

Floor plan labels: Patio, MBr 16-7x16-0 vaulted clg, Brk fst 14-9x13-0 vaulted clg, Great Rm 19-6x23-10 vaulted clg, Kitchen 14-4x12-11 vaulted clg, Br 2 12-0x11-0, Menu Desk, Dn, Laundry, Entry, Dining 12-0x15-0 tray clg, Br 3 12-0x11-5, Study 14-4x11-0 vaulted clg, Porch, Garage 22-4x20-4, 53'-8", 69'-0"

SMARTtip

Art in Pools

The tiled walls and floor of a pool make great canvases for art, so incorporate a serious or whimsical design. Also, make the stairs wide and shallow to form a wading area for kids.

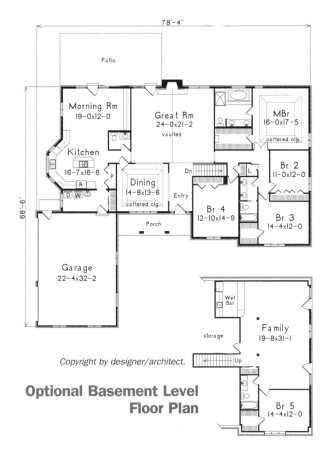

Plan #211011

Dimensions: 84' W x 54' D

Levels: 1

Square Footage: 2,791

Bedrooms: 3 or 4

Bathrooms: 2

Foundation: Slab or crawl space

Materials List Available: Yes

Price Category: F

Images provided by designer/architect.

CAD FILE AVAILABLE • CAD

Copyright by designer/architect.

Floor plan labels: game rm 22 x 16, 12' clg; ice; bar; porch; wic; br 2 15 x 12; sto 10x7; util; w/d; carousel atrium; morn. rm 12' clg; lin 10' clg; bath; books; br 3 12 x 11; clo; 3 car garage 31 x 22; br/ov; kit; family 20 x 20, 12' clg; library /br 4 12 x 11; porch; courtyard; work bench; ref; pan; dining 14 x 12, 12' clg; foy; por; living/ sitting 16 x 12, 12' clg; clo; books; optional; mbr 18 x 12; skylight; bath; wic

---

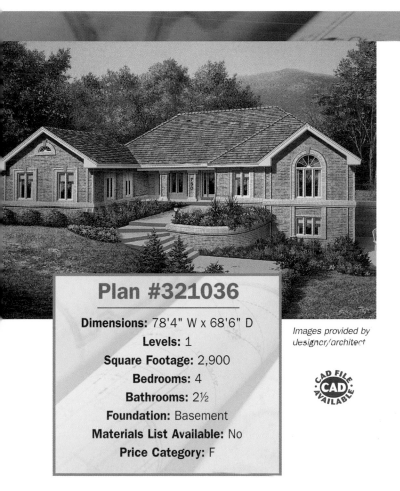

Plan #321036

Dimensions: 78'4" W x 68'6" D

Levels: 1

Square Footage: 2,900

Bedrooms: 4

Bathrooms: 2½

Foundation: Basement

Materials List Available: No

Price Category: F

Images provided by designer/architect

CAD FILE AVAILABLE • CAD

Floor plan labels: 78'-4"; Patio; Morning Rm 19-0x12-0; Great Rm 24-0x21-2 vaulted; MBr 16-0x17-5 coffered clg.; Kitchen 16-7x16-6; 68'-6"; Dining 14-8x13-6 coffered clg.; Dn; Br 2 11-0x12-0; Entry; Br 4 12-10x14-9; Garage 22-4x32-2; Porch; Br 3 14-4x12-0

Copyright by designer/architect.

Basement labels: Wet Bar; Family 19-8x31-1; storage; Up; Br 5 14-4x12-0

Optional Basement Level Floor Plan

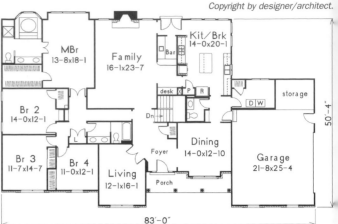

Copyright by designer/architect.

Plan #321011

Images provided by designer/architect.

Dimensions: 83' W x 50'4" D
Levels: 1
Square Footage: 2,874
Bedrooms: 4
Bathrooms: 2½
Foundation: Basement
Materials List Available: Yes
Price Category: F

CAD FILE AVAILABLE

SMARTtip

Drilling for Kitchen Plumbing

Drill holes for plumbing and waste lines before installing the cabinets. It is easier to work when the cabinets are out in the middle of the floor, and there is no danger of knocking them out of alignment when creating the holes if they are not screwed to the wall studs or one another yet.

Copyright by designer/architect.

Optional Bonus Space Floor Plan

Plan #151108

Images provided by designer/architect.

Dimensions: 84'6" W x 58'6" D
Levels: 1
Square Footage: 2,742
Bedrooms: 4
Bathrooms: 2½
Foundation: Crawl space, slab, or basement
CompleteCost List Available: Yes
Price Category: F

CAD FILE AVAILABLE

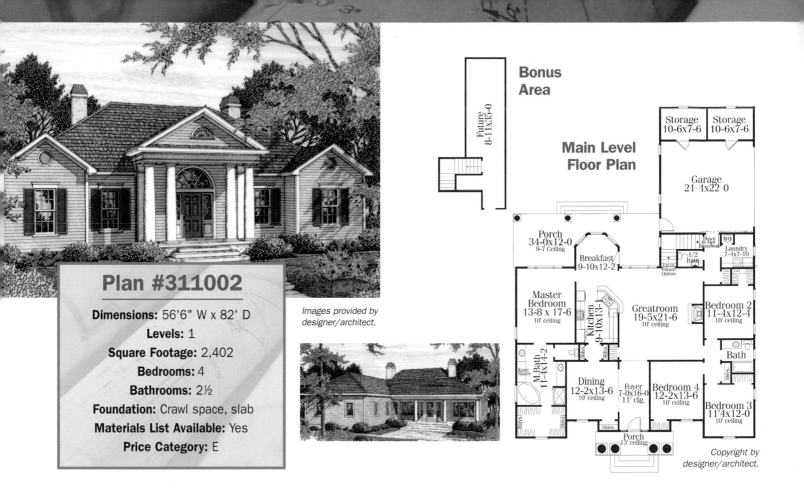

Plan #311002

Dimensions: 56'6" W x 82' D

Levels: 1

Square Footage: 2,402

Bedrooms: 4

Bathrooms: 2½

Foundation: Crawl space, slab

Materials List Available: Yes

Price Category: E

Images provided by designer/architect.

Bonus Area

Main Level Floor Plan

Future 8-11x35-0

Storage 10-6x7-6

Storage 10-6x7-6

Garage 21-4x22-0

Porch 34-0x12-0 9-7 Ceiling

Breakfast 9-10x12-2

Laundry 7-4x7-10

1/2 Bath

Master Bedroom 13-8 x 17-6 10' ceiling

Kitchen 9-10x13

Greatroom 19-5x21-6 10' ceiling

Bedroom 2 11-4x12-4 10' ceiling

Bath

M.Bath 11-4x14-2

Knee Space

Dining 12-2x13-6 10' ceiling

Foyer 7-0x16-0 11' clg.

Bedroom 4 12-2x13-6 10' ceiling

Bedroom 3 11'4x12-0 10' ceiling

Porch 13' ceiling

Copyright by designer/architect.

Plan #111018

Dimensions: 67' W x 79' D

Levels: 1

Square Footage: 2,745

Bedrooms: 4

Bathrooms: 3½

Foundation: Basement

Materials List Available: No

Price Category: G

Images provided by designer/architect.

Bedroom 15'9"x 13'1"

Breakfast 13'5"x 11'7"

Patio

Porch

Master Bedroom 14'5"x 18'7"

Bath

Kitchen 13'9"x14'

Living 20'x 19'3"

WIC

Bedroom 12'1"x 13'1"

Dress

WIC

Utility

Dining 12'7"x 16'1"

Foyer

Master Bath

Storage 12'1"x 6'3"

Bedroom 14'7"x 13'1"

Porch

Two-Car Garage 21'3"x 22'3"

Copyright by designer/architect.

Images provided by designer/architect. Living Room

Plan #111004

Dimensions: 76' W x 85' D

Levels: 1

Square Footage: 2,698

Bedrooms: 4

Full Bathrooms: 3½

Foundation: Crawl space or slab

Materials List Available: No

Price Category: G

If you've been looking for a home that includes a special master suite, this one could be the answer to your dreams.

Features:

• **Living Room:** Make a sitting area around the fireplace here so that the whole family can enjoy the warmth on chilly days and winter evenings. A door from this room leads to the rear covered porch, making this room the heart of your home.

• **Kitchen:** An island with a cooktop makes cooking a pleasure in this well-designed kitchen, and the breakfast bar invites visitors at all times of day.

• **Utility Room:** A sink and a built-in ironing board make this room totally practical.

• **Master Suite:** A private fireplace in the corner sets a romantic tone for this bedroom, and the door to the covered porch allows you to sit outside on warm summer nights. The bath has two vanities, a divided walk-in closet, a standing shower, and a deluxe corner bathtub.

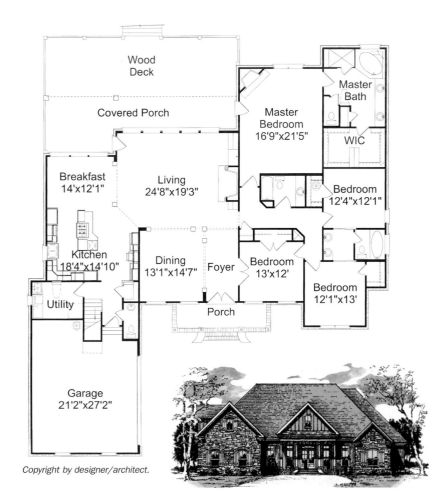

Copyright by designer/architect.

Kitchen

Dining Room

Master Bath

Master Bath

SMARTtip

How to Quit Smoking — Lighting Your Fireplace

Before attempting to light a wood fire, make certain that the damper is open all the way. This allows a good draft (flow of air up the chimney) to prevent smoke from blowing back into the room. To ensure a good draft—particularly if your home is well insulated —open a window a bit when lighting a fire.

The opposite of draft is downdraft, which occurs when cold air flows down the chimney and into the room. If the fireplace is properly designed and maintained, the smoke shelf will prevent backpuffing from downdraft most of the time by redirecting cold air currents back up the chimney. The open damper also helps prevent backpuffing.

Also, build a fire slowly to let the chimney liner heat up, which will create a good draft and minimize the chances of downdraft.

Don't wait until fall to inspect the chimney. Do this job, or call a chimney sweep, when the weather is mild. Because some repairs take a while to make, it's best to have them done when the fireplace is not normally in use. If you do the inspection yourself, wear old clothes, eye goggles, and a mask.

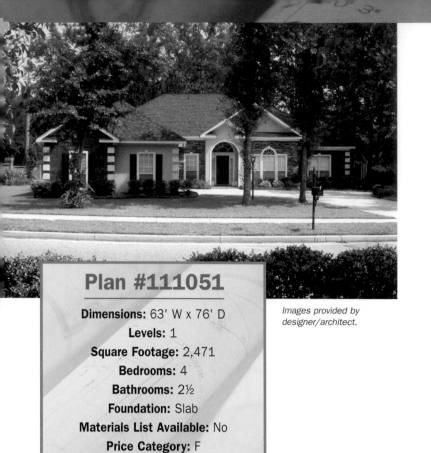

Plan #111051

Dimensions: 63' W x 76' D

Levels: 1

Square Footage: 2,471

Bedrooms: 4

Bathrooms: 2½

Foundation: Slab

Materials List Available: No

Price Category: F

Images provided by designer/architect.

Copyright by designer/architect.

Plan #201063

Dimensions: 74'10" W x 70'10" D

Levels: 1

Square Footage: 2,697

Bedrooms: 4

Bathrooms: 3

Foundation: Crawl space, slab

Materials List Available: Yes

Price Category: F

Images provided by designer/architect.

Copyright by designer/architect.

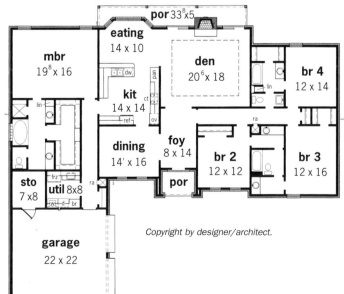

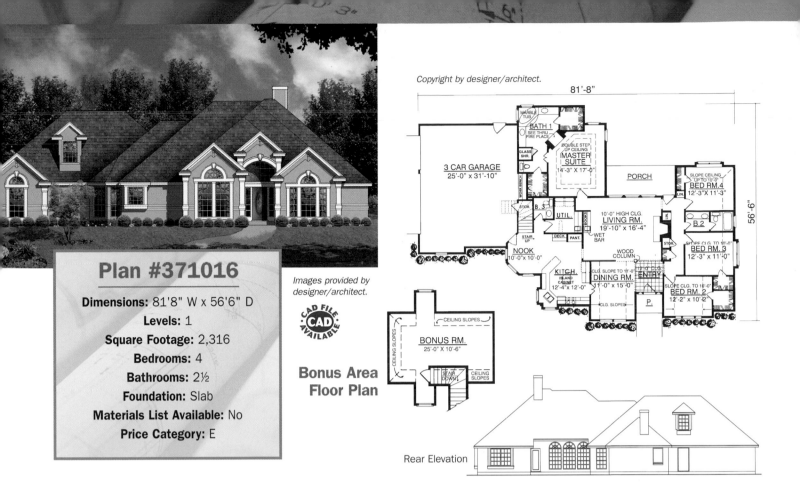

Copyright by designer/architect.

81'-8"

56'-6"

3 CAR GARAGE 25'-0" x 31'-10"

MASTER SUITE 14'-3" X 17'-0"

PORCH

BED RM. 4 12'-3" X 11'-3"

BATH 1

SEE THRU FIRE PLACE

MARBLE TUB

GLASS SHR.

WORK BENCH

DOUBLE STEP UP CEILING

SLOPE CEILING UP TO 10'-0"

STOR.

B. 3

UTIL.

LIVING RM. 19'-10" X 16'-4"

B. 2

SLOPE CLG. TO 10'-0"

BED RM. 3 12'-3" X 11'-0"

STAIR UP

DECK PANT.

WET BAR

STOR.

NOOK 10'-0"x 10'0"

WOOD COLUMN

ENTRY

SLOPE CLG. TO 10'-0"

KITCH. ISLAND CABINET 12'-4" X 12'-0"

DINING RM. 11'-0" X 15'-0"

CLG. SLOPE TO 11'-0"

BED RM. 2 12'-2" X 10'-2"

P.

CLG. SLOPES

Images provided by designer/architect.

CAD FILE AVAILABLE

Plan #371016

Dimensions: 81'8" W x 56'6" D

Levels: 1

Square Footage: 2,316

Bedrooms: 4

Bathrooms: 2½

Foundation: Slab

Materials List Available: No

Price Category: E

Bonus Area Floor Plan

CEILING SLOPES

CEILING SLOPES

CEILING SLOPES

CEILING SLOPES

BONUS RM. 25'-0" X 10'-6"

STAIR DOWN

Rear Elevation

Plan #151040

Dimensions: 70' W x 51'10" D

Levels: 1

Square Footage: 2,444

Bedrooms: 4

Bathrooms: 2½

Foundation: Crawl space, slab (basement option for fee)

CompleteCost List Available: Yes

Price Category: E

Images provided by designer/architect.

CAD FILE AVAILABLE

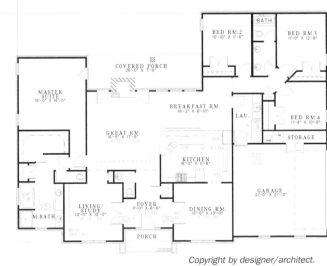

70'-0"

BED RM. 2 10'-10" X 11'-6"

BED RM. 3 11'-0" X 12'-8"

BATH

COVERED PORCH 26'-0" X 7'-0"

MASTER SUITE 15'-0" X 16'-0"

BREAKFAST RM. 16'-2" X 8'-10"

LAU.

BED RM. 4 11'-4" X 10'-8"

GREAT RM. 16'-5" X 17'-6"

KITCHEN 16'-0" X 11'-9"

STORAGE

M. BATH

LIVING/ STUDY 13'-0" X 13'-0"

FOYER 11'-0" X 6'-6"

DINING RM. 13'-0" X 13'-0"

GARAGE 21'-0" X 21'-10"

PORCH

Copyright by designer/architect.

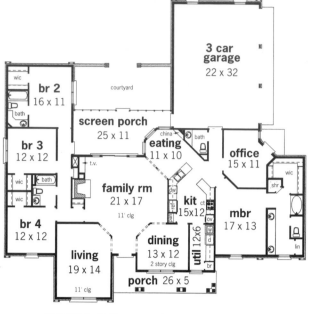

Plan #211062

Dimensions: 96'6" W x 43' D

Levels: 1

Square Footage: 2,719

Bedrooms: 4

Bathrooms: 2½

Foundation: Slab

Materials List Available: Yes

Price Category: F

Images provided by designer/architect.

Copyright by designer/architect.

Plan #151046

Dimensions: 63'4" W x 59'10" D

Levels: 1

Square Footage: 2,525

Bedrooms: 3

Bathrooms: 2

Foundation: Crawl space, slab, or basement

CompleteCost List Available: Yes

Price Category: E

Images provided by designer/architect.

Copyright by designer/architect.

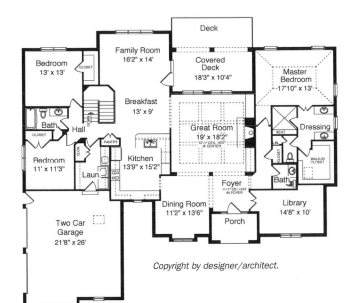

Plan #161158

Dimensions: 72' W x 64'2" D
Levels: 1
Square Footage: 2,679
Bedrooms: 3
Bathrooms: 2½
Foundation: Basement
Materials List Available: Yes
Price Category: F

Images provided by designer/architect.

Copyright by designer/architect.

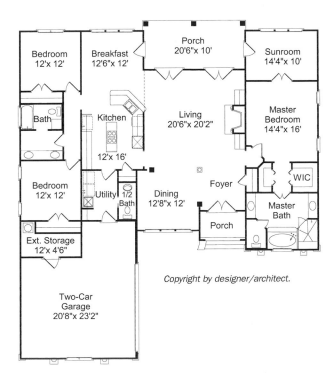

Plan #111017

Dimensions: 61' W x 70' D
Levels: 1
Square Footage: 2,323
Bedrooms: 3
Bathrooms: 2½
Foundation: Monolithic slab
Materials List Available: No
Price Category: F

Images provided by designer/architect.

Copyright by designer/architect.

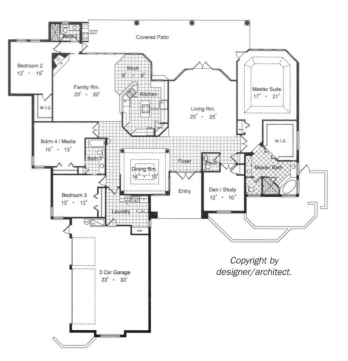

Images provided by designer/architect.

Copyright by designer/architect.

Plan #661258

Dimensions: 86'8" W x 94'8" D

Levels: 1

Square Footage: 3,743

Bedrooms: 4

Bathrooms: 3½

Foundation: Slab

Materials List Available: No

Price Category: H

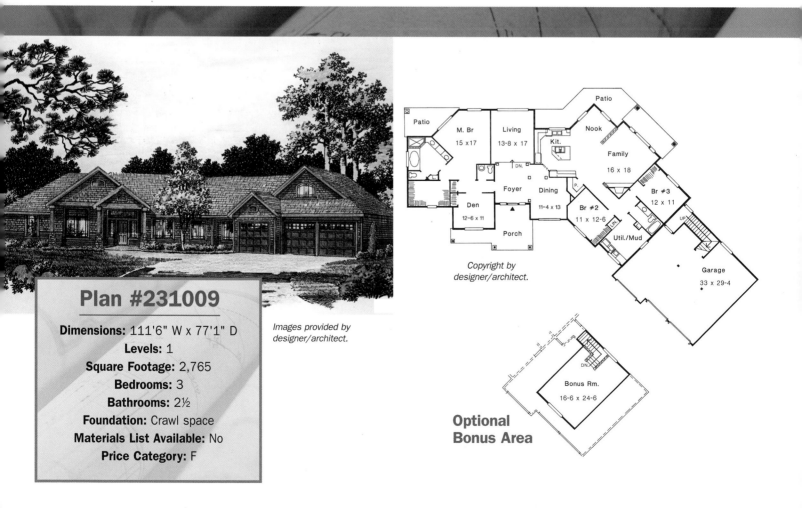

Plan #231009

Dimensions: 111'6" W x 77'1" D

Levels: 1

Square Footage: 2,765

Bedrooms: 3

Bathrooms: 2½

Foundation: Crawl space

Materials List Available: No

Price Category: F

Images provided by designer/architect.

Copyright by designer/architect.

Optional Bonus Area

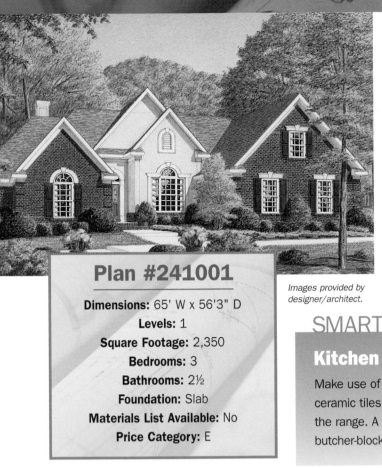

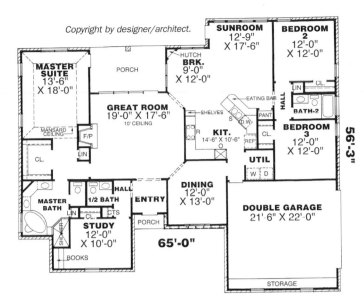

Copyright by designer/architect.

Images provided by designer/architect.

Plan #241001

Dimensions: 65' W x 56'3" D

Levels: 1

Square Footage: 2,350

Bedrooms: 3

Bathrooms: 2½

Foundation: Slab

Materials List Available: No

Price Category: E

SMARTtip

Kitchen Counters

Make use of counter inserts to help with the cooking chores. For example, ceramic tiles inlaid in a laminate counter create a heat-proof landing zone near the range. A marble or granite insert is tailor-made for pastry chefs. And a butcher-block inlay is a great addition to the food prep area.

Copyright by designer/architect.

Images provided by designer/architect.

Plan #221001

Dimensions: 87' W x 60' D

Levels: 1

Square Footage: 2,600

Bedrooms: 3

Bathrooms: 2½

Foundation: Basement

Materials List Available: No

Price Category: F

Rear Elevation

Kitchen

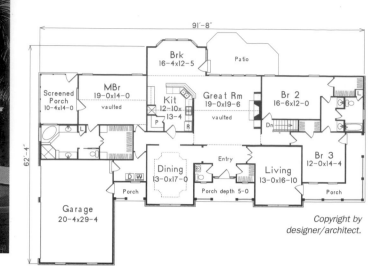

Copyright by
designer/architect.

Plan #321004

Dimensions: 91'8" W x 62'4" D

Levels: 1

Square Footage: 2,808

Bedrooms: 3

Bathrooms: 2½

Foundation: Basement

Materials List Available: Yes

Price Category: F

Images provided by designer/architect.

SMARTtip

Ornaments in a Garden

Placement is everything with ornaments in a garden. Some elements are best sitting by themselves. Others are better when they are part of a cohesive whole, perhaps placed in the greenery at a corner or flanking a structure.

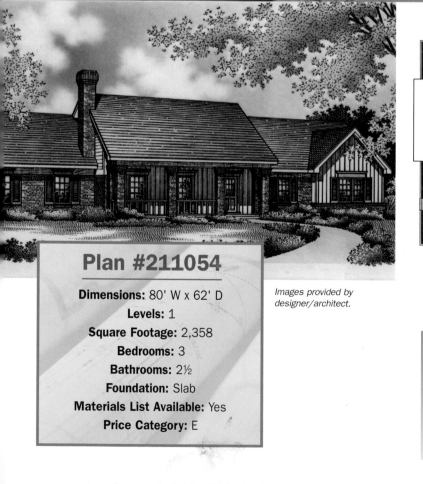

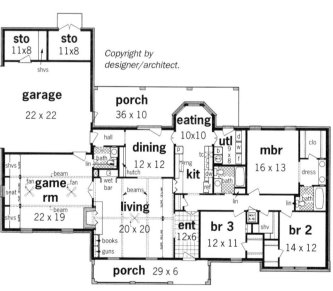

Copyright by
designer/architect.

Plan #211054

Dimensions: 80' W x 62' D

Levels: 1

Square Footage: 2,358

Bedrooms: 3

Bathrooms: 2½

Foundation: Slab

Materials List Available: Yes

Price Category: E

Images provided by designer/architect.

SMARTtip

Dressing Up a Simple Fireplace

Painting a wood surround with a faux marble or faux bois (wood) is inexpensive. Adding a simple, prefabricated wooden shelf mantel can add lots of architectural character.

Plan #151845

Dimensions: 84'10" W x 69'4" D

Levels: 1

Square Footage: 3,003

Bedrooms: 5

Bathrooms: 4

Foundation: Crawl space, slab; basement or walkout for fee

CompleteCost List Available: Yes

Price Category: G

Images provided by designer/architect.

CAD FILE AVAILABLE

Bonus Area

Copyright by designer/architect.

Plan #351153

Dimensions: 75'6" W x 70'10" D

Levels: 1

Square Footage: 2,750

Bedrooms: 4

Bathrooms: 3½

Foundation: Basement, crawl space, or slab

Materials List Available: Yes

Price Category: F

Images provided by designer/architect.

CAD FILE AVAILABLE

Bonus Area

Copyright by designer/architect.

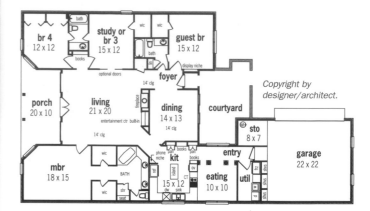

Plan #211057

Dimensions: 50' W x 86' D

Levels: 1

Square Footage: 2,366

Bedrooms: 4

Bathrooms: 3

Foundation: Slab

Materials List Available: No

Price Category: E

Images provided by designer/architect.

CAD FILE AVAILABLE

SMARTtip

Using a Hand Miter Box

Because hand-powered miter boxes generally are much lighter than electric-powered models, you need to clamp them securely to a workbench to avoid shifting that could alter the cut.

Plan #211065

Dimensions: 72' W x 70' D

Levels: 1

Square Footage: 3,158

Bedrooms: 4

Bathrooms: 3

Foundation: Crawl space

Materials List Available: Yes

Price Category: G

Images provided by designer/architect.

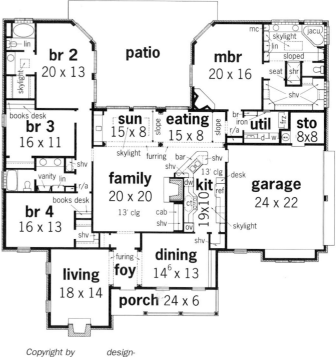

Copyright by designer/architect.

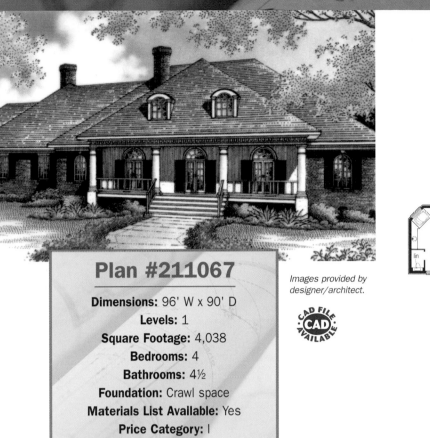

Plan #211067

Dimensions: 96' W x 90' D

Levels: 1

Square Footage: 4,038

Bedrooms: 4

Bathrooms: 4½

Foundation: Crawl space

Materials List Available: Yes

Price Category: I

Images provided by designer/architect.

CAD FILE AVAILABLE

Copyright by designer/architect.

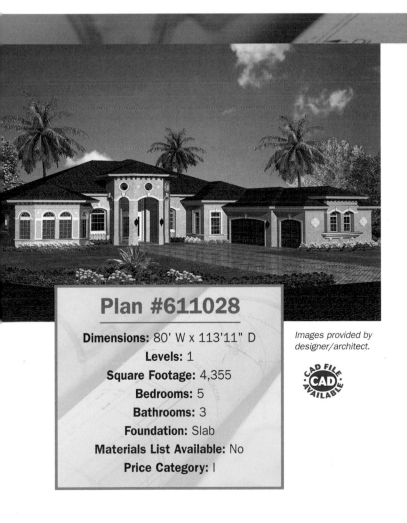

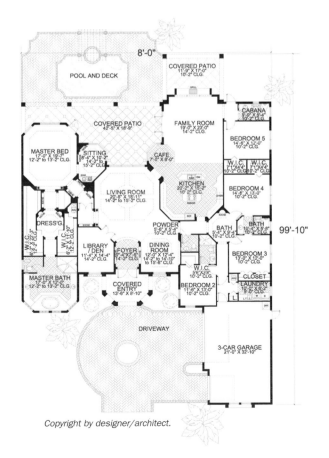

Plan #611028

Dimensions: 80' W x 113'11" D

Levels: 1

Square Footage: 4,355

Bedrooms: 5

Bathrooms: 3

Foundation: Slab

Materials List Available: No

Price Category: I

Images provided by designer/architect.

CAD FILE AVAILABLE

Copyright by designer/architect.

Plan #121196

Dimensions: 71' W x 67' D

Levels: 1

Square Footage: 2,512

Bedrooms: 3

Bathrooms: 3

Foundation: Slab; basement for fee

Material List Available: Yes

Price Category: E

Images provided by designer/architect.

Bonus Area Floor Plan

Copyright by designer/architect.

ATTIC

OPTIONAL GAMEROOM
19'6" X 16'

Plan #201061

Dimensions: 64'10" W x 54'10" D

Levels: 1

Square Footage: 2,387

Bedrooms: 4

Bathrooms: 2½

Foundation: Crawl space, slab

Materials List Available: Yes

Price Category: E

Images provided by designer/architect.

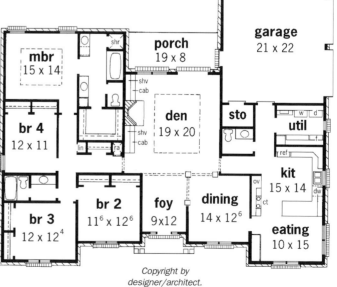

Copyright by designer/architect.

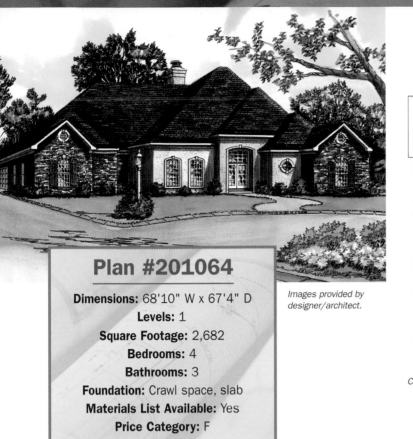

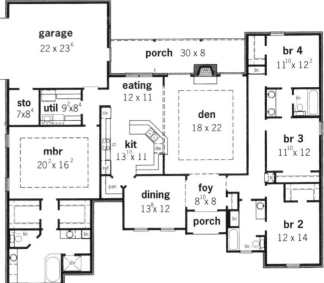

Plan #201064

Dimensions: 68'10" W x 67'4" D

Levels: 1

Square Footage: 2,682

Bedrooms: 4

Bathrooms: 3

Foundation: Crawl space, slab

Materials List Available: Yes

Price Category: F

Images provided by designer/architect.

Copyright by designer/architect.

garage 22 x 23⁶

porch 30 x 8

br 4 11¹⁰ x 12²

sto 7x8⁴

util 9²x8⁴

eating 12 x 11

den 18 x 22

br 3 11¹⁰ x 12

mbr 20²x 16²

kit 13¹⁰ x 11

br 2 12 x 14

dining 13⁸x 12

foy 8¹⁰x 8

porch

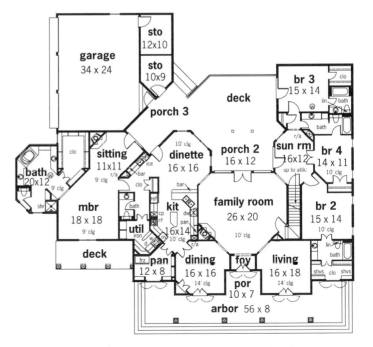

Plan #211068

Dimensions: 98' W x 90' D

Levels: 1

Square Footage: 3,960

Bedrooms: 4

Bathrooms: 4½

Foundation: Crawl space

Materials List Available: Yes

Price Category: H

Images provided by designer/architect.

CAD FILE AVAILABLE

garage 34 x 24

sto 12x10

sto 10x9

deck

br 3 15 x 14

porch 3

deck

bath 20x12

sitting 11x11 9' clg

dinette 16 x 16

porch 2 16 x 12

sun rm 16x12

br 4 14 x 11

mbr 18 x 18 9' clg

kit 16x14 10' clg

family room 26 x 20 10' clg

br 2 15 x 14

util iron

pan 12 x 8

dining 16 x 16 14' clg

foy

por 10 x 7

living 16 x 18 14' clg

deck

arbor 56 x 8

Copyright by designer/architect.

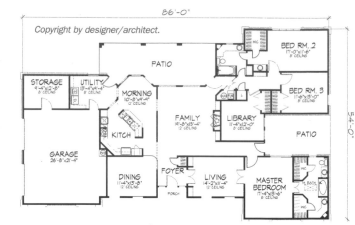

Copyright by designer/architect.

86'-0"

54'-0"

BED RM. 2
17'-0"x11'-6"
8' CEILING

BED RM. 3
11'-6"x15'-0"
8' CEILING

PATIO

STORAGE
9'-4"x12'-8"
8' CEILING

UTILITY
15'-4"x9'-4"
8' CEILING

MORNING
10'-8"x9'-4"
12' CEILING

FAMILY
19'-8"x15'-4"
12' CEILING

LIBRARY
11'-4"x12'-0"
8' CEILING

KITCH.

PATIO

GARAGE
26'-8"x21'-4"

DINING
11'-4"x13'-8"
12' CEILING

FOYER

LIVING
14'-4"x11'-4"
12' CEILING

MASTER
BEDROOM
17'-4"x13'-6"
8' CEILING

PORCH

Plan #271081

Dimensions: 86' W x 54' D

Levels: 1

Square Footage: 2,539

Bedrooms: 3

Bathrooms: 2

Foundation: Slab

Materials List Available: No

Price Category: E

Images provided by designer/architect.

SMARTtip

Determining Curtain Length

Follow length guidelines for foolproof results, but remember that they're not rules. Go ahead and play with curtain and drapery lengths. Instead of shortening long panels at the hem, for instance, take up excess material by blousing them over tiebacks for a pleasing effect.

Plan #351151

Dimensions: 69'2" W x 65'6" D

Levels: 1

Square Footage: 2,369

Bedrooms: 3

Bathrooms: 2½

Foundation: Basement, crawl space, slab

Materials List Available: Yes

Price Category: E

Images provided by designer/architect.

Copyright by designer/architect.

Master
Bedroom
13'-6" x 15'-8"
10' Clg. Ht.
(Trayed Clg.)

Closet or
Retreat
10'-0" x 7'-0"

M. Bath
10'-0" x
16'-6"

Utility
9'-2" x 7'-8"
Utility Sink

Closet
9'-8" x 5'-2"

Bedroom 3
12'-8" x 12'-6"
9' Clg. Ht.

Covered Porch
17'-0" x 6'-6"

Breakfast
14'-0" x 10'-2"
9' Clg. Ht.

Hall

1/2
Bath

Great Room
17'-0" x 20'-0"
11' Clg. Ht.
(Trayed Clg.)

Kitchen
14'-0" x 12'-0"

Hall Bath
8'-10" x 5'-4"

Hall

Two Car Garage
23'-10" x 24'-6"

Bedroom 2
12'-6" x 12'-8"
9' Clg. Ht.

Foyer
8'-2" x 8'-0"
10' Clg. Ht.

Dining
12'-0" x 11'-6"
10' Clg. Ht.

Flex Space
10'-6" x 11'-4"
10' Clg. Ht.

Covered Porch
9'-2" x 4'-0"

Bonus Area

Unfinished
Bonus Room
12'-0" x 11'-6"
8' Clg. Ht.

Plan #211010

Dimensions: 81' W x 84' D

Levels: 1

Square Footage: 2,503

Bedrooms: 3

Bathrooms: 2½

Foundation: Slab

Materials List Available: Yes

Price Category: E

Images provided by designer/architect.

CAD FILE AVAILABLE

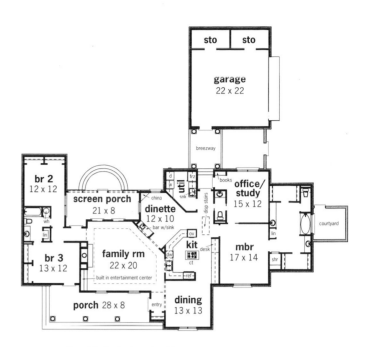

Copyright by designer/architect.

Plan #541028

Dimensions: 77' W x 58' D

Levels: 1

Square Footage: 2,737

Bedrooms: 4

Bathrooms: 2½

Foundation: Basement; crawl space, slab, or walkout for fee

Materials List Available: No

Price Category: F

Images provided by designer/architect.

CAD FILE AVAILABLE

MAIN FLOOR PLAN

Copyright by designer/architect.

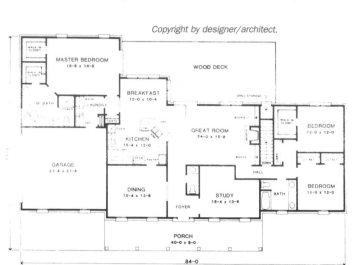

Copyright by designer/architect.

Plan #301003

Dimensions: 84' W x 55'8" D

Levels: 1

Square Footage: 2,485

Bedrooms: 3

Bathrooms: 2½

Foundation: Crawl space, basement

Materials List Available: Yes

Price Category: E

Images provided by designer/architect.

SMARTtip

Making Mitered Returns

Cut the small return piece from a substantial board that you can hold safely and securely against the saw fence.

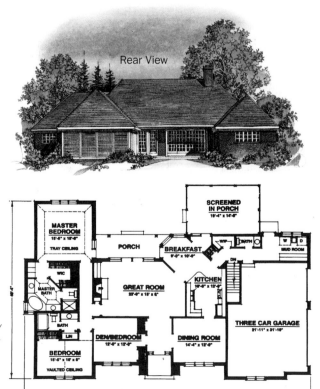

Rear View

Plan #291004

Dimensions: 77'4" W x 54'8" D

Levels: 1

Square Footage: 2,529

Bedrooms: 3

Bathrooms: 2½

Foundation: Basement

Materials List Available: No

Price Category: E

Images provided by designer/architect.

Copyright by designer/architect.

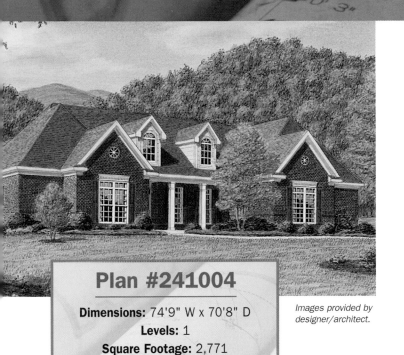

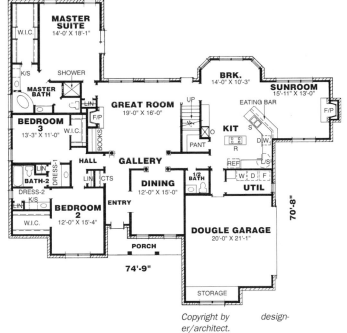

Plan #241004

Dimensions: 74'9" W x 70'8" D

Levels: 1

Square Footage: 2,771

Bedrooms: 3

Bathrooms: 2½

Foundation: Slab

Materials List Available: No

Price Category: F

Images provided by designer/architect.

Copyright by designer/architect.

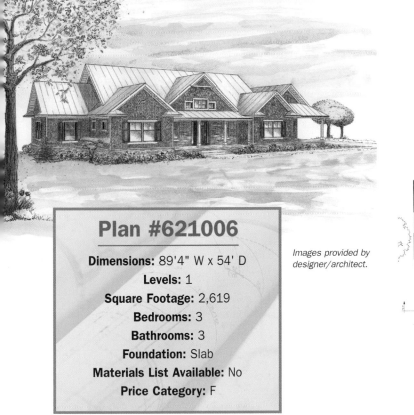

Plan #621006

Dimensions: 89'4" W x 54' D

Levels: 1

Square Footage: 2,619

Bedrooms: 3

Bathrooms: 3

Foundation: Slab

Materials List Available: No

Price Category: F

Images provided by designer/architect.

Copyright by designer/architect.

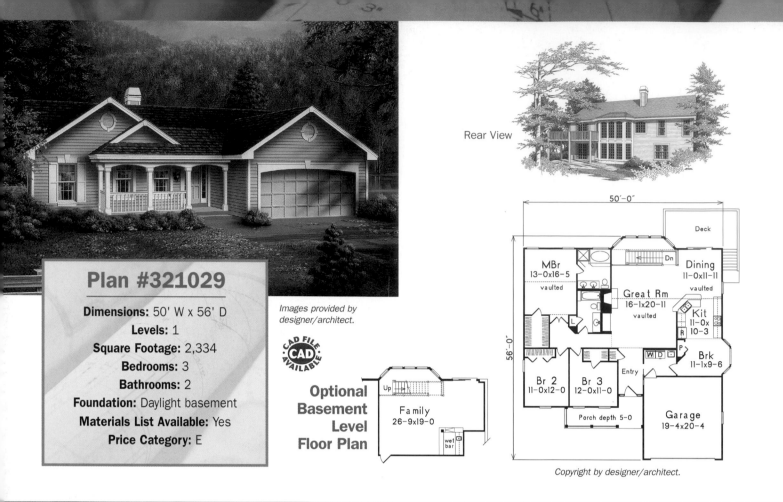

Plan #321029

Dimensions: 50' W x 56' D

Levels: 1

Square Footage: 2,334

Bedrooms: 3

Bathrooms: 2

Foundation: Daylight basement

Materials List Available: Yes

Price Category: E

Images provided by designer/architect.

CAD FILE AVAILABLE

Rear View

Optional Basement Level Floor Plan

Family 26-9x19-0

Up

wet bar

50'-0"

Deck

MBr 13-0x16-5 vaulted

Dining 11-0x11-11 vaulted

Dn

Great Rm 16-1x20-11 vaulted

Kit 11-0x 10-3

R

Br 2 11-0x12-0

Br 3 12-0x11-0

Entry

WD

Brk 11-1x9-6

P

56'-0"

Porch depth 5-0

Garage 19-4x20-4

Copyright by designer/architect.

Plan #611025

Dimensions: 76'9" W x 94'11" D

Levels: 1

Square Footage: 3,593

Bedrooms: 4

Bathrooms: 3½

Foundation: Slab

Material List Available: No

Price Category: H

Images provided by designer/architect.

CAD FILE AVAILABLE

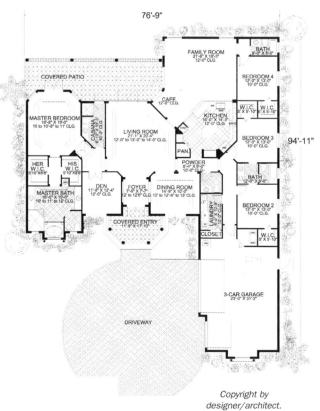

76'-9"

COVERED PATIO

FAMILY ROOM 21'-6" X 18'-3" 12'-0" CLG

BATH 8'-4" X 5'-0"

BEDROOM 4 12'-0" X 13'-0" 10'-0" CLG

CAFE

MASTER BEDROOM 16'-9" X 19'-0" 10' to 10'-8" x 11' CLG

CABANA

LIVING ROOM 21'-1" X 20'-4" 12'-0" to 13'-0" or 14'-0" CLG

KITCHEN 16'-0" X 14'-3" 12'-0" CLG

W.I.C.

W.I.C.

BEDROOM 3 12'-0" X 13'-0" 10'-0" CLG

94'-11"

HER W.I.C.

HIS W.I.C.

PAN.

POWDER

BATH 12'-0" X 6'-0"

MASTER BATH 16'-0" X 19'-0" 10' to 11' to 12' CLG

DEN 11'-8" X 12'-4" 12'-0" CLG

FOYER 7'-9" X 7'-7"

DINING ROOM 12' X 12'-6" 13' CLG

LAUNDRY

BEDROOM 2 12'-0" X 13'-0" 10'-0" CLG

COVERED ENTRY

CLOSET

W.I.C.

3-CAR GARAGE 23'-0" X 31'-2"

DRIVEWAY

Copyright by designer/architect.

Let Us Help You
Plan Your Dream Home

Whether you've always dreamed of building your own home or you can't find the right house from among the dozens you've toured, our collection of affordable plans can help you achieve the home of your dreams. You could have an architect create a one-of-a-kind home for you, but the design services alone could end up costing up to 15 percent of the cost of construction—a hefty premium for any building project. Isn't it a better idea to select from among the hundreds of unique designs shown in our collection for a fraction of the cost?

What does Creative Homeowner Offer?

In this book, Creative Homeowner provides hundreds of home plans from the country's best architects and designers. Our designs are among the most popular available. Whether your taste runs from traditional to contemporary, Victorian to early American, you are sure to find the best house design for you and your family. Our plans packages include detailed drawings to help you or your builder construct your dream house. **(See page 310.)**

Can I Make Changes to the Plans?

Creative Homeowner offers three ways to help you achieve a truly unique home design. Our customizing service allows for extensive changes to our designs. **(See page 311.)** We also provide reverse images of our plans, or we can give you and your builder the tools for making minor changes on your own. **(See page 314.)**

Can You Help Me Manage My Costs?

To help you stay within your budget, Creative Homeowner has teamed up with the leading estimating company to provide one of the most accurate, complete, and reliable building material take-offs in the industry. **(See page 312.)** If that is too much detail for you, we can provide you with general construction costs based on your zip code. **(See page 314.)** Also, many of our plans come with the option of buying detailed materials lists to help you price out construction costs.

How Can I Begin the Building Process?

To get started building your dream home, fill out the order form on page 315, call our order department at 1-800-523-6789, or visit ulti mateplans.com. If you plan on doing all or part of the work your-self, or want to keep tabs on your builder, we offer best-selling build-ing and design books available at www.creativehomeowner.com.

Our Plans Packages Offer:

"Square footage" refers to the total "heated square feet" of this plan. This number does not include the garage, porches, or unfinished areas. All of our home plans are the result of many hours of work by leading architects and professional designers. Most of our home plans include each of the following:

Frontal Sheet

This artist's rendering of the front of the house gives you an idea of how the house will look once it is completed and the property landscaped.

Detailed Floor Plans

These plans show the size and layout of the rooms. They also provide the locations of doors, windows, fireplaces, closets, stairs, and electrical outlets and switches.

Foundation Plan

A foundation plan gives the dimensions of basements, walk-out basements, crawl spaces, pier foundations, and slab construction. Each house design lists the type of foundation included. If the plan you choose does not have the foundation type you require, our customer service department can help you customize the plan to meet your needs.

Roof Plan

In addition to providing the pitch of the roof, these plans also show the locations of dormers, skylights, and other elements.

Exterior Elevations

These drawings show the front, rear, and sides of the house as if you were looking at it head on. Elevations also provide information about architectural features and finish materials.

Interior Elevations and Details

Interior elevations show specific details of such elements as fireplaces, kitchen and bathroom cabinets, built-ins, and other unique features of the design.

Cross Sections

These show the structure as if it were sliced to reveal construction requirements, such as insulation, flooring, and roofing details.

Frontal Sheet

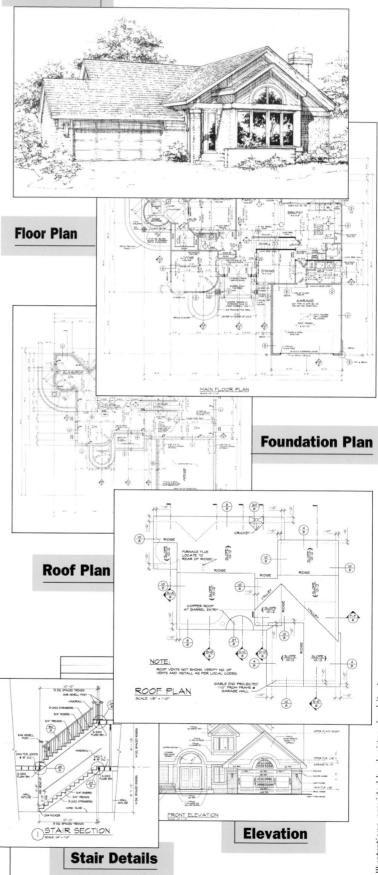

Floor Plan

Foundation Plan

Roof Plan

Cross Sections

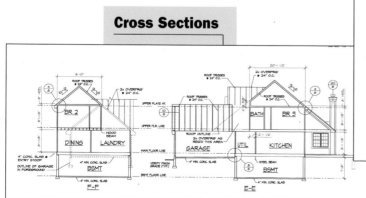

Stair Details

Elevation

Illustrations provided by designer/architect

Customize Your Plans in 4 Easy Steps

1 **Select the home plan** that most closely meets your needs. Purchase of a reproducible master is necessary in order to make changes to a plan.

2 **Call 1-800-523-6789 to place your order.** Tell our sales representative you are interested in customizing your plan. To receive your customization cost estimate, our modification company will contact you (via fax or email) requesting a list or sketch of the changes requested to one of our plans. There is a $50 nonrefundable consultation fee for this service. If you decide to continue with the custom changes, the $50 fee is credited to the total amount charged.

3 **Fax or email your request** to our modification company. Within three business days of receipt of your request, a detailed cost estimate will be provided to you.

4 **Once you approve the estimate,** a 75% retainer fee is collected and customization work begins. Preliminary drawings typically take 10 to 15 business days. After approval of the design, the balance of your customization fee is due before modified plans can be shipped. You will receive five sets of blueprints, a reproducible master, or CAD files, depending on which package was purchase.

Modification Pricing Guide

Categories	Average Cost For Modification
Add or remove living space	Quote required
Bathroom layout redesign	Starting at $150
Kitchen layout redesign	Starting at $120
Garage: add or remove	Starting at $600
Garage: front entry to side load or vice versa	Starting at $300
Foundation changes	Starting at $220
Exterior building materials change	Starting at $200
Exterior openings: add, move, or remove	$75 per opening
Roof line changes	Starting at $600
Ceiling height adjustments	Starting at $280
Fireplace: add or remove	Starting at $90
Screened porch: add	Starting at $300
Wall framing change from 2x4 to 2x6	Starting at $250
Bearing and/or exterior walls changes	Quote required
Non-bearing wall or room changes	$65 per room
Metric conversion of home plan	Starting at $495
Adjust plan for handicapped accessibility	Quote required
Adapt plans for local building code requirements	Quote required
Engineering stamping only	Quote required
Any other engineering services	Quote required
Interactive illustrations (choices of exterior materials)	Quote required

Note: Any home plan can be customized to accommodate your desired changes. The average prices above are provided only as examples of the most commonly requested changes, and are subject to change without notice. Prices for changes will vary according to the number of modifications requested, plan size, style, and method of design used by the original designer. To obtain a detailed cost estimate, please contact us.

Before Customization

After

Turn your dream home into reality with

UltimateEstimate

When purchasing a home plan with Creative Homeowner, we recommend you order one of the most complete materials lists in the industry.

1 | What comes with an Ultimate Estimate?

Quote

- Basis of the entire estimate.

- Detailed list of all the framing materials needed to build your project, listed from the bottom up, in the order that each one will actually be used.

Comments

- Details pertinent information beyond the cost of materials.

- Includes any notes from our estimator.

Express List

- A version of the Quote with space for SKU numbers listed for purchasing the items at your local lumberyard.

- Your local lumberyard can then price out the materials list.

Construction-Ready Framing Diagrams

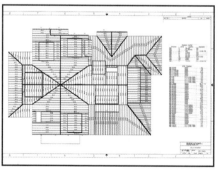

- Your "map" to exact roof and floor framing.

Millwork Report

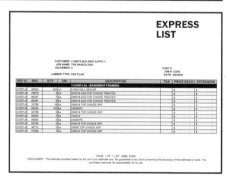

- A complete count of the windows, doors, molding, and trim.

Man-Hour Report

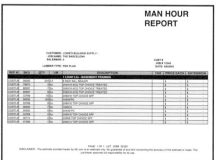

- Calculates labor on a line-by-line basis for all items quoted and presented in man-hours.

CRE▲TIVE
HOMEOWNER®

◆2 Why an Ultimate Estimate?

Accurate. Professional estimators break down each individual item from the blueprints using advanced software, techniques, and equipment.

Timely. You will be able to start your home-building project quickly — knowing the exact framing materials you need to order from your local lumberyard.

Detailed. Work with your local lumberyard associate to complete your quote with the remaining products needed for your new home.

◆3 So how much does it cost?

Pricing is determined by the total square feet of the home plan — including living area, garages, decks, porches, finished basements, and finished attics.

Square Feet Range	UE Tier*	Price
Up to 5,000 total square feet	XB	$299.00
5,001 to 10,000 total square feet	XC	$499.00

*Please see the Plan Index to determine your plan's Material Take-off Tier (MT Tier).
Note: All prices subject to change.

Call our toll-free number (800-523-6789), or visit ultimateplans.com to order your Material Take-off.

◆4 What else do I need to know?

Call our toll-free number (800-523-6789), or visit
ultimateplans.com to order your Ultimate Estimate.

Turn your dream home into reality.

Decide What Type of Plan Package You Need

How many Plans Should You Order?

Standard 8-Set Package. We've found that our 8-set package is the best value for someone who is ready to start building. The 8-set package provides plans for you, your builder, the subcontractors, mortgage lender, and the building department.

Minimum 5-Set Package. If you are in the bidding process, you may want to order only five sets for the bidding round and reorder additional sets as needed.

1-Set Study Package. The 1-set package allows you to review your home plan in detail. The plan will be marked as a study print, and it is illegal to build a house from a study print alone. It is a violation of copyright law to reproduce a blueprint without permission.

Buying Additional Sets

If you require additional copies of blueprints for your home construction, you can order additional sets within 60 days of the original order date at a reduced price. The cost is $45.00 for each additional set. For more information, contact customer service.

Reproducible Masters

If you plan to make minor changes to one of our home plans, you can purchase reproducible masters. These plans are printed on bond or vellum paper that is easy to alter. They clearly indicate your right to modify, copy, or reproduce the plans. Reproducable mastrs allow an architect, designer, or builder to alter our plans to give you a customized home design. This package also allows you to print as many copies of the modified plans as you need for the construction of one home.

CAD (Computer Aided Design) Files

CAD files are the complete set of home plans in an electronic file format. Choose this option if there are multiple changes you wish made to the home plans and you have a local design professional able to make the changes. Not available for all plans. Please contact our order department or visit our website to check the availability of CAD files for your plan.

Mirror-Reverse Sets/Right-Reading Reverse

Plans can be printed in mirror-reverse—we can "flip" plans to create a mirror image of the design. This is useful when the house would fit your site or personal preferences if all the rooms were on the opposite side than shown. As the image is reversed, the letter-ing and dimensions will also be reversed, meaning they will read backwards. Therefore, when ordering mirror-reverse drawings, you must order at least one set of right-reading plans. A $50.00 fee per plan order will be charged for mirror-reverse (regardless of the number of mirror-reverse sets ordered). Some plans are available in right-reading reverse, this feature will show the plan in reverse, but the writing on the plan will be readable. A $150.00 fee per plan order will be charged for right-reading reverse (regardless of the number of right-reading reverse sets ordered). Please contact our order department or visit our website to check the availibility of this feature for your chosen plan.

EZ Quote: Home Cost Estimator

EZ Quote is our response to one of the most frequently asked questions we hear from customers: "How much will the house cost me to build?" EZ Quote: Home Cost Estimator will enable you to obtain a calculated building cost to construct your home, based on labor rates and building material costs within your zip code area. This summary is useful for those who want to get an idea of the total construction costs before purchasing sets of home plans. It will also provide a level of comfort when you begin soliciting bids. The cost is $29.95 for the first EZ Quote and $19.95 for each additional one. Available only in the U.S. and Canada.

Materials List

Available for most of our plans, the Materials List provides you an invaluable resource in planning and estimating the cost of your home. Each Materials List outlines the quantity, dimensions, and type of materials needed to build your home (with the exception of mechanical systems). You will get faster, more-accurate bids from your contractors and building suppliers. A Materials List may only be ordered with the purchase of at least five sets of home plans.

CompleteCost Estimator

CompleteCost Estimator is a valuable tool for use in planning and constructing your new home. It provides more detail than a materials list and will act as a checklist for all items you will need to select or coordinate during your building process. CompleteCost Estimator is only available for certain plans (please see Plan Index) and may only be ordered with the purchase of at least five sets of home plans. The cost is $125.00 for CompleteCost Estimator.

Ultimate Estimate (See page 312.)

Order Toll Free by Phone	**Order Online**	**Canadian Customers**
1-800-523-6789	**www.ultimateplans.com**	**Order Toll Free 1-800-393-1883**
By Fax: 201-760-2431		

Orders received 3PM ET, will be processed and shipped within two business days.

Mail Your Order
Creative Homeowner
Attn: Home Plans
24 Park Way
Upper Saddle River, NJ 07458

Mail Your Order (Canada)
Creative Homeowner Canada
Attn: Home Plans
113-437 Martin St., Ste. 215
Penticton, BC V2A 5L1

Before You Order

Our Exchange Policy

Blueprints are nonrefundable. However, should you find that the plan you have purchased does not fit your needs, you may exchange that plan for another plan in our collection within 60 days from the date of your original order. The entire content of your original order must be returned before an exchange will be processed. You will be charged a processing fee of 20% of the amount of the original order, the cost difference between the new plan set and the original plan set (if applicable), and all related shipping costs for the new plans. Contact our order department for more information. Please note: reproducible masters may only be exchanged if the package is unopened and CAD files cannot be exchanged and are nonrefundable.

Building Codes and Requirements

All plans offered for sale in this book and on our website (www.ultimateplans.com) are continually updated to meet the latest International Residential Code (IRC). Because building codes vary from area to area, some drawing modifications and/or the assistance of a professional designer or architect may be necessary to comply with your local codes or to accommodate specific building site conditions. We strongly advise you to consult with your local building official for information regarding codes governing your area.

Multiple Plan Discount

Purchase 3 different home plans in the **same order** and receive **5% off** the plan price.

Purchase 5 or more different home plans in the **same order** and receive **10% off** the plan price.

(Please Note: Study sets do not apply.)

Blueprint Price Schedule

Price Code	1 Set	5 Sets	8 Sets	Reproducible Masters	CAD	Materials List
A	$400	$440	$475	$575	$1,025	$85
B	$440	$525	$555	$685	$1,195	$85
C	$510	$575	$635	$740	$1,265	$85
D	$560	$605	$665	$800	$1,300	$95
E	$600	$675	$705	$845	$1,400	$95
F	$650	$725	$775	$890	$1,500	$95
G	$720	$790	$840	$950	$1,600	$95
H	$820	$860	$945	$1,095	$1,700	$95
I	$945	$975	$1,075	$1,195	$1,890	$105
J	$1,010	$1,080	$1,125	$1,250	$1,900	$105
K	$1,125	$1,210	$1,250	$1,380	$2,030	$105
L	$1,240	$1,335	$1,375	$1,535	$2,270	$105

Note: All prices subject to change

Ultimate Estimate Tier (UE Tier)

MT Tier*	Price
XB	$299
XC	$499

* Please see the Plan Index to determine your plan's Ultimate Estimate Tier (UE Tier).

Shipping & Handling

	1-4 Sets	5-7 Sets	8+ Sets or Reproducibles	CAD
US Regular (7–10 business days)	$18	$20	$25	$25
US Priority (3–5 business days)	$25	$30	$35	$35
US Express (1–2 business days)	$40	$45	$50	$50
Canada Express (3-4 business days)	$100	$100	$100	$100
Worldwide Express (3–5 business days)			** Quote Required **	

Note: All delivery times are from date the blueprint package is shipped (typically within 1-2 days of placing order).

Order Form
Please send me the following:

Plan Number: _____ **Price Code:** _____ (See Plan Index.)

Indicate Foundation Type: (Select ONE. See plan page for availability.)
- ❏ Slab
- ❏ Crawl space
- ❏ Basement
- ❏ Walk-out basement
- ❏ Optional Foundation for Fee _____ $_____
  (Please enter foundation here)

*Please call all our order department or visit our website for optional foundation fee

Basic Blueprint Package | Cost
- ❏ Reproducible Masters — $_____
- ❏ 8-Set Plan Package — $_____
- ❏ 5-Set Plan Package — $_____
- ❏ 1-Set Study Package — $_____
- ❏ Additional plan sets:
  ___ sets at $45.00 per set — $_____
- ❏ Print in mirror-reverse: $50.00 per order — $_____
  *Please call all our order department or visit our website for availibility
- ❏ Print in right-reading reverse: $150.00 per order — $_____
  *Please call all our order department or visit our website for availibility

Important Extras
- ❏ Ultimate Estimate (See Price Tier above.) — $_____
- ❏ Materials List — $_____
- ❏ CompleteCost Materials Report at $125.00 — $_____
  Zip Code of Home/Building Site _____
- ❏ EZ Quote for Plan #_____ at $29.95 — $_____
- ❏ Additional EZ Quotes for Plan #s_____ at $19.95 each — $_____

Shipping (see chart above) — $_____
SUBTOTAL — $_____
Sales Tax (NJ residents only, add 7%) — $_____
TOTAL — $_____

Order Toll Free: 1-800-523-6789   By Fax: 201-760-2431
Creative Homeowner
24 Park Way
Upper Saddle River, NJ 07458

Name _____
(Please print or type)

Street _____
(Please do not use a P.O. Box)

City _____ State _____

Country _____ Zip _____

Daytime telephone ( ) _____

Fax ( ) _____
(Required for reproducible orders)

E-Mail _____

Payment   ❏ Bank check/money order. No personal checks.
Make checks payable to Creative Homeowner

❏ VISA   ❏ MasterCard   ❏ American Express   ❏ Discover

Credit card number _____

Expiration date (mm/yy) _____

Signature _____

Please check the appropriate box:
❏ Building home for myself   ❏ Building home for somone else

SOURCE CODE **CD150**

Copyright Notice

All home plans sold through this publication are protected by copyright. Reproduction of these home plans, either in whole or in part, including any form and/or preparation of derivative works thereof, for any reason without prior written permission is strictly prohibited. The purchase of a set of home plans in no way transfers any copyright or other ownership interest in it to the buyer except for a limited license to use that set of home plans for the construction of one, and only one, dwelling unit. The purchase of additional sets of the home plans at a reduced price from the original set or as a part of a multiple-set package does not convey to the buyer a license to construct more than one dwelling.

Similarly, the purchase of reproducible home plans (sepias, mylars) carries the same copyright protection as mentioned above. It is generally allowed to make up to a maximum of 10 copies for the construction of a single dwelling only. To use any plans more than once, and to avoid any copyright license infringement, it is necessary to contact the plan designer to receive a release and license for any extended use. Whereas a purchaser of reproducible plans is granted a license to make copies, it should be noted that because blueprints are copyrighted, making photocopies from them is illegal.

Copyright and licensing of home plans for construction exist to protect all parties. Copyright respects and supports the intellectual property of the original architect or designer. Copyright law has been reinforced over the past few years. Willful infringement could cause settlements for statutory damages to $150,000.00 plus attorney fees, damages, and loss of profits.

Index

For pricing, see page 311.

Plan #	Price Code	Page	Total Finished Area Square Feet	Materials List	CompleteCost	Ue Tier
161007	C	93	1,611	Y	N	XB
161008	D	179	1,860	N	N	XB
161009	C	146	1,651	Y	N	XB
161010	C	135	1,544	Y	N	XB
161013	C	143	1,509	Y	N	XB
161014	C	147	1,698	Y	N	XB
161026	D	204	2,041	N	N	XB
161026	D	205	2,041	N	N	XB
161028	H	259	3,570	Y	N	XC
161056	G	281	3,171	Y	N	XC
161066	D	256	2,078	Y	N	XB
161072	D	230	2,183	Y	N	XC
161073	D	159	1,895	N	N	XB
161079	B	47	1,498	Y	N	XB
161081	B	37	1,390	Y	N	XB
161085	D	197	1,979	N	N	XB
161158	F	295	2,679	Y	N	XC
161160	E	231	2,230	Y	N	XB
161161	C	144	1,569	Y	N	XB
161180	E	259	2,437	Y	N	XB
161225	E	285	2,591	Y	N	XB
171002	B	68	1,458	Y	N	XB
171003	D	227	2,098	Y	N	XB
171004	E	220	2,256	Y	N	XB
171006	C	137	1,648	Y	N	XB
171008	C	146	1,652	Y	N	XB
171009	C	113	1,771	Y	N	XB
171010	D	168	1,972	Y	N	XB
171013	G	269	3,084	Y	N	XC
171015	D	217	2,089	Y	N	XB
181021	B	13	1,124	Y	N	XB
181147	B	50	1,360	Y	N	XB
181215	A	17	929	Y	N	XB
181218	A	18	946	Y	N	XB
191003	C	148	1,785	N	N	XB
191009	D	227	2,172	N	N	XB
191027	E	261	2,354	N	N	XB
201004	B	13	1,121	Y	N	XB
201014	B	49	1,237	Y	N	XB
201023	B	49	1,390	Y	N	XB
201024	B	59	1,324	Y	N	XB
201032	C	85	1,556	Y	N	XB
201061	E	302	2,387	Y	N	XB
201063	F	292	2,697	Y	N	XB
201064	F	303	2,682	Y	N	XB
201069	F	267	2,735	Y	N	XB
201084	D	216	2,056	Y	N	XB
201087	C	124	1,672	Y	N	XB
211002	C	126	1,792	Y	N	XB
211003	D	190	1,865	Y	N	XB
211009	E	261	2,396	Y	N	XB
211010	E	305	2,503	Y	N	XB
211011	F	287	2,791	Y	N	XB
211029	C	123	1,672	Y	N	XB
211037	D	138	1,800	Y	N	XB
211039	D	190	1,868	Y	N	XB
211040	D	113	1,800	Y	N	XB
211048	D	243	2,002	Y	N	XB
211049	D	202	2,023	Y	N	XB
211050	D	178	2,000	Y	N	XB
211051	D	226	2,123	Y	N	XB
211054	E	298	2,358	Y	N	XB
211055	E	279	2,394	Y	N	XB
211057	E	300	2,366	N	N	XB
211058	E	280	2,564	N	N	XB
211059	E	218	2,299	N	N	XB
211061	F	280	2,655	Y	N	XB
211062	F	294	2,719	Y	N	XB
211065	G	300	3,158	Y	N	XB
211067	I	301	4,038	Y	N	XC
211068	H	303	3,960	Y	N	XB
211086	C	116	1,704	Y	N	XB
221001	F	297	2,600	N	N	XC
221003	D	163	1,802	N	N	XB
221004	C	149	1,763	N	N	XB
221008	C	84	1,540	N	N	XB
221011	C	136	1,756	N	N	XB
221013	B	19	1,495	N	N	XB
221014	D	191	1,906	N	N	XB
221015	D	187	1,926	N	N	XB
221016	B	68	1,461	N	N	XB
221018	D	241	2,007	N	N	XB
221020	D	166	1,859	N	N	XB
231009	F	296	2,765	N	N	XC
241001	E	297	2,350	N	N	XB
241002	D	212	2,154	N	N	XB
241004	F	307	2,771	N	N	XB
241005	C	133	1,670	N	N	XB
241006	C	136	1,744	N	N	XB
241007	D	243	2,036	N	N	XB
241008	E	251	2,526	N	N	XB
251001	B	56	1,253	Y	N	XB
251002	B	59	1,333	Y	N	XB
251003	B	63	1,393	Y	N	XB
251006	D	161	1,849	Y	N	XB
271060	C	88	1,726	N	N	XB
271073	D	192	1,920	N	N	XB
271074	E	284	2,400	N	N	XB
271076	D	244	2,188	N	N	XB
271077	C	142	1,786	N	N	XB
271081	E	304	2,539	N	N	XB
281011	B	58	1,314	Y	N	XB
291002	C	121	1,550	N	N	XB
291004	E	306	2,529	N	N	XC
301002	D	163	1,845	Y	N	XB
301003	E	306	2,485	Y	N	XC
301005	D	192	1,930	Y	N	XB
311001	D	223	2,085	N	N	XC
311004	D	245	2,046	Y	N	XC
311006	E	256	2,465	Y	N	XC
311010	D	178	1,997	Y	N	XB
311011	D	172	1,955	Y	N	XB
311013	C	137	1,698	Y	N	XB
311019	E	257	2,506	Y	N	XC
321001	C	97	1,721	Y	N	XB
321002	B	42	1,400	Y	N	XB
321003	C	130	1,791	Y	N	XB
321004	F	298	2,808	Y	N	XC
321005	E	286	2,483	Y	N	XC
321006	D	186	1,977	Y	N	XB